DATE DUE

DE 18 '98,			
MY 10 '99			
JY 21 '99			

DEMCO 38-296

$\mathcal{D}$isplaying Women

$\mathcal{D}$isplaying Women

Spectacles of Leisure
in Edith Wharton's New York

Maureen E. Montgomery

Routledge   New York   London

For Mary and Joseph Montgomery

Published in 1998 by
Routledge
29 West 35th Street
New York, NY 10001

Published in Great Britain by
Routledge
11 New Fetter Lane
London EC4P 4EE

Copyright © 1998 by Routledge

Printed in the United States of America on acid-free paper.

Library of Congress Cataloging-in-Publication Data

Montgomery, Maureen E.
    Displaying women : spectacles of leisure in Edith Wharton's New York / Maureen E. Montgomery.
        p. cm.
    Includes bibliographical references and index.
    ISBN 0-415-90566-6 (hbk. : acid-free paper). — ISBN 0-415-90565-4 (pbk. : acid-free paper)
        1. Wharton, Edith, 1862–1937—Knowledge—New York (State)—New York.
    2. Women and literature—New York (State)—New York. 3. Upper class—New York (State)—New York—History. 4. Wharton, Edith, 1862–1937—Characters—Women. 5. New York (N.Y.)—In literature. 6. Upper class in literature. 7. Leisure in literature. 8. Women in literature. I. Title.
    PS3545.H16Z747 1998
813'.52—dc21   97-31983
                                                                                CIP

British Cataloging-in-Publication Data forthcoming

Contents

List of Illustrations

1. *New York World*, 20 January 1895, p. 20.
2. "Fifth Avenue," William Thomas Smedley, *Life and Character: Drawings by W. T. Smedley* (New York: Harper and Bros., 1899), p. 44.
3. "Everyman to his taste," Charles Dana Gibson, *Gibson's New Cartoons: A Book of Charles Dana Gibson's Latest Drawings* (New York: Charles Scribner's Sons, 1916), n.p.
4. Costumes in tableaux vivants, *Vogue*, 12 February 1910, p. 10. Courtesy of The Winterthur Library: Printed Book and Periodical Collection.
5. "Is a caddy always necessary?" Charles Dana Gibson, *The Best of Charles Dana Gibson*, edited with a biography and introduction by Woody Gelman (New York: Bounty Books, 1969), p. 9.
6. "Wireless Telegraphy," *The Best of Charles Dana Gibson*, edited with a biography and introduction by Woody Gelman (New York: Bounty Books, 1969), p. 69.
7. "Aunt Jane," Charles Dana Gibson, *Gibson's New Cartoons: A Book of Charles Dana Gibson's Latest Drawings* (New York: Charles Scribner's Sons, 1916), n.p.
8. "Household Decoration," Charles Dana Gibson, *Gibson's New Cartoons: A Book of Charles Dana Gibson's Latest Drawings* (New York: Charles Scribner's Sons, 1916), n.p.
9. "Le Matin après le Bal," A. A. Anderson, *Vogue*, 5 December 1907, n.p. Courtesy of The Winterthur Library: Printed Book and Periodical Collection.
10. "New York's Latest Fad—The Michaux Cycle Club," drawing by T. de Thulstrup, *Harper's Weekly*, 19 January 1895, p. 65.
11. "The Announcement of Her Engagement," Charles Dana Gibson, *Gibson's New Cartoons: A Book of Charles Dana Gibson's Latest Drawings* (New York: Charles Scribner's Sons, 1916), n.p.
12. Advertisement for Scandinavian Fur and Leather Co., *Vogue*, 12 October 1905, p. 413. Courtesy of The Winterthur Library: Printed Book and Periodical Collection.
13. "Leap Year," Charles Dana Gibson, *Gibson's New Cartoons: A Book of Charles Dana Gibson's Latest Drawings* (New York: Charles Scribner's Sons, 1916), n.p.
14. Cover, *Town Topics*, 6 August 1903. Courtesy of Henry Francis Du Pont Winterthur Museum.

Acknowledgments

This study has its origins in a discussion with Carroll Smith-Rosenberg that took place during a miserable winter in Canterbury at a time when she was a visiting fellow in my department. After the publication of my doctoral dissertation, the question "What next?" loomed large. It seemed a demanding question then, all the more so because of my recent relocation to New Zealand and the geographical distance between my new home and the archives in the United States. I thank Carroll for giving me both the incentive and the encouragement to pursue my professional identity as an "Americanist."

My next important stimulus (and a major source of material support) came from a visit to New Zealand later that same year of a visiting Fulbright Scholar, Cecilia Macheski, who shares my passion for Edith Wharton's writings and who just so happens to live not all that far from The Mount, Wharton's home from 1902 to 1913. A research and travel grant from the Department of History at the University of Canterbury meant that my project could begin in earnest. Support for the next phase came from a University of Canterbury research grant and a fellowship at the New York State Archives. In this connection, I wish to thank Jim Corsaro, Elaine Clark, and Billy Aul for their gracious assistance. While in Albany I also made frequent trips to the Albany Institute of History and Art, where I was kindly aided by Mary Schifferli and Prudence Backman and, more recently, by Sandra Markham. My host, Cecilia Macheski, whose hospitality knows no bounds, took me touring around New York State and the Berkshires, visiting the various summer homes of wealthy New Yorkers from the turn of the century and enjoying the local fare. Thanks to conference leave and research grants from my department, American Studies, there have been several trips since, more archives plundered, and more red wine consumed. Cecilia Macheski's colleagues at LaGuardia Community College, her family, and her friends have also been materially and intellectually supportive of my project: Marian Arkin, Sandra Hanson, Danny and Clellie Lynch, Russell Needham and Leonard Vogt, Jeremiah Rusconi, and Helen Macheski.

In 1992 I was granted a year's study leave from the University of Canterbury and spent a more extensive period in the New York archives. During this trip I visited many places that had been used as settings by Martin Scorsese in his film *The Age of Innocence*. In fact, I even spent a month in a Brooklyn brownstone apartment on a street used in the movie. At this time, I made several trips out to the Rye Historical Society and greatly enjoyed being a solitary researcher in the company of the wonderfully friendly and helpful staff there. Three months were then spent as a fellow at the Henry Francis DuPont Winterthur Museum, Delaware, in luxurious surroundings. This was a very fruitful time for my research and thinking, and I particularly wish to thank Neville Thompson and Pat Elliott for their gracious assistance and Mary Corbin Sies for her support and encouragement. I gained a different perspective on studying everyday life in turn-of-the-century New York through my contact with the staff and students at Winterthur. At this stage, I needed one last foray into the archives before I could settle down to write, and on this occasion I was the recipient of the generous hospitality of Steve and Hasia Diner in Washington, D.C. While much of the research was conducted in the United States, I must also acknowledge the kind assistance of the staff at the University of Canterbury Library over the past seven years as well as that of the staff at the Victoria University Library in Wellington.

Over the years, my graduate students have been subjected to various manifestations of this project in my Gender, History, and Fiction class, and I thank them for their contributions to our lively discussions of Wharton's novels. Other audiences have also been recipients of various stages of my thinking, and in this connection I would especially like to thank Jean Lown and the members of the Women and Gender Research Institute and Women Studies Program at Utah State University; Rosemary Du Plessis and the Department of Sociology at the University of Canterbury; Clare Simpson and the Department of Leisure Science at Lincoln University; Ellen Dubois and the Women's Studies and American Studies Programs at the University of California at Los Angeles; Mary Ryan, Tom Laqueur, and the Department of History at the University of California at Berkeley; Karen Offen and members of the Women and Gender Research Institute at Stanford University; John and Joy Kasson and the American Studies Program at the University of North Carolina at Chapel Hill; John David Smith and the History Department at North Carolina State University; Eric Sandeen and the American Studies Program at the University of Wyoming; and Leonore Davidoff and the Social History Seminar Group at the University of Essex. I have also gained from the discussions and insights arising from giving papers at the following conferences: meetings of the Australian Victorian Studies Association at Auckland in 1993, Hobart in 1994, and La Trobe in 1995; and Rod Phillip's Family History Conferences at Carleton University in 1992, 1994, and 1997.

At Routledge I would like to thank Brendan O'Malley and Brian Phillips for their support and attentive responses to my queries; Sue Warga for her assiduous copy-editing; and Cecelia Cancellaro, formerly of Routledge, who was my initial editor.

To Clare Simpson and Rosemary Du Plessis I owe special thanks for undertaking to read parts of the manuscript and for their warm and generous support over the years. Cornelia Sears generously gave of her time to assist with proofreading during the hottest week of the summer. I am also especially grateful to the following for their help and encouragement: Terry Austrin, Constance Carroll, Nabila Jaber, Chigusa Kimura-Steven, Sharon Mazer, Maureen Molloy, and Michele Slatter. And I owe a special debt to Gwen Standring for her support, particularly since I took on the headship of my department. The love and support of my parents, as ever, played a crucial role, and to them I dedicate this book.

To my husband, Rodney Foster, I wish to express my deepest appreciation of his intellectual perspicacity, his fine editorial skills, and his scholarly contributions to the making of this book. And even more than this, I wish to acknowledge his unstinting support of and faith in this project.

Introduction

At the turn of the century, "Saunterings," the weekly society column in *Town Topics*, a gossipy society magazine, provided prolonged lamentations on the sins of New York's high society. Indeed, since the establishment of the magazine in 1885, the writer of the column, "The Saunterer," had set himself up as a censor of society. Through his network of informants, the Saunterer had "eyes" in different places—he was a panoptical figure surveying social life in the metropolis. He was also a merchant dealing in information, gossip, rumor, and innuendo, and in his hands the currency of gossip was transformed into profit and power. In his most pessimistic mood, he would describe New York society as a circus, a grotesque form of human life where "money-making and festal enjoyment" were the "prime motives of existence." For the Saunterer, the city was both repellent and bewitching: "a mass of fascinating evils that can ruin any weak nature." In 1890, for example, he complained that what he called "the woman habit" was a threat to the "lofty mental development and domestic grace in our young people," responsible, in fact, for "nine-tenths" of the misery and crime in the city.[1] Prostitutes were everywhere, he claimed, "feminine flesh" costing "from one cent to a hundred thousand dollars a pound." And if his readers doubted his word, they could go and see for themselves: "Start at Murray Hill and pass from there through upper Broadway and Sixth avenue to Water street, and at every turn stands the woman with the devilish eyes and mercenary soul."[2] Just over a year later, he again complained that vice was rampant in the metropolis, pointing his finger at those with great wealth and luxury who overindulged themselves in sensual gratification outside of marriage.[3] His particular *bêtes noires* in this regard were adultery, alcoholism, prostitution, and homosexuality.[4]

The Saunterer read the street as a boulevard promenader; he was a man-about-town, frequenting clubs, restaurants, and theaters, taking in the sights and listening at keyholes. His eyes penetrated the shadowy corners in ballrooms, his ears listened for *faux pas* and indiscretions. He appraised public space and evaluated people's behavior and appearance both in terms of polite conventions and with regard to the gender, class, racial, and ethnic boundaries of New York's high society. In his surveillance of public space he was a sexual voyeur, keen to pick up on society men's peccadilloes and ruthless in his condemnation of women's improprieties.

In April 1895 the Saunterer treated his readers, in four consecutive paragraphs, to a particularly florid rant on the public revelation of female flesh. The first two paragraphs began with an attack on the Reverend Charles Parkhurst, minister of a fashionable Fifth Avenue church, for instigating raids on the city's brothels, raids that had subsequently forced prostitutes out onto the streets. Preferring to keep "immoral conditions" "veiled," that is, in the relative privacy of brothels, the Saunterer deplored the creation of a public spectacle of "unescorted ladies with the boot heels that click and the skirts that climb . . . brought into the open street and illuminated by electricity."[5] He then proceeded, in the third paragraph, to discuss the appearance on the Boulevard and Riverside Drive of genteel women on bicycles, wearing bloomers that showed their knees and revealed their curves. As if this were not startling enough, the bloomer costume, he predicted, would soon be replaced by small, elastic breeches. Worse still: "Women bicyclists will be wearing tights within a year." And why? Because "woman is in a progressive mood nowadays and will not remain content with half measures. . . . Youthful and beauteous womanhood is going to emancipate itself by means of the bicycle. It has charms to exhibit and is bound to exhibit them." But such a public exhibition of the female form would not, declared the Saunterer in his fourth paragraph, evoke much public outcry. And here was the rub: A liberal police force and a permissive public would hardly find such a "parade" shocking when they were so tolerant of female nudity on the stages of Bowery theaters in "living pictures":

> At present the youth of New York may gaze each night in the year upon female nakedness presented in the most tempting and sensual shape that ingenious men can devise. Under the name of art the most amazing visions of living, breathing, palpitating nudity . . . is deliberately spread before innocent eyes, and the moral damage thereby is, I maintain, beyond computing.

Prostitution the Saunterer was prepared to condone, provided it was conducted discreetly, but he drew the line at female nudity on the stage, the latter being a blatant example of the commodification of female flesh. For him, the toleration of such commercial entertainment signified widespread degeneracy that would contaminate the respectable community. And, in a final flourish, he anticipated that, while the appearance of nude revuists on bicycles was unlikely, the highways would nevertheless soon see women cyclists in flesh-colored tights simulating nudity—in other words, "bicycle Godivas."

This censure of society women by the Saunterer stands out because of its moralistic tone, its use of sexual imagery, its treatment of sexual deviance, and the leap in logic in linking women cyclists to prostitutes and performers in salacious living pictures. It also raises a number of questions. Why, for example, in the view of the Saunterer, does the act of respectable women cycling signify the potential for moral degeneracy? Why does he infer a parallel between the behavior of prostitutes, women cyclists, and women in nude revues? Why does he superimpose onto women cyclists what he regards as most threatening in the metropolis, that is, naked women? His construction of sexual danger from the presence of prostitutes in the streets or the pornographic style of entertainments in the theaters is fairly predictable, but by framing his discussion of women cyclists with examples drawn from the world of commercialized sex, he draws this third group into the category of sexual deviance, confirming bourgeois men's suspicion that "beneath each woman's respectability lay a potential 'whore.'"[6] If we go back to his opening paragraph, we can see that the Saunterer cannot abide streetwalkers, but he is prepared to concede that "leapfrog in private is not so generally demoralizing as soliciting in public."[7] What has previously been hidden behind closed doors is now in public view and, what is worse, in "respectable places, such as restaurants and theatres." He reiterates his concern about the public display of the female form in his next paragraph, which focuses on women cyclists. By immediately going on to discuss women cyclists after commenting on streetwalkers, the Saunterer infers an analogy between prostitutes appearing on the streets and respectable women's appearance in a new and startling form as bicyclists, wending their way through city traffic with unprecedented independence and mobility. He makes his comparison between these two groups of women even more emphatic, however, by referring to the unveiling of their bodies:

> The female limb is to gradually succeed in exhibiting itself abundantly in New York . . . [with] the swift disappearance of drapery and revelation of curves. . . . We are becoming very intimate with the sections of metropolitan beauty that have heretofore been secluded. That which was recently shy and shrinking is now bold and blooming. The sacred bulge is on view. The sculptured mystery is being brilliantly revealed.

The Saunterer's description of the display of "limbs," not to mention "the sacred bulge," and "curves," by "the gentle straddlers of wheels" is intended to equate to the "spectacular ankles" of prostitutes and their "skirts that climb." While the "bewildering exposure" was to be admired, he suggests, "we must dread what it is sure to lead to." And what it must lead to is made abundantly clear in his paragraph on living pictures, namely the shedding of long skirts and the donning of bloomers, which is tantamount to the total loss of all modesty. So total is this loss that, unlike the prostitutes, the women who performed in erotic living pictures are not even referred to as human. They are more repugnant than the "unescorted ladies" (his euphemism for prostitutes); the Saunterer deindividualizes them into the abstraction "female nakedness."

The sequencing of these paragraphs dealing with prostitutes, women bicyclists, and living pictures in a society magazine registers a profound unease with the presence of women in public space, one that is expressed in explicitly sexual terms and linked specifically to commodification. Boundaries have been transgressed. Neither fallen women nor respectable ones have kept to their allotted space, secluded from the street in private abodes. The worst is therefore to be feared. The moral damage to "innocent [male] eyes" from sexually dangerous women not only emanates from the theaters but is also present in the streets and now emanates from respectable women too. Women on bicycles, moving conspicuously in the streets, are, contrary to the codes of etiquette governing their behavior in public places, drawing attention to themselves. The leap in logic that the Saunterer consequently makes is that with respectable women now displaying their bodies, all women have become prostitutes.[8]

What appears to motivate the Saunterer as a society columnist is a perceived need—all the more urgent in an era of commercialized sex—to remind women from the respectable classes that the dividing line between them and those women who were denied respect was a very thin one indeed. He therefore took it upon himself to direct ridicule at society women on bicycles and sexualize their appearance in a bid to dissuade other women from following the fashion. In certain respects, this was not atypical of bourgeois white male culture in the United States at that time and its efforts to maintain the status quo in gender relations. During this same period similar epithets were flung at white women suffragists, who were also regarded as stepping outside their domestic role in seeking the vote.[9] All in all, it seems that the 1890s were a troublesome time for men who were used to negotiating metropolitan space with confidence. Bourgeois women were testing the spatial boundaries of an urban topography that had been so conveniently arranged for men of the white Protestant establishment. As such, women riding bicycles on public thoroughfares were just one manifestation of the encroachment by women upon public space, claiming their share of the entertainment and self-gratification offered by the new palaces of amusement and new forms of recreation.

The Saunterer's concerns about increasingly ambiguous gender and sexual boundaries in New York City at the turn of the century illustrate many of the difficulties facing society women as they attempted to negotiate a world in which material possessions increasingly connoted social status. On the one hand, society women who "took up the wheel" signified, in fairly conventional terms, leisure (cycling as a form of recreation), wealth (before bicycles became

WHAT WE ARE COMING TO.

THE BICYCLE RACE OF UP-TO-DATE WOMEN IN THE NEAR FUTURE

widely available), and fashion (women's cycling as a novel activity).[10] It was expected of them that they assert their class identity in these terms. On the other hand, the sight of women on bicycles suggested independence, mobility, and emancipation, which, taken together, threatened the traditional confinement of society women to domestic space and to those public places where social interaction was carefully regulated. It was one thing for society women to cycle within the confines of a private club or at the fashionable hour in Central Park, but to cycle down a popular thoroughfare in bloomers in 1895 was to contest the codes of etiquette governing women's behavior in public places. Throughout the nineteenth century, albeit implicitly, these codes had incessantly stressed the need to wear modest street dress and to move inconspicuously in order to avoid being misrecognized as a prostitute. In view of this, the full significance of the Saunterer's strategy becomes apparent: Society women riding bicycles in the street did not conform to the code of gentility. In fact, the Saunterer was acting as a censor of the behavior of those who set the fashion for the rest of society.

The Saunterer was not alone, however, in expressing alarm at the appearance of women cyclists in the mid-1890s. In January 1895, a cartoon caricaturing society women on bicycles appeared on the society page in the *New York World* alongside the column "The Week in Society," which featured a story about a fifteen-day women's bicycle race at the exclusive Michaux Club.[11] This cartoon was a transgressive image of women, a bizarre, carnivalesque depiction ridiculing society women in particular but, at the same time, betraying a deep unease with the notion of independently mobile women in public. It reveals a widely felt anxiety evident in the 1890s: an anxiety about gender transgression, the fear that women, especially by riding bicycles astride, were adopting masculine behavior. Together, the Saunterer's article and the *World's* cartoon of society women cyclists connote difficulties that American society generally was having in coming to terms with the major transformation that the United States was undergoing in the late nineteenth and early twentieth centuries. This process of modernization included changes in gender roles as well as changes in patterns of heterosocial relations. Other significant dimensions of this transformation involved commercialization, the development of consumer capitalism, the changing relationship between the public and private spheres, the growth of the print media, the decline of Victorian moral standards and formality, and the decline of gentility. At times, and certainly with respect to gender relations, the Saunterer represented those conservative forces that resisted modernization by trying to maintain the old ideals and traditions on which American gentility had been founded. At the same time, however, society journalism itself played a role in the process of modernization.

Leisure and the Leisure Class

The subject of this book is the public world of New York society women. It covers various aspects of women's lives at the turn of the century in terms of how they negotiated the larger transformation of American culture and society, as well as in terms of the intersection of class and gender interests. In particular, it explores how women's appearance and activities signified leisure with the express intention of laying claim to high social status, and how these women were, in turn, represented in the dominant discourses of journalism and etiquette. This study therefore seeks to make explicit the diverse meanings ascribed to New York society women's activities at the turn of the century in shaping and defining an upper-class identity. Leisure is the key to this upper-class identity precisely because it was an important marker of class. Moreover, the popular designation for the elite was "the leisure class."[12]

Authors of etiquette manuals looked upon leisure as something integral to the existence of society and essential to the United States's view of itself as a civilized nation, that is to say, a society led by a group of cultivated people who were knowledgeable about manners and the finer things in life. The very notion of leisure implied that certain people had time in which to pursue activities that conferred gentility. It also signified that such people did not have to engage in manual labor and that their time was not regulated by the demands of remunerative labor. This notion of leisure was, in fact, derived from the practices of the European aristocracy and was therefore firmly rooted in conceptions of class. Indeed, the American bourgeoisie had difficulties with the fact that Europeans failed to take seriously its claims to having a leisure class and a society. As one turn-of-the-century etiquette manual typically noted:

> An American traveller, when once rallied upon the fact that there was no aristocracy in his country, replied: "Pardon me, you forget our women!"
>
> It was gallantly said, and characteristic of the chivalry that has always been so marked a trait of American manhood.
>
> It is the stock reproach among Europeans towards us—this lack of aristocracy—which politely but thinly veils their conviction that we are a nation of rich and prosperous parvenus. . . . We believe the outward and visible signs of aristocracy are shown in perfect breeding, charm of manner, and unfailing courtesy, of which the inward grace is an instinctive refinement that is not merely a decorative attribute.[13]

Maud Cooke made even more explicit this notion that women in the United States represented the whole of the upper class when she asserted: "Women are our only leisure class." She firmly attributed refinement to women: "It is women who create society . . . and it is largely to women with their leisure, and their tact, that we must look to create and sustain the social fabric."[14] This interpretation of American social affairs clearly heightened the value both of women's role in high society and of their active contribution to the advance or maintenance of their families' social status. Nevertheless, the female domination of society still meant that the American leisure class was vulnerable to criticism from those who saw European court society as representing the highest ideal.

Expatriate novelist Henry James was one of the major critics of social arrangements in U.S. high society. In James's view, the American upper class could never measure up to its European counterpart, and in both his fiction and nonfiction he refers to the conspicuous absence from high society of the male head of the household.[15] In *The American Scene*, for example, he explores this state of affairs in some detail with reference to New York and Washington, D.C. He contrasts "the general European spectacle, the effect . . . of a large, consummate economy, traditionally practised . . . [and] arranged exactly to supply functions, forms, the whole element of custom and perpetuity, to any massiveness of private ease" to the "floundering" social organism of America's "vast commercial democracy," where only the women labor to find out "what civilization really *is*." The American businessman may, James contends, "never hope to be anything *but* a businessman" and thus is forced to abdicate "the boundless gaping void of 'society'" to women. In seizing upon this opportunity, women "represent the situation as perfectly normal," whereas for James it is entirely "unnatural."[16] There is clearly a discrepancy, then, between the representation of society in American etiquette manuals, which promoted the role of women in sustaining the "social fabric" and claimed that American society was capable of refinement and civilization, and James's insistence that the American social spectacle lacked men of leisure and history.

Mrs. Sherwood, a New York resident and noted authority on matters of etiquette, was mindful of European criticisms of U.S. society and especially those of Henry James when she drew her American readers' attention to "our bumptiousness, our spreadeagleism, and our too great familiarity and lack of dignity." She advised her readers to take on board some of these criticisms in the interest of self-improvement and to avoid being "held up as savages." But, at the same time, she exhorted Americans to decide for themselves on points of etiquette that would be in tune with America's distinctive political institutions and history, because "they are a part of our great nation, of our republican institutions, and of that continental hospitality which gives a home to the Russ, the German, the Frenchman, the Irishman, and the 'heathen Chinee.'"[17] This quotation is representative of an ongoing concern about national identity that underscored the discourse of turn-of-the-century etiquette manuals. This formulation of national identity was, moreover, still rooted in an Anglo-American and racist construction of "civilization." At a time of intense concern about "racial 'fitness' and culture," the possibility of being equated with "savages" carried the damning implication in the mind of the white Anglo-Saxon bourgeoisie that the United States had not sufficiently "progressed along the path of civilization." Furthermore, because women were seen as carrying the burden of maintaining high society, the "American woman"—that is, the white Anglo-Saxon Protestant *haute bourgeoise*—was also regarded as responsible for demonstrating America's "racial fitness."[18]

Etiquette discourse racialized "civilization," and this went hand in hand with the maintenance of a white Anglo-Saxon Protestant elite confronted with the growing ethnic diversification of America's population and the challenge of wealthy Jewish families to the de facto segregation practiced by high society. In the late nineteenth and early twentieth centuries, class and racial boundaries alike were policed. At the turn of the twentieth century, then, the identity of the American leisure class—that is, the ways in which the leisure class defined itself and presented itself to the world at large—was intricately connected to the issues of national identity, ethnicity, and gender relations. Indeed, identity was also shaped by the growing authority of scientific discourses on race and the hierarchy of races on a scale ranging from civilization to savagery.[19]

The notion of an American leisure class emerged in the late nineteenth century with the multiplication of vast fortunes gained from industrialization. As Richard Bushman has noted, the "self-appointed aristocrats of the post–Civil War era" with "their mansions, their airs, their pretensions were the natural outgrowth of the aristocratic genteel culture that the American middle class had appropriated from its former rulers."[20] The "leisure" of the "leisure class," then, constituted activities that were displayed to others or written about in newspapers, such as formal sociability, going to art galleries, the theater, and the opera, recreation and travel. The wealth of the leisure class was signified through such activities as well as through the conspicuous consumption of expensive material objects: houses, carriages, clothes, and so on. Such display "performed a hegemonic function," not unlike that of the World's Fairs at this time, in propagating "the ideas and values of the country's political, financial, corporate, and intellectual leaders."[21] In turn-of-the-century New York, the nature of leisure as activity as well as the scale and practice of consumption changed significantly with increasing competition for elite status. This was the subject of Thorstein Veblen's *The Theory of the Leisure Class* (1899), in which he argued that leisure was intentionally displayed to others because it connoted gentility, refinement, specialized knowledge, civilization, cultivation, wealth, and breeding. He also argued that it was by and large the responsibility of leisure-class women and their servants to convey these things to the public at large.

Many society women took up the challenge to become more public in the conspicuous display of wealth, thus making use of the wide range of resources available to them in the metropolis: fashionable ballrooms and restaurants, the services of press agents, and so on. Some of these women became celebrities, the minute details of their daily lives reported in the society columns of newspapers and in magazine articles. They were held up as leaders—leaders of society, of fashion, of taste, of gentility. On the other hand, if they were found wanting, censorship was swift. In fact, engaging in the public world led to all sorts of problems for society women. Traditional social conventions required women to behave and dress inconspicuously in public places, but the demands of high-society life required society women to seek notice and publicity. To cope with this contradiction, therefore, display and publicity had to be carefully managed.

A major concern in this study, then, is with how women in the New York social elite shaped a leisure-class identity for themselves and their families in the new age of the mass-circulation print media. From the 1880s on, the "mediazation" of high society had irrevocably altered the public/private boundaries between the private lives of the wealthy and the commercial world.[22] High society found itself commodified into so many inches of news columns that helped to sell champagne and aids for indigestion, as well as to rent rooms in resort hotels. Its activities were frequently written about and photographed, with articles being mass-produced and circulated throughout the nation. The wealthy could well appreciate the enhancement of their claims to social leadership afforded by such publicity, but it was precisely this kind of publicity that was more difficult to control and that gave rise to new kinds of vulnerability.

Women Displaying Leisure

As has already been indicated, the notion of leisure connoted gentility, refinement, and respectability, so those who aspired to bourgeois social status had to
put in evidence their command of leisure time. Because the male half of the
American bourgeoisie was, by and large, a working bourgeoisie, it was therefore left to the women of the family to carry the marker of class by displaying
leisure. In late-nineteenth-century New York this display of leisure moved to
the public realm because of the intensification of social competition as wealthy
newcomers were drawn to the metropolis, and this brought about a significant
shift in the conceptualization of the woman of leisure for the bourgeoisie.
Traditionally the bourgeois male had preferred to restrict women's access to the
public realm; bourgeois status had been predicated upon the ability of the male
to support his wife and family, thus relieving them of any necessity to engage in
paid work. In the more segregated world of the bourgeoisie prior to 1870, it
was the woman of leisure at home who had been regarded as an important
symbol of class. But for the urban *haute bourgeoisie* in the late nineteenth century, the home was proving to be a somewhat inadequate arena for the display
of wealth and leisure, and therefore public spaces were brought into service by
way of supplementation.

The expansion of women's role in the public display of leisure had important ramifications for the construction of leisure-class femininity because
women's display of leisure was no longer limited to putting on fine clothes and
promenading on Fifth Avenue or in a carriage in Central Park at the fashionable
hour. Instead, society women were on display in boxes at the opera or various
shows at Madison Square Garden; they dined in fashionable restaurants; their
portraits appeared in newspapers; and their social activities were recorded in
detail. Large general entertainments well attended by the press ensured that
women would be seen and that their names would appear in newspaper reports
the following day, but the competition at large gatherings was intense and
heightened the pressure on women to attract the right kind of publicity. By the
1880s much more was at stake, with growing competition for high social status
and the emergence of society journalism. Displays of wealth became more blatant: Women donned "ropes of pearls" and wore the latest Parisian fashions.
Fancy-dress balls and *tableaux vivants* were entertainments that permitted
women wide scope for drawing attention to themselves, by dressing up as a
well-known historical or mythological figure or as a figure in a painting.
Putting on novel entertainments such as minstrel shows staged in private theaters or silver-service dinners for dogs guaranteed instant publicity, and possibly
ridicule.[23]

During the period in question, the whole nature of leisure changed for the
urban *haute bourgeoisie* in New York. With specific regard to women, it came to

have less to do with "cultivated" pursuits in private settings, such as reading, singing, small-scale hospitality, and visiting artists' studios, or with traveling to see the sights of ancient European civilizations, but instead had more to do with public display and spectacle. In the eighteenth century the "ideal" woman of leisure engaged in activities that either "improved the mind," such as reading sermons, or enhanced the interior décor of the home, as, for example, by embroidering fire screens. Admonitory tales about either women with too much "free time" on their hands or others who participated in unproductive occupations such as gambling, reading romances, or gossiping painted an image diametrically opposed to that of the woman of virtue. Moreover, women who spent their time idly and self-indulgently were considered disorderly and even dangerous.[24] In the late nineteenth century, the leisure that women displayed was no longer restricted to the home and came to involve large outlays on leisure goods and services. The increasingly public nature of leisure enjoyed in heterosocial settings, such as restaurants, cabarets, or skating clubs, gave women greater access to public space, and this was combined with a greater mobility due to the availability of mechanized transport. Women had to work hard at displaying leisure and making sure that the display was noticed, particularly as newspaper scrutiny raised the ante. But while there was increasing surveillance of women at leisure and mounting pressure to make their leisure signify distinction, the other side to this was that women were able to have fun, indulge new desires, enjoy the attention and admiration that came from display, and have access to resources in order to put on an effective "show."

Women's participation in leisure activities can be seen, then, as being potentially emancipatory and, paradoxically, as providing further opportunities for domination and control. Clearly, it was acceptable for women to display their husband's wealth through legitimate forms of high-class entertainments, and innovations in leisure had to attain legitimacy on the grounds that they advanced class interests in order for women to partake in them. As such, the choices made by women as to which leisure activities they pursued were made within a context of gender inequalities.[25] Yet though leisure was an area of contestation between men and women, it may nevertheless be argued that New York society women were able to explore new ways of expressing their femininity through leisure. At the turn of the century, the increased emphasis on appearance opened up to women a whole realm of activities, specialized knowledge, and skills where choices could be made. As sociologist Dorothy Smith has argued with reference to current times, "The production of appearance calls for thought, planning, the exercise of judgement, work, the use of resources, skills. Behind appearance and its interpretation is secreted a subject who is fully an agent."[26] Society women in turn-of-the-century New York would have been brought up to know, or would have later learned, how to produce an effect concomitant with their definition as respectable, heterosexual, leisure-class women. And, as Smith might well argue, they would have known how to put into practice the dominant discourses of femininity, would have known how to reproduce the "ideal"—or at least something evidently approaching it. If, as Smith says, women nowadays "work" at their appearance, then clearly it can be claimed that women in turn-of-the-century New York "worked" at signifying leisure. Although this work was itself not directly visible in form, it would have been "consciously planned" and would have taken a great deal of time. Moreover, it is in this backstage setting, behind the scenes, Smith argues, that women are "active and effective, making decisions, finding pleasure, having fun."[27]

Society women were not, on the whole, reluctant participants in the changes affecting the nature and meaning of leisure and leisure-class lifestyle at the turn of the century. It appears, rather, that they welcomed opportunities to engage in the more heterosocial world of public places, while at the same time some venues of commercialized leisure encouraged women's participation because it lent respectability to their enterprises and increased the number of their wealthy patrons. Leisure activities enabled women of the *haute bourgeoisie* to gain access to the city, perhaps more significantly than did either voluntary or paid work. There can be no doubt, then, that leisure helped to legitimize women's presence in public space.

Leisure as Performance

The dramaturgical metaphor of "performance" has been widely deployed by historians of everyday life and material culture to elucidate the meanings of social interaction. In the work of Richard Bushman, Karen Halttunen, and John Kasson on American gentility, this notion of "performance" has been used to analyze the ways in which, in the past, people defined both themselves and their social relations. All three scholars have drawn attention to the exaggerated emphasis that was placed upon behavior, appearance, and possessions in societies that were undergoing rapid change. John Kasson and Karen Halttunen, for example, allude to a crisis in social identity in nineteenth-century urban America and to the turning of social aspirants en masse to etiquette manuals for advice on how to negotiate "the anonymous 'world of strangers'" and "to establish the legitimacy of their claims to genteel standing."[28] As Halttunen explains:

> In what was believed to be a fluid social world where no one occupied a fixed social position, the question "Who am I?" loomed large; and in an urban social world where many of the people who met face-to-face each day were strangers, the question "Who are you really?" assumed even greater significance.[29]

According to Halttunen, by the late nineteenth century the second of her typological questions was less of a concern, for instead of posing a threat to the "social forms and rituals" of polite society, the confidence man had by then become a "kind of model for ambitious young Americans to emulate." In other words, in corporate America "the art of manipulating others to do what you want them to do . . . was far more valuable."[30]

It is tempting to ask, therefore, whether there was a "growing theatricality of middle-class culture in the 1850s and 1860s," as Halttunen contends, or rather, whether a different *kind* of theatricality emerged as the techniques of theatricality themselves were transformed.[31] Historians of the colonial and Victorian periods use the concept of theatricality. What is often not clear, however, is whether the construction of theatricality they use relates to the world of the theater relevant to the period they are studying or to that at the time of writing. After all, dramaturgical principles change over time, and our comprehension of illusions and their role in everyday life also changes. There is, nevertheless, something of a consensus among these historians, who have all drawn upon the work of sociologist Erving Goffman and his idea that gentility is a performance and that "houses, yards, carriages, costume, posture, manners were all part of the show."[32] But as Goffman himself warned: "The claim that all the world's a stage is sufficiently commonplace for readers to be familiar with its limitations and tolerant of its presentation, knowing that at any time they will easily be able to demonstrate to themselves that it is not to be taken too seriously." However, the use of dramaturgical terms as metaphors for describing and interpreting social interaction always runs the risk of conflating the terms of theatrical illusion with real life; furthermore, the pervasiveness of such metaphors is so compelling that the differences can be overlooked. In addition, Goffman maintained that the dramaturgical perspective is only one of several that can be utilized.

According to Goffman's theory of the presentation of self in everyday life, the individual deploys techniques to "give off expressions," techniques that are "more theatrical and contextual, . . . non-verbal, [and] presumably unintentional," and these are used "on and off the stage." Like actors in the theater, individuals in "real life" want to convey a certain definition of themselves and their context. Within the realist/naturalist tradition at least, actors want the audience to believe that they are a particular character, and to be consistent with this projection they affect appropriate gestures and postures and wear appropriate costumes. There is a high degree of conscious intentionality in their performance, which is accepted as "real" by the audience as long as the illusion is sustained. In "real life," individuals may also intend that those whom they encounter accept that they have a particular kind of personality with specific social and cultural attributes. This may also involve a high degree of conscious intentionality. What is conveyed may, in fact, be either true or false, and Goffman's analysis is an attempt to understand how individuals, or groups of individuals, "define the situation" in everyday life.[33] This kind of analysis can also be applied to the New York leisure class at the turn of the century and, in particular, to the ways in which social aspirants conveyed to each other and to society at large messages of self-definition. Rituals, social practices, and the use of material culture all conveyed expressions about forms of social identity that were class-, race-, and gender-specific. It is therefore possible to ascertain how these "messages" were received by the wider public through examining, *inter alia,* newspaper and magazine articles and other forms of social commentary.

Discourse and Counterdiscourse

In exploring the social experiences of women in New York society at the turn of the century, I have brought together different types of texts (or genres).[34] These texts, which range from newspapers to society magazines, from private correspondence to published memoirs, from contemporary novels to social commentary, all produce social meanings that have shaped my interpretation of social and, especially, gender relations in turn-of-the-century New York. Some texts bear directly on each other, while others are brought together for the first time in this study. What I have attempted to do in making connections between different types of texts is to draw attention to possible ways in which they deal with similar material, to suggest ways in which these texts reinforce or contest each other as well as ways in which they influence social practices. At the same time, social practices influence both the composition, or revision, of texts such as etiquette manuals, which were (and are) constantly updated and reissued, and the production of newspapers, which report, for example, on innovative social practices.

One particular framework I have used in making connections between texts is that of discourse and counterdiscourse.[35] It is, however, important to stress that particular types of texts need not fall neatly into either category—nor necessarily remain there. Not all newspapers, for example, reproduce dominant ideologies all of the time. Nevertheless, the oppositional concepts of discourse and counterdiscourse are useful for the purposes of this study because they can be employed to draw attention to the ways in which some texts take up and circulate dominant meanings about femininity, while others contest those meanings and produce alternatives. But these oppositional concepts are limited in taking account of texts such as newspapers or etiquette manuals, which can, at one time, represent dominant values in U.S. culture and, at another, support changes that have serious repercussions for dominant values. This, however, should come as no great surprise, because dominant values, or dominant discourses, are never homogeneous, let alone fixed, particularly during periods of major social, economic, and cultural transformation. So while etiquette discourse may on the whole have reinscribed traditional meanings of femininity, it also enabled women to negotiate social change and gain improvements in their access to public space. Likewise, society columns usually reinforced the dominant construction of gender relations but also, through publicizing the activities of society women, could lead these same women to be more influential in their milieu and assist them in their efforts to maintain or lay claim to high social status.

And yet for each step forward there seems to have been a corresponding step backward. For example, etiquette manuals strongly encouraged self-surveillance through making readers believe that they were constantly under scrutiny by others. In effect, codes of etiquette placed powerful constraints on women's behavior in public, especially insofar as they reinscribed the dominant nineteenth-century categorization of women as either respectable or fallen. Nineteenth-century American etiquette was predicated upon the concept of respectability, and even though etiquette manuals advised women on how to safeguard their respectability, women still did not have absolute control over the way in which their behavior and appearance were interpreted by others. Indeed, the development of mass-circulation daily newspapers, and of society journalism in particular, extended the process of surveillance because of the capacity of the press to publicize infractions of codes of gentility, resulting in the kind of publicity that could have ramifications far greater than if the transgressor had just been seen by one or two individuals. While society journalism could greatly assist in the promotion of a society hostess's campaign for high status, therefore, it also provided the means for greater surveillance through the activities of reporters and the fact that payment might be made for information.

Women participated on both sides of the debate about femininity and what constituted acceptable genteel behavior. Their opinions were expressed in a variety of text types such as diaries, letters, memoirs, etiquette manuals, and fiction. Those women who were able to articulate their position in print were able to make significant interventions in the generation of meanings about women. Women were not merely "bearers of meaning"; they were also "makers of meaning."[36] One of the most significant interventions came from novelist Edith Wharton, herself a member of New York's social elite, who wrote about New York society at the turn of the century. Inevitably, her work represents certain interests, above all those of what Bourdieu would call the "dominated fraction" within New York society, that grouping that prided itself on its "cultural capital." At the same time, however, Wharton was critical of the society in which she grew up, and she used her skills as a writer of fiction to contest some of the past and contemporary social relations that kept women in a subordinate position. In some respects, therefore, her fiction constitutes a counterdiscourse that challenges the meanings given to femininity and gender relations by the news media and by consumer capitalism in general. And it is significant, moreover, that it was fiction that provided Wharton with the discursive space in which she could challenge dominant discourses. For although some of her novels were best-sellers, which might suggest that she aimed at a popular market, she clearly aspired to being a serious writer and wanted to produce the kinds of novels that would stand for cultural values she held in high esteem. She was not about to participate in the mass culture of women's magazines, newspapers, or popular fiction. And indeed, there are ways in which her literary work provides important insights into the predicament of women in New York's high society.[37]

Chapters 1 and 2 look at the "mechanics" of high society, the rituals involved in demarcating a social elite anxious to distinguish itself from the many hundreds of wealthy families converging on New York City after 1865. The emphasis in these early chapters is upon the period from 1870 to the late 1890s, when Mrs. Astor was an undisputed leader of New York society and social formality was at its peak. Chapter 3 considers the way in which the home was brought into service as a base for the increasingly publicized sociability of New York's leisure class. The remaining three chapters focus on society women and the public world of high society. Chapter 4 expands on issues raised at the beginning of this introduction with regard to the mobility and sexualization of women in public space. Chapter 5 further develops issues of the sexualization of women in the realm of commercialized entertainments. Chapter 6 examines the impact of newspaper publicity upon women leaders in society and considers how they adapted to publicity as a permanent feature of their lives.

1

The Social Calendar

Shortly before midnight on New Year's Eve 1904 the streets around Times Square and Forty-second Street were thronged with merrymakers and revelers. Pouring out of the restaurants and cafés along the Great White Way and emerging from the subway, the crowds converged on Times Square to see the fireworks display that heralded the dawning of the new year. The *New York Times* had recently acquired the land bounded by Broadway, Seventh Avenue, and Forty-second Street and had built a skyscraper to house its expanding operations. The newspaper claimed pioneering status for itself because of the subsequent northward move of commerce and entertainment and praised its owners' foresight in choosing what was to become a central Manhattan location amid theaters, hotels, restaurants, retail stores, and office buildings.[1] In 1907 Adolph Ochs, the publisher of the *New York Times*, set up a "time ball" that would descend down the outside of the Times Building on the stroke of midnight.[2] This new, gaudier commemoration of the new year, one befitting the electrical age, permanently took over from the old tradition of welcoming in the new year to the pealing of the bells at Trinity Church on lower Broadway, and of course the celebration of the new year at Times Square has now become an annual ritual relayed by television to millions of people across the United States.

This shared public celebration of New Year's Eve at Times Square began in the years just after the adoption of standardized time throughout the world. Indeed, this was a celebration of time itself, in Times Square, a location named after a mass-circulation daily newspaper that in its name declared its allegiance to public time. New Year's Eve was commemorated both by ritualistic celebration and by reports in the newspapers that were distributed only a few hours later—even before some of the revelers had crawled into bed. Moreover, because traditionally the passing of the old year was considered to be a time for retrospection, a time for reviewing the year's events, newspapers and weeklies published special editions or sections that brought together accounts of events considered particularly significant.

While New Year's Eve brought New Yorkers from all walks of life together in public celebration, New Year's Day itself was celebrated privately. Up until the early 1880s in New York, the Dutch custom of men calling on women still prevailed. Men would dash around in sleighs all day until late in the evening distributing small gifts. In one Dutch-American household, each male caller was presented at the door with four *nieuwjahrskoeks* (New Year cakes) and, if he called during luncheon or dinner, he was expected to help himself to oyster stew, chicken croquettes, and salad. Each family had its own special recipes for sweets and cakes, but most popular of all with the men were the servings of punch and, for "appreciative older men," glasses of madeira. Some men made at least a hundred calls but "were always ready for another glass to keep out the cold and give strength for more."[3] Keeping open house all day and supplying food and drink to male callers was exhausting for both the hostess and her household. In the 1890s New Year's Eve took precedence as the preferred time for commemoration of the new year, and hotels and restaurants provided venues for its celebration. One New York society columnist suggested that this new fad, which had become "a fixed feature of metropolitan life" by 1907, was perhaps a reaction to the "home celebration of Christmas." On the other hand, it might be "just a fancy to be bohemian, to forget all cares and responsibilities, and pass the most solemn hour of the year amid strangers or in strange surroundings."[4] Whatever the motivation, the celebration of New Year's Eve illustrated an underlying trend in New York's high society to discard rigid gendered roles and private sociability and engage in heterosociability in commercial venues.[5]

This chapter provides a brief overview of the structure and function of New York's social life with regard to the various seasons and rituals that constituted the everyday routine of participants in high society. Particular consideration is given to the way in which social customs and codes of etiquette were invested with authority and the aura of tradition. Women of the *haute bourgeoisie* actively engaged in a busy social round of obligations and events in which they represented their husband's or father's interests. Examination of such activities offers glimpses into the kinds of social practices overlooked in most studies of the New York elite. Parlors, dining rooms, ballrooms, and the opera were social spaces in which gender and class relations were enacted and performed.

The Seasons

Every year on the fifteenth of October Fifth Avenue opened its shutters, unrolled its carpets and hung up its triple layer of window-curtains.

By the first of November this household ritual was over and society had begun to look about and take stock of itself. By the fifteenth the season was in full blast, Opera and theatres were putting forth their new attractions, dinner-engagements were accumulating, and dates for dances being fixed. And punctually at about this time Mrs. Archer always said that New York was very much changed.[6]

The annual New York social calendar developed over the years into a finely detailed schedule of events, of departures and arrivals worthy of a train timetable in the great age of railroads. Maintaining a fixed annual schedule, year in and year out, was a virtue in the eyes of a social leader such as Mrs. Astor. New Yorkers could set their clocks by her movements. Indeed, for most of the years during which Mrs. Astor held sway over the rapidly moving currents of New York society, her rigid adherence to routine provided it with a certain stability, if not predictability. Only the observation of mourning rituals was sufficient excuse for an alteration to Mrs. Astor's program. In 1905, when she was about to give what would be her last ball in her Fifth Avenue home, the *World* paid tribute to Mrs. Astor in a full-page item in its magazine section. In particular, it drew attention to her "amazing system":

> From the day that she married until this Mrs. Astor has been a woman of amazing system. Her dances are always upon Mondays, her state dinners always upon Thursdays. She has had the same butler, Thomas Haig, since 1876. She sails for Europe on the first steamer after Ash Wednesday. She keeps the same apartment in Paris. She returns always in the same week in June. Her Newport villa, Beechwood, is always open on the same date. She comes to town in the same week in October. And so each year is rounded out.[7]

In fact, what Mrs. Astor did and when she did it became benchmarks for New York society.

The mobility afforded by steam travel enabled New Yorkers to spend a season in different parts of the country, if not the world. They moved like migratory birds, in flocks and at certain times of the year. Cold weather in February prompted early departures for points south, especially Florida. Unbearably hot weather in the summer drove businessmen out of the city to seaside resorts to join their families or friends already established there for the season. The advent of the automobile further increased the possibilities of travel, particularly opening up the environs of Manhattan and making popular the "suburban season" at places such as Tuxedo, New York, or Lakewood, New Jersey.

In the 1870s and 1880s the year was basically divided into two main seasons, winter and summer. The winter season was marked by the opening of the opera season, initially at the Academy of Music and then, after 1883, at the Metropolitan Opera House. It was a period of formal entertainments, particularly coming-out receptions for débutante daughters in December and balls and dinners after Christmas. Those in society might remain in town until the summer months, when townhouses were closed and families moved to summer resorts. In the intervening period there was Lent, when entertainments were of a quieter nature and women gathered in each other's houses for sewing circles. After Easter there was a rush of weddings before society scattered to various summer retreats or abroad. By the 1900s and 1910s the New York winter season was foreshortened, with society dispersing early in January for warmer climes. Weddings, accordingly, were brought forward to accommodate the changing patterns of social migration.

Newport was the premier summer resort for much of the period in question. Here New Yorkers rented or owned "cottages" where they would spend two months or more. The scarcity of hotels in Newport afforded them the peace and quiet of a resort without the hustle and bustle of a seaside town readily accessible to a wide range of people—until, that is, the day of the excursionist dawned. According to some society columnists, by the turn of the century Newport's attractions began to pall and other resorts found favor with New York's elite, notably Southampton, Long Island. By the mid-1890s social life in Newport had become so formal that its original attractions as a watering place where one could relax and enjoy gentle recreation, had been marred, for some, by the expectations of society hostesses. One way of getting away from the demands of hostesses desperate for unattached men to make up the numbers in their cotillions was to escape to the Adirondack Mountains.

The establishment of a winter season in New York and a summer season in Newport was a part of the process of centralization and control. It grew out of the increasing concentration of wealthy families in New York after the Civil War, a development related to the rise of New York as the national center of banking and finance and as the headquarters of major business corporations. By establishing a regular program of social events, and thereby guaranteeing the presence of a sufficiently large proportion of the wealthy and well-connected families, social leaders could lay claim to the exercise of power and influence and enhance both their social and economic status. According to one eulogy on the death of Mrs. Astor in 1908 that appeared in a society magazine, her emergence as a social leader had helped to bring order to a "heterogeneous collection of people" and she had "controlled, in a way, the sentiment, beliefs and ideas on social life and customs of a certain number of families and individuals," people who came together frequently. The eulogy continued: "These people had common meeting places both in Winter and Summer; they saw each other frequently, their children grew up together, attended the same schools, and met each other at the same comparatively large balls of the Winter season, such as the Patriarchs and Assemblies, and at smaller dances in half a dozen large private houses."[8]

In this process of defining the social season around the opera, the theater, and formal entertainments in private homes or rented public space, New York society was understood to be aping other metropolitan centers, notably those of western Europe. Society leaders were accused of acquiescing to the standards of effete aristocratic systems and going against the grain of democratic America. Undoubtedly there were strong European influences in the way that New Yorkers shaped and defined their social entertainments, partly because Parisian and London societies constituted models for elite formation and behavior, and partly because New York's elite was keen to establish parity with European metropolitan elites.

As previously noted, Mrs. Burton Kingsland asserted that it was "the stock reproach" of Europeans, in refusing to accredit American elites with equal status, to point to the absence of an aristocracy in the United States.[9] From a traditional European perspective, leisured gentlemen were a prerequisite for the existence of an aristocracy, although by the late nineteenth century even this requirement was under revision in London and Paris. By comparison, men in New York's high society were, by and large, active businessmen and professionals. Yet it would appear from the scheduling of formal entertainments and the seasonal shifts that few concessions were made to the demands made by men's work. In fact, as one society columnist put it with reference to cotillions, the work schedules of men were distinctly incompatible with the social calendar:

> The truth is that the men are beginning to find out that the pleasure of going to bed at four or five o'clock and getting up at 7:30 is very much overrated, and they wisely stay at home. A few foolish women, in order to be fashionable, began a couple of years ago, to arrive at 12 o'clock, and other equally foolish women took to copying them. . . . Nine men out of ten are in business or follow a profession, and must be at their offices about nine, or at latest, ten o'clock; yet the women expect them to dance until daybreak and to enjoy it.[10]

In the 1870s and 1880s New York society women persisted nevertheless in their adoption of polite European conventions in order to press home their social claims and to complement their husband's business interests, however awkwardly.[11] This meant, for example, that the optimum time for mixed sociability was after business hours, and, accordingly, dinners and dances became important ways of bringing people together to consolidate social and business ties. The conjunction of business interests with formal sociability in New York was not lost on those observing the metropolitan scene. As one columnist alleged, being a member of the exclusive committee that put on the annual Patriarchs series of subscription balls "entitles you to the privilege of inviting any business acquaintances you may have from whom you think you can extract a few dollars in a purely 'business connection,' in return for the invitation."[12]

The incompatibility of high society with business hours was, essentially, a conflict between public and private time. Men's activities were governed by an encroaching sense of public time dictated by the workplace, whereas women's time continued to be governed by the reproductive life cycle and the traditional construction of women's lives as revolving around family concerns. Emile Durkheim's sociological distinction between "private time" and "time in general," that is, time that has a social origin as opposed to the individual experience of time, is instructive here. Durkheim argued that the division of time into days, weeks, months, and years corresponded to the periodic recurrence of rites, feasts, and public ceremonies, and that these established rhythms came to be uniformly imposed as a framework for all temporal activities. "A calendar," Durkheim claimed in 1912, "expresses the rhythm of the collective activities, while at the same time its function is to assure their regularity."[13] It is clear, therefore, how broad acceptance of a social calendar enabled high society in New York and elsewhere to function successfully while, at the same time, claiming authority over certain activities and denying sanction to others.

With the passage of time, society gradually made more concessions to the demands of business while also laying claim to both public time and public space. The formality of high society in the era of Mrs. Astor and the Four Hundred did not sit well with the businessman, and complaints about the absence, or lack, of men at balls reached a peak by the mid-1890s. Subsequently, informal entertainments, such as country-house weekends, became popular both during the winter season and at other times of the year. Heterosociability in general was promoted by a more mobile society, with the advent of the automobile enabling men to motor out into the country for the weekend and giving women greater access to places of commercialized entertainment in the city. On the other hand, greater mobility also meant that high society became more decentralized, so the traditions and rituals that had once helped to give cohesion to a fast-expanding urban elite in the 1870s and 1880s were weakened.

The Winter Season
The development of a regular calendar of events, which those with social aspirations were expected to attend, was one way of establishing traditions at a time of social upheaval and unprecedented social mobility. The annual repetition of activities helped to assert both order and control at a time of flux. Attending the opera, for example, on opening night and thereafter on Friday nights for the rest of the season was a key social activity that helped to define those who were members of the inner circle. As a cultural activity implying that those involved had a knowledge of music and were well educated, the opera conveyed a con-

siderable range of cultural significance. Henry James captured the onerous burden placed upon the opera in New York:

> The Opera . . . plays its part as the great vessel of social salvation, the comprehensive substitute for all other conceivable vessels; the *whole* social consciousness thus clambering into it, under stress, as the whole community crams into the other public receptacles, the desperate cars of the Subway or the vast elevators of the tall buildings. The Opera, indeed, as New York enjoys it, one promptly perceives, is worthy, musically and picturesquely, of its immense function; the effect of it is splendid, but one has none the less the oddest sense of hearing it, as an institution, groan and creak, positively almost split and crack, with the extra weight thrown upon it—the weight that in worlds otherwise arranged is artfully scattered, distributed over all the ground.[14]

The social importance of the opera was recognized by the old elite, who tried to restrict access to the boxes at the Academy of Music, New York's premier auditorium for opera during the 1870s. But the small and incommodious Academy of Music, with its meager eighteen boxes and its stubborn patrons, was soon superseded. A powerful new elite group of corporate financiers and industrial entrepreneurs, including men such as J. P. Morgan, built a much larger opera house, the Metropolitan, with three tiers of thirty-six boxes each —more than enough to satisfy contemporary demand. The spaciousness of the new auditorium enabled the opera to maintain its centrality to the social life of New York throughout the period.

December became firmly established as the month for coming-out receptions for débutante daughters, while the winter season "proper," centered around large, formal entertainments, commenced after the new year. During this period, dinners and assemblies featured prominently as forums for introducing daughters into society. The Patriarchs' Balls, one of the best known series of subscription balls in the late nineteenth century, attracted mothers with daughters to bring out. The Junior Cotillions were also popular for débuts. Various subscription balls were organized as a series of two or three meetings, the first usually occurring in December and subsequent ones after New Year's. They provided a public forum for the introduction of daughters into society and were particularly welcomed by those of new wealth who preferred such public venues to optimize opportunities for making social contacts.

The annual ball held by Mrs. Astor was another attempt to establish a tradition and provide a focal point for society.[15] It was regarded as marking the climax of the season and generally took place on either the first or second Monday in January. However, when Mrs. Astor moved her residence uptown to 842 Fifth Avenue from Fifth Avenue and Thirty-fourth Street to make way for the building of the original Waldorf-Astoria, she was able to increase the space for her entertainments because she could throw open the adjoining doors to her son's mansion, thus creating an enormous ballroom unsurpassed by any other in Manhattan. As a private ball, Mrs. Astor's "dinner and dance" assisted in the shaping and defining of the innermost circles of high society. But the one event that cut across coteries and sets was the Charity Ball. This public ball, held in early February, signaled the end of the winter season proper and the onset of Lent, which began, of course, officially on Ash Wednesday.

Social events during Lent were far less public, less "general," and less showy than those during the winter season. The Lenten period was a time when society took stock of itself while enjoying some respite from the daily, if not nightly, formal entertainments of the winter season. In 1895, with tongue in cheek, the *New York Times* society columnist marked the change in society's attitude toward the penitential interlude: "The sackcloth of old has been bundled into old trunks and the ashes have been swept away in order to clear the floor for modern diversions." Following the cessation of formal entertainments, to be sure, the usual outward observance of Lent was maintained, but

> one need not employ opera glasses with magnifying lenses to see that other doors than those of churches swing on easy hinges during Lent. In fact, society—that chameleonlike contingent—regards Lent more from a hygienic than a religious standpoint. Following a season of midnight suppers and early morning dances, Lent affords forty days of rest much needed by stomach and limb; but since pleasure is the order of the day, and the love of it has tuned up every nerve and fibre to the highest pitch, rest without recreation is intense weariness to the flesh, and a program of gayety is prepared highly satisfactory to those who are fasting.[16]

Social events during Lent were accorded legitimacy on the grounds of fundraising for various charitable enterprises. Such causes seemed to justify society's enjoying itself by essentially carrying on with the same rituals that had marked the winter season. Likewise, during the First World War, large social events continued to occur, so that the season was barely different from former years, but justification for such conspicuous enjoyment was always provided in the form of fund-raising, either for some group of orphans in war-torn France or Belgium, or for impoverished groups at home.

The Summer Season
For years Newport had been a popular watering place for southerners, but it was not until after the Civil War that the resort entered the most conspicuous phase of its social career. In the 1870s more and more New York millionaires built their summer "cottages" along Bellevue and Ocean View Avenues. The flamboyant architecture of Newport's summer palaces deliberately invoked a

European aristocratic past, with the copying of Italian Renaissance palaces, French châteaux, and English Gothic structures. Despite the grandiose marking of New Yorkers' presence in Newport, it was women and children who predominated in the summer colony. Newport did have the advantage, however, of being close enough to New York City to enable businessmen to visit for an extended weekend if unable, or unwilling, to tear themselves away either from their work or from the pleasures of the city.

The lack of hotels in Newport helped to keep away those who might have come just to see the passing show, thereby maintaining a fairly exclusive environment for the enjoyment of summer pleasures. The summer colonists jealously guarded their privacy, particularly at Bailey's Beach, where changing rooms could only be purchased at a cost of $1,500. Photography was not allowed at Bailey's Beach, but in 1902 the *New York World*'s Sunday magazine broke with this ban and displayed a double-page spread of photographs of "millionaires and their families in the round of their pleasures."[17] Part of the relief of being out of Manhattan was to be away from the detailed scrutiny of the crowds, but even by the ocean the wealthy could not relax entirely. Indeed, for some, relaxation did not figure at all, for standards of propriety, decorum, and exclusiveness had to be maintained, so that a pervasive formality was part of social life in Newport. Florence Howe Hall, daughter of Julia Ward Howe, described Newport's summertime *moeurs* for readers of the *Ladies Home Journal* and in doing so emphasized both how tasteful the display of refinement and culture and how expensive the social life in the resort was. She also pointed out that Newport residents did not bathe at Easton's, the public beach, as they found "the publicity of the bathing beach . . . very unpleasant . . . especially as they not only have to endure being stared at by all their friends, but by an army of people of all sorts—including domestics and Negroes—some of whom one would rather prefer not to meet in the water, even though one may be thoroughly Democratic in principle."[18] This illustrates what Brook Thomas has identified about published views on privacy in the late nineteenth century, namely that some Americans felt uneasy about defending privacy for fear of sounding undemocratic.[19] Nevertheless, Hall's statement affirms that taboos against mingling across class and racial lines were implicated in the desire of the wealthy for privacy. In fact, E. L. Godkin, editor of *The Nation*, made this perfectly clear in 1890 in his contribution to the debate on the right to privacy, when he claimed that "privacy is a distinctly modern product, one of the luxuries of civilization, which is not only unsought for but unknown in primitive or barbarous societies."[20]

Newport had its own social routine. In 1905 the *New York Times*'s Sunday magazine section offered readers its version of "How Newport Spends Its Day." It asked whether Newport's routine was merely "a repetition of the treadmill of society—one tiring round of luncheons, dinners and dances." The article informed the uninitiated (including potential sightseers) as to what the fashionable venues were called and when society frequented them, providing such examples as Bailey's Beach between 11:00 A.M. and 1:00 P.M. and the casino prior to noon. Informal luncheons were said to be the "delight" of Newport matrons and to take place between 1:30 and 2:30 P.M., followed by a nap and then some vigorous activity, such as tennis or squash at the Casino, yachting, or polo—to work up an appetite for tea at 5:00 P.M. Between 6:00 and 7:00 P.M. was the time for promenading in carriages, followed by an hour in which to rest and get ready for dinner. After-dinner entertainments included dances, moonlight sails, or drives for the young, while there were always bridge parties for the less energetic.[21]

The fragmentation in the 1890s and 1900s of New York's society into competing sets was manifested in the diversity of places that prominent families chose to spend their summers. The development of Long Island, and particularly of Southampton, with its country homes and exclusive golf and country clubs, attracted numerous people away from Newport. In the early nineteenth century Saratoga had been popular among the social elite of New York and the South, but in the post–Civil War years it was favored mostly by the racing set, including prominent New Yorkers the Whitneys. The Spencer Trasks and other society figures had homes there, but, with its capacious hotel facilities, Saratoga was too democratic a resort for the likes of people who preferred the exclusive ambience of Newport. Nevertheless, the peak of the August racing season was well attended by high society.

The height of the summer season in Newport found many New Yorkers getting away from it all among the mountains and lakes of the Adirondacks. Indeed, the Adirondacks, with their fine fishing resorts, became a mecca for the sportsman. Camping and living rough had its attractions for both men and women, and for those preferring something less rugged, there were lodges and summer homes that provided the basic comforts and amenities of urban dwelling. Formality had no place here, enabling men and women to don casual clothes. The new vogue of the "outdoors life" at the turn of the century was manifested in a number of different ways, from al fresco dining or garden parties to sports such as golf, tennis, skating, and tobogganing, depending on the season. Country houses within easy reach of New York City by either railroad, boat, or automobile permitted the prolonged enjoyment of this outdoors life. Men could stay at their clubs in town on weeknights and come up on weekends.

The Suburban Season

Symptomatic of this enthusiasm for the outdoors was the development of a "suburban" season in the autumn. In this connection, the chief social centers were Lenox, Massachusetts, and Tuxedo. Lenox already had an established summer colony of families with country homes nestled among the tree-studded Berkshires, and, just as at Newport, there were some who stayed for much longer than the summer season. There were some formal social gatherings in the form of dances, but the emphasis was on the enjoyment of country sports such as hunting, shooting, fishing, riding, cycling, and swimming. Stockbridge was another popular Berkshires resort. There the U.S. diplomat and lawyer Joseph Choate had a summer home that had been designed by Stanford White. Indeed, with its front door opening onto a large hall that was utilized as a living room, the interior design of the house embodied the new fashion of country living. On the other hand, the large country estates along the Hudson River, such as those owned by the Ogden Millses and the Frederick W. Vanderbilts, were much more formal in design. These homes were also close enough to the city for English-style country-house weekends. For some, such estates were their main residential base, with smaller establishments maintained in town. Tuxedo Park, founded by Pierre Lorillard IV in 1886, was a popular private "resort" just north of Manhattan. It brought together just over twenty families, each with a "cottage" on five-acre sections within a six-hundred-thousand-acre private estate.[22] Elite New Yorkers took up residence mostly in the autumn, through to Thanksgiving, and again during the midwinter holiday at Christmas and New Year's. Dinners and dances were held at the Tuxedo Club. Although well established while the railroad was the main form of travel, Tuxedo came into its own with the advent of the automobile.

European Seasons

Long before the "jet set" came into being, high society was a remarkably mobile entity, and with ongoing improvements in transportation, the social calendar was divided up into smaller segments of time to be spent in different places. Americans moved around Europe enjoying social seasons at different locations, in London and Paris in the spring or in Rome and on the French Riviera in the winter. For some New Yorkers a common itinerary was to travel to Europe in late spring to participate in the Parisian or London seasons, spend the summer months touring Italy or visiting a German spa such as Baden Baden, and then return to Paris in early autumn to pick up their orders from the ultrafashionable couturiers in the rue de la Paix, cross the Channel, and embark at Liverpool on a steamer headed back to New York.[23] There were colonies of long-term American residents as well as transient Americans in most of the fashionable cities and resorts in western Europe. Americans were integrated into London society more than in any other European city because of strong kinship ties created by the large number of transatlantic marriages.[24]

Daytime Rituals

Just as the year was divided into social seasons, so too was the day divided into discrete temporal segments for particular activities. Daytime social rituals were predominantly homosocial, as the common pattern was for men to socialize downtown or in their clubs while women entertained at home. Women's establishment of a daily routine reduced the unpredictability of life; it lessened the chances for embarrassment such as might result if a call was made on someone when they were likely to be dressed for housework. Society women conformed to a large degree to such daily routines, encouraged as they were by etiquette and household manuals that advocated routines. They learned to advertise the hours when they were "at home" in order to control undesired interruptions. They left cards with their friends indicating which afternoon of the week they were "at home," an expression that euphemistically implied that they were available to callers. Some women even advertised their hours in newspapers.

Three of the everyday social rituals that dominated women's lives for much of this period merit particular attention: luncheons, teas, and, most important of all, calling. As an occasion for female sociability, luncheon provided women with opportunities for networking, whether for social or philanthropic purposes. In addition, elaborate luncheons in private dwellings served to establish, or maintain, a woman's claim to being "in" society. Like luncheons, teas were a predominantly female social ritual, but because they took place in the late afternoon, there was always the added possibility of entertaining male guests. Teas could serve a number of different purposes and encapsulated a wide variety of different social occasions. They could be large entertainments, such as the formal débutante tea, or more intimate gatherings, such as "the cozy fireside tea," which was advocated as something more conducive to male attendance because of its informality. Hotels and restaurants, such as Sherry's, began to realize the potential of this female market and encouraged women to partake in the tea hour at their establishments.

But of all of the everyday rituals of the winter season, calling was the most commonly practiced form of female sociability. Women spent an inordinate amount of time calling and leaving cards; indeed, some women allegedly had visiting lists containing over five hundred names, which meant that some form of method had to be introduced to ensure that social blunders did not occur.[25] Prominent hostesses therefore made use of methods associated more with the world of business than with that of society, employing secretaries to handle their correspondence and organize their daily routine. Prior to the advent of the telephone, when it was not possible to ascertain immediately whether someone was available or not, the social networking performed by women in maintaining contacts with friends and kin was voluminous. It involved both letter writing and calling which were fundamental means of communication in the preelectronic age. It was generally understood that formal calls were made between 3:00 and 5:00 P.M. and then only for fifteen minutes, with men being permitted to call a little later, or on Sundays, in order to accommodate their business schedules.

In fact, calling was central to the maintenance of social networks. All invitations to private entertainments and all major changes in one's life's circumstances (for example, getting engaged, returning from an extended trip out of town, returning from a honeymoon, and so on) required personal calls. Calling was an elaborate and highly formal ritual governed by myriads of rules that were detailed and explained in etiquette manuals. Both the space devoted to the fine art of calling and leaving cards and the ever-increasing intricacies of calling etiquette reflect the social importance of this everyday ritual in women's lives. Nevertheless, it was seen by some as wasteful: "The system of calling is one that wastes much time, and is rather senseless. But there seems to be no other institution to take its place; and as a code of signals it has its uses. Without it, it is difficult to see how lists would be recruited for invitations, or any entertaining done in order."[26] When a married woman called she left her husband's card as well as her own, and this was understood to imply that the husband was participating in the courtesy of the call. Mothers would also leave the cards of sons. As Mrs. Frank Learned explained in her manual *The Etiquette of New York Today* (1906), a husband "is not supposed to have leisure for calling and is exempt from such duties, but his existence is thus recognized socially."[27] However, Mrs. Burton Kingsland, a frequent contributor to etiquette manuals and to the *Ladies Home Journal*, was forthright in her opinion on this matter:

> There are those who scoff at the custom of leaving the husband's card, and call it senseless, alleging that it is absurd that when a man is at his office his card should imply that he has been accompanying his wife on a round of social calls. It deceives no one, but neither is it intended to. It is merely a rather stupid attempt to preserve a married man's social recognition among his own and his wife's acquaintances, since nothing is expected of him in the matter of calls.[28]

The introduction of the telephone in the 1880s did not immediately displace the activity of calling. Social conservatives regarded the telephone as intrusive and threatening. In fact, one etiquette manual stressed that the use of the telephone for anything other than an informal engagement was "hopelessly vulgar" and should be the "last resort."[29] Whereas domestic servants and hallways had served as buffers between the outside world and the private domestic world, telephones gave people direct access to the interior of the home (though of course servants could be, and were, required to answer the phone and directed to say, as before, that their mistress was or was not "at home.") It was, moreover, the growing trend toward informality in social relations and the relaxation of formal etiquette that relieved women of the burdens of calling, although clearly the use of the telephone and the automobile reduced the amount of time that had to be spent in this way and greatly accelerated communication. Irrespective of the introduction of the telephone, calling was beginning to diminish in importance in the 1890s because of competing demands on women's time and because of the trend toward more informal communication.

Nightlife

In contrast to daytime social events in New York, events that largely revolved around women's sociability, most forms of nighttime entertainment were attended by both women and men. Up until at least the turn of the century, nightlife during New York's winter season was dominated by the subscription ball, the opera, and elaborate private dinners.

The subscription ball was a veritable institution of American high society, peaking in popularity during the first half of the period under review. It constituted a highly formalized form of entertainment the organization of which was carefully controlled, such control denoting an attempt to impose exclusivity and a rigid demarcation of social boundaries. The popularity of the subscription ball can be attributed to the rapid growth of New York society and the need for large venues where dancing and dining could be effected in comfort and, above all, in luxury.[30] New York City's most famous subscription ball was the Patriarchs' Ball, which dominated the metropolitan scene between the 1870s and the late 1890s. The standard procedure for such an event was for a group of subscribers to come together and plan for either one ball or for a series of them, whereby each subscriber would put up a sum of money and then be allotted a specified number of invitations. This sharing of the expense and organization allowed for large "general" entertainments, as they were called. Very few individuals had either the resources or facilities for large entertainments, and the subscription ball played an important part in giving cohesion to the social elite at a time of expansion.[31] The Patriarchs' Ball began with a committee of twenty-five men in 1872[32] and had a female equivalent in the Ladies' Assemblies, a series of winter balls run by a committee of women.[33] The most popular venues for balls were Delmonico's, Sherry's, and the Waldorf-Astoria Hotel. By the 1900s, however, newspapers widely reported that society had broken up into cliques, with more than one large ball being given on the same night—something that broke with New York tradition—and by 1920 only the Charity Ball had survived as the one general entertainment that still brought the various factions together. However, the Charity Ball was a public event, unlike the subscription balls which could be regarded as "semipublic" in the sense that they took place in a hired public space but guests were admitted by invitation only.

Up until the 1910s a regular feature of both subscription and private balls was the cotillion or german. This was a formal dance, a kind of formal parade, with set figures, planned and rehearsed well in advance. General dancing would prevail until midnight, at which point a supper was served and then the cotillion would begin. "Favors," consisting of small gifts of such things as ribbons, purses, or cigarette holders, were distributed by the dancers to those seated around the ballroom. Some favors were exceedingly elaborate and costly, having been imported from Europe. Details of these favors almost always appeared the next day in the press or in the following Sunday's papers.

Throughout the period from 1870 to 1920, the opera and the theater were the two main commercial venues for nighttime heterosociability. The opera had been central to the development of New York's high society in the latter half of the nineteenth century, but from the 1870s onward, the institution was a contested site. On the one hand, there was a determined effort by New York's elite, as well as by impresarios and conductors, to sacralize the opera as a high-culture form to be enjoyed exclusively by disciplined, informed, and socially homogeneous audiences.[34] On the other hand, there was a struggle between the older and newer socioeconomic elites over access to the boxes at the Academy of Music, New York's premier auditorium for opera, because boxes provided a forum for high society to "perform the obligatory rituals of public display."[35] Attendance at the Academy on Monday and Friday, the fashionable nights, bestowed distinction and announced one's class affiliation and one's access to material wealth and cultural knowledge. The fashionable arrived late and left early, women in expensive ball gowns and jewelry clearly announcing the main priority of their evening's entertainment. Women's appearance in "shimmering fabrics" and décolletage both emphasized their sexuality and testified to men's wealth and power. It was customary, furthermore, for débutantes to attend the opera before going on to private balls. The opera was thereby incorporated into the rituals of the marriage market and the processes that reproduced class.

Dining also became a key social ritual in the development of New York's high society. Private dinners were one of the most important forms of sociability for conferring social acceptance and cementing social bonds. In old New York the home had been a significant center for maintaining social, business, and kinship networks, and dinners had therefore played a key role in sustaining and strengthening such ties. Edith Wharton described her parents' social life at that time as "mild and leisurely" and as centering around "stately and ceremonious" or "intimate and sociable" dinners.[36] Dinners functioned as access rituals for newcomers, who were confronted with the intricacies of seating arrangements, tableware, and multiple courses as well as rules governing introductions, conversation, and leave-taking. The well-known etiquette authority Mrs. Sherwood extolled the delights of dining at home, delights that were all too often glossed over by busy men who bolted down their food instead of engaging in the sociability afforded by a table of carefully selected guests. A sorry sight were the "hard-worked, rich men in America," "bored to death by the gilded and over-burdened splendour of their wives' dinners," who sat like "poor dyspeptics" unable to eat. In an effort to make dinners appeal to both men and women, she proclaimed that "dinners are intended to be recreations, and recreations of inestimable value. The delightful contrast that they offer to the labours of the day, the pleasant, innocent triumph they afford to the hostess . . . all this refreshes the tired man of affairs and invigorates every creature."[37] For Mrs. Sherwood, then, there was a fine art to entertaining, something totally missed by those who thought that a good dinner consisted of sending a check to Delmonico's "for a heavy feed" and putting on a "sumptuous" display.[38]

The concern expressed by social conservatives such as Mrs. Sherwood about society's emphasis on display and outward appearance was a response to the transformation of elite social life into a more public affair during the 1880s and 1890s. Many of the forms of sociability long practiced by old New York had by then moved out of the home to more public venues, thus allowing for large-scale entertainments. Central to this transformation was Delmonico's restaurant and ballroom, which were heavily utilized by fashionable society for key social events such as the Patriarchs' Ball. Between 1876 and 1897 Delmonico's occupied premises on Twenty-sixth Street opposite Madison Square, extending its facilities to meet the recent demand for large, elegant venues for dining and dancing. It was during this period of New York's social history that Delmonico's was closely associated with Mrs. Astor and the Four Hundred, and therefore with the era of formality. After 1897, however, when social life was becoming more informal, it had serious competitors, notably the Waldorf-Astoria Hotel, and had to relocate in that year to Fifth Avenue and Forty-fourth Street in order to continue attracting clientele from the upper circles of New York society.[39]

From the mid-1890s on, New York's high society had begun to experiment with a different kind of nightlife, one that was confined neither to the home nor to large general entertainments. It was conducted, moreover, with a keen eye for opportunities for display. Uptown restaurants favored by the fashionable elite tapped into and advanced this desire for display. Indeed, Lloyd Morris credits the Waldorf-Astoria Hotel, which opened in 1897, with bringing about "profound changes in the tastes, manners and customs of Americans." The Palm Garden was its premier restaurant, for which formal evening attire was required, and according to Morris, a table there was coveted as much by "the rich and well born" as an opera box at the Metropolitan. Leading up to the restaurant was a three-hundred-foot-long corridor lined with "luxurious chairs and sofas," aptly known as "Peacock Alley," where the public could survey in comfort the promenade of the rich and famous on their way to dine.[40] Once seated, diners remained on public view because the walls of the restaurant were made of glass, constituting therefore a huge, live, windowlike display. Meanwhile, floor-to-ceiling mirrors offered patrons an opportunity to see their fellow diners.[41] "Here," as Henry James commented in 1907, "was a conception of publicity *as* the vital medium organized with the authority with which the American genius for organization . . . alone could organize it."[42] Indeed, Lewis Erenberg has argued that the hotel's proprietor, George C. Boldt, "engineered the growing emergence of the wealthy from the sanctity of their private homes to the public opulence of his hotel dining rooms" and encouraged the wealthy to pursue a more public social life. Boldt was not without rivals or imitators; a whole host of sumptuous restaurants—such as Martin's, Maxim's, Rector's, and Shanley's—sprang up in the 1890s and 1900s along the Great White Way and around Times Square.[43]

In 1895 the *New York Times* published a series of articles investigating why so many people were dining out in restaurants and clubs. Prominent socialite Chauncey Depew put it down to the fact that many families could quite simply not afford to keep a French chef, butler, and housekeeper—something that required an annual income of $100,000—and so it was easier for those people who needed "to reciprocate the attentions" they had received in society to do so at the Waldorf or Delmonico's.[44] Louis Sherry, the famous restaurateur, claimed that "home dinners" took too much time and trouble and that most Americans did not know what a good dinner was anyway.[45] And Laurence McCormick of the Waldorf attributed the frequent visits of New Yorkers to large hotels and restaurants to a desire for change. Women, in particular, he said, "come to see and be seen. Possibly they may have new gowns which they like to wear."[46] A common thread that runs through much of the women's commentary quoted in these *Times* articles is that New Yorkers were becoming "homeless." This term was used to signify the lack of time spent in the home. Mrs. Russell Sage, wife of a New York millionaire, was quoted as saying: "I shall be sorry if we, as a race, get to living in the homeless way that some people do, going to a restaurant for this and a hotel for that."[47] References to home-lessness were still appearing in newspaper articles on society ten years later. In 1905 the *New York World* published the evening schedule of the "homeless rich," those who lived in apartments and went around all night from one restaurant to the next, eating one course in each of them. The published sched-ule, or menu, began with oysters at Martin's, followed by consommé at the Waldorf, fish at Sherry's, roast duck at Delmonico's, an unnamed course at the Café Beaux Arts, and dessert at François's, above the Garrick Theater. Such people were said to live in "gilded dyspepsia mills."[48]

The opening up of fashionable restaurants in the vicinity of Broadway and Times Square after 1890 signaled a more significant change in patterns of high-class heterosociability. To begin with, the bird-and-bottle suppers in Broadway restaurants had, in the main, brought together society or wealthy men with actresses, not elite women, so that when society women began to encroach upon this "male" territory, it was considered "very fast" to do so. Even as late as the 1910s a society magazine had found it newsworthy to report that society leader Mrs. Tessie Oelrichs had been seen dining noisily with another woman and two men, to whom they were not related, at a little "bohemian" Italian café in Greenwich Village, an establishment said to be frequented by "artists and models, musicians, and milliners." The women were described as having worn black gowns while the men had been in ordinary business clothes, the implication being that the men were of a lower social class.[49] The fact that society reporters very rarely mentioned it when married society men were seen dining with actresses from popular musical comedies makes it clear that a double standard was applied to women in public space after dark. For even though there was a greater likelihood of society men engaging in extramarital liaisons outside their social class than there was of society women doing so, the potential for marital infidelity is inferred by the mere remarking of Mrs. Oelrichs's presence in a "bohemian" restaurant. The correspondence of the high-society débutante Elsie Clews contains letters from Stanford White, a man who was known to enjoy late suppers with actresses and who was one of the most notorious men about town at the time. Several of these letters refer to arrangements for dinner parties, some at fashionable restaurants like Martin's, others at White's tower apartment at Madison Square Garden. Among the letters alluding to a "Tower dinner" on April Fool's Day is a reference to the difficulties that one of Elsie's unmarried friends, Helen Ripley Benedict, was having with her parents. White writes that Helen's parents "are on to the April first racket and won't let her come; but the shindig will take place as soon as she can elude their vigilance and make another date."[50] Elsie herself had to negotiate with her mother ways of being able to spend time with Stanford White, and this usually involved setting up parties with friends from her own social set.

At around this time, then, society women "played with their identity" in new ways, exploring the boundaries of bourgeois respectability in places where they might be mistaken for prostitutes.[51] This is implied in Edith Wharton's novel *The Custom of the Country* (1913). The female protagonist, Undine Spragg, is portrayed as craving crowds and as particularly enjoying "the image of her own charm mirrored in the general admiration." Her "conception of enjoyment," as her second husband, Ralph, discovers to his cost, is "publicity, promiscuity—the band, the banners, the crowd, the close contact of covetous impulses." Parisian life appeals especially to Undine: the dressmakers, "the crowded lunches at fashionable restaurants," people sipping tea at sunset "on a crowded terrace above the Seine," dinners at the Nouveau Luxe or Café de Paris, after-theater suppers in a lamp-hung restaurant in the Bois, or "a tumultuous progress through the midnight haunts where 'ladies' were not supposed to show themselves, and might consequently taste the thrill of being occasionally taken for their opposites."[52] In Wharton's novel, then, crowded spaces of leisure and amusement not only are represented as socially promiscuous, with ample opportunities for the display of wealth to a broadly constituted spectatorship, but are also potentially areas for sexual promiscuity. But Paris is not the only city where wealthy men indulge their sexual appetites by crossing class lines. Earlier in the novel, when Undine is at the Metropolitan Opera House, the New York socialite Peter Van Degen suggests to her that they get together for "a jolly little dinner" at the Café Martin and "a cheerful show afterward." However, as soon as Undine learns that Mrs. Van Degen will not be a member of the party because she doesn't go to restaurants, her sense of respectability is profoundly insulted: "If Mrs. Van Degen didn't go to restaurants, why had he supposed that *she* would?"[53] Sex and class are portrayed as intertwined.

"New Year's Day"

Although old New York is represented by Edith Wharton in her fiction as preferable to the sham society that displaced it, it is nevertheless portrayed with ambivalence. In her collection of four novellas, *Old New York* (1924), Wharton focuses on the ultraconservative society of bourgeois New York. This is a society that rigidly distinguishes between what is respectable and moral and what is not, and therefore has little compassion either for those who fail to follow conventions or who fall on hard times. Financial misfortune is regarded as a moral failing comparable to financial misdemeanor. As for a woman who transgresses the strict code of female chastity, there is little space for rehabilitation if she is seen in the wrong place at the wrong time. Looking back, shortly after the First World War, on the middle decades of the nineteenth century, Wharton was acutely aware of the historical nature of her enterprise. As she told her close friend Bernard Berenson, the art dealer: "Before the war you could write fiction without indicating the period, the present being assumed. The war has put an end to that for a long time, and everything will soon have to be timed with reference to it. In other words, the historical novel with all its vices will be the only possible form for fiction."[54] Looking back from an even greater temporal distance, at the time of writing her memoirs in the 1930s, Wharton thought of how the "little low-studded rectangular New York" of her youth, "hidebound in its deadly uniformity of mean ugliness," had become "as much a vanished city as Atlantis" and how its "social organization" had been "swept to oblivion with the rest."[55] In both *The Age of Innocence* (1921) and *Old New York* Wharton attempted to recapture something of that lost city and to reevaluate the present in view of the transformation of American society in the previous fifty years, and especially with regard to the historical chasm created by the First World War.

If traditionally the ringing in of the new year and ringing out of the old was supposed to prompt the act of retrospection, then the title of the last novella in *Old New York*, "New Year's Day," reinforces the overall intention of the four stories as a commemoration of the passage of time. The old New York of

Wharton's fiction is shown as having roots in the Anglo-Dutch colonial past when English and Dutch settlers came to the New World to make money. The descendants of these colonists are portrayed as having fought in the Revolution and established their fortunes in shipbuilding, the seafaring trade, and banking.[56] The story's reference to the Dutch custom of celebrating New Year's Day is intended to evoke this colonial past, and the fall of the custom into disuse by the late nineteenth century is yet another marker of the passing of an age.

"New Year's Day" opens with a family reunion at the Parrett household on West Twenty-third Street. Grandmamma Parrett has given up the tradition of receiving on New Year's Day but refuses to join the rest of society in its exodus out of the city. Instead she gathers her extended family around her for luncheon. As if to symbolize the elder Parretts's clinging to old ways, their house is no longer in a fashionable residential district, fashion having moved "Parkward," while its chocolate-colored façade overlooks the "noble edifice of white marble" of the once-fashionable Fifth Avenue Hotel. While the Parretts are lunching, the hotel catches fire and the whole family rushes to watch the event from the drawing room window. As a time of family celebration, New Year's Day is an unlikely time for an adulterous couple to meet at a downtown hotel. It is therefore the incongruity of seeing Lizzie Hazeldean, a married society woman, in a "conspicuously plain" dress outside the Fifth Avenue Hotel in the middle of the day next to a well-known "man of the world," which confirms for the Parrett-Wesson clan that an illicit affair is being conducted under their noses. In fact, it transpires that Lizzie Hazeldean is a marginal figure in New York society. She is the penniless daughter of a disgraced preacher, "Rector of a fashionable New York church," but has been rehabilitated through her adoption by one of her father's rich parishioners, Mrs. Mant. Indeed, she has been "rescued" a second time, on this occasion by a young lawyer, Charles Hazeldean, a nephew of Mrs. Mant's, just as Mrs. Mant was about to throw Lizzie out of the house. Lizzie accepted Hazeldean's offer of marriage and married him in haste. Such circumstances have already consigned Lizzie to the margins of old New York, and on seeing her exit the Fifth Avenue Hotel in the company of Henry Prest, the Wesson-Parrett clan is quick to assume adultery has already taken place.[57]

The novella goes on to tell of the death of Charles Hazeldean from a weak heart soon after the day of the hotel fire and of the ostracization of his wife from society. It is revealed, however, that adultery was not the "sin" Lizzie had committed; rather, she had prostituted herself in order to get money to help her ailing husband, whom she loved deeply. In the genteel formulation of the male narrator: "She had known of no way of earning money except by her graces." Lizzie herself does not mince words when she tells Prest: "You thought I was a lovelorn mistress; and I was only an expensive prostitute." Prest rejects this self-definition: "Mistress! Prostitute! Such words were banned. No one reproved coarseness of language in women more than Henry Prest." Worse still for him is the implication that he has been "duped" into thinking she loved him. "Oh, well, yes: a woman *can*—so easily!" says Lizzie. Prest still offers to marry her because he has compromised her, but Lizzie rejects the opportunity to "regularize" their "attachment" and chooses "cold celibacy" for the rest of her life.[58]

In opting for a lonely widowhood in the *demimonde,* Lizzie gives proof of her love for her husband. More important, however, she chooses independence—something hard to acquire for a woman in her situation. The precariousness of her position is brought home to her first of all as Mrs. Mant's ward, when this lady falls out with her. In marrying Charles, she remains a dependant; he too provides her with status and money. This dependency on her husband is further underscored when ill health prevents him from working and his income seriously declines. In these circumstances she chooses to sell herself. It is an act of self-sacrifice that puts her beyond the pale of respectable society, and she refuses rehabilitation involving a state of dependency upon Prest. Her choices throughout her adult life are severely limited and involve different kinds of sacrifice: pride, money, independence, society, honor, and "virtue." In representing Lizzie's choices in this way, Wharton indicts old New York for condemning women to a position of dependency. It takes away or at best reduces their freedom of choice, their power to define themselves and their actions. The ramifications of such a critique are to call into question the nature of marriage in such a society. Is not marriage itself a form of prostitution when so little choice is afforded women? When this novella is read in conjunction with her earlier novel *The House of Mirth*, this conclusion is reinforced. Moreover, a society that prides itself on honor and respectability but that allows women little opportunity to provide for themselves bears responsibility for the prostitution of women.

Lizzie remains outside of respectable society for the rest of her life. Unlike Hester Prynne, the most famous adulteress in American literature, she does not live an exemplary life as such; she frequently entertains men, and the only women who visit her in her home are ones who do so "infrequently" and "furtively," seeking to test the boundaries of respectable behavior. She has a reputation for being a "fast widow" and does nothing to counter it. On the other hand, like Hester Prynne she more than expiates her "sin" by a "rigidity of conduct."[59] In its own way old New York is as much a closed society as the Puritan colony, one in which status and identity depend on conformity to the rules of the community. Both have well-defined categories of anomalies and outsiders, both maintain "strong boundaries between purity and impurity," and in both "all moral failings are at once sins against religion and the community."[60] Both "groan and creak" with the inevitability of changes that undermine their social cohesion.

. . .

The New York season took on its most elaborate form during the era of Mrs. Astor and the Four Hundred. The organization of social events by the elite was deliberately designed to bring order to the social flux of urban growth and, above all, to facilitate, however inadequately, the bonding of a disparate group of well-to-do people in commerce and the professions.[61] Mrs. Astor's Four Hundred combined traditional rituals of exclusion with conspicuous public display. Aided by the new mass-circulation dailies and society journals,[62] "self-appointed" leaders of society asserted the exclusiveness of "the elect" and enhanced their power by making inclusion something worth aspiring to.[63] It is perhaps no coincidence that the formalization of New York's high society should have followed a similar path to that of English society earlier in the century, at a time when London was likewise under siege from the forces of industrialization.[64] As Richard Bushman has eloquently argued, there is, nevertheless, a specifically American slant to this narrative. Bushman places into perspective the aristocratization of American society in the late nineteenth century as "the logical fulfilment of the refining process," a process he dates as beginning circa 1690. Republicanism, he claims, left American society with "a truncated culture whose zenith and ultimate realization lay outside their borders," but gentility "required a top for society" and the "self-appointed aristocrats of the post–Civil War era" provided just that, a place where American architecture, decor, manners, and art could achieve "grandeur and high finish."[65]

By the mid-1890s, however, the formality of Mrs. Astor's social regime came under increasing attack from those seeking a more relaxed mode of sociability. The advent of commercialized entertainments, the growth of high society, improvements in modes of transportation—all of these decentralized continuing attempts to maintain social exclusivity. This had profound ramifications for women's role in society. On the one hand, the development of heterosociability gave women more access to public forms of entertainment and recreation, but, on the other, women ceded the power and influence they had exercised in more formal, more home-based forms of social life.

2

The Female World of
Ritual and Etiquette

Both the expansion and the formalization of New York society and the season
after the Civil War were directly related to the city's rapid demographic and
economic growth. The convergence upon New York of newly enriched families and individuals, in addition to the emergence of New York's own nouveaux riches, put considerable stress upon existing social structures. Prevailing
methods of social placing used by New York's elite proved inadequate with the
increase in geographic and social mobility, and so more elaborate methods were
introduced in order to preserve its power and status. At the same time, some
degree of flexibility was necessary to prevent the elite's complete and utter displacement by those with superior financial resources, and so in the 1870s and
1880s the social mechanisms that were put in place allowed for a controlled
merger of old and new wealth.

By means of the rituals of society and the season, women took primary
responsibility for countering the destabilizing effects of social flux and urban
expansion. As Maud Cooke pointed out in her etiquette manual:

> In this country the burden of social work rests upon women, while in all
> European countries, men, young and old, statesmen, officials, princes, ambas-
> sadors, make it one of the duties of life to visit, leave cards and take up all the
> numerous burdens of the social world.
>
> Here it is the lady of the house that does all this. Husbands, fathers, sons, are
> all too much engrossed in the pursuit of business or pleasure to spend time in
> these multifarious cares.[1]

Just as the bourgeois home in general was conceptualized as a haven from the marketplace, so too, at this level of society, was the home viewed as something of a breathing space free from the forces of change bringing social disruption in their wake. In other words, the home was a place where some choices could be exercised as to the desirability of acceding to change. At first it seemed as though women had made real gains in the control that they were given over the management of household affairs, social life, and child-rearing. Indeed, authors of etiquette manuals insisted that deference be shown to women as a sign that the United States had a civilized society. The expression of such deference was therefore an indicator of the increase in symbolic power that women had gained as a result of the home becoming the "primary site of genteel activity."[2] But even the home was overwhelmed by the effects of urban expansion and technological innovation. As the century drew to a close, the whole style of social life began to change in response to an emerging culture of consumer capitalism and as a result of the opening up of public space with the advent, for example, of electricity and the automobile. The center of power had now shifted away from the private space of the home to the public sphere and, in particular, to places of commercialized entertainment, access to which was more difficult to control.

Prior to 1870 New York society was still small enough for social controls to operate out of a family-based network, but rapid population expansion after the Civil War necessitated an extension of these controls as well as new means to implement them. One example of this is the way in which personal visits by women to each other at home, the foundation of female sociability and networking, were replaced with the leaving of a card. This was symptomatic in the 1870s and 1880s of the displacement of personal and intimate forms of sociability by less personal and larger entertainments. To manage larger visiting lists, hostesses organized reception days so that they could group their acquaintances' visits—a strategy akin to that detailed in late-twentieth-century manuals on time management.[3] Certainly the amount of advice written on this subject suggests that there was a great deal of confusion about the "proper" thing to do and that some women were finding it difficult to adapt to the demands of modern society. It was at about this time, too, that critiques of their attempts to emulate the British aristocracy began to appear in the daily and periodical press. In examining some of the criticism leveled at society women, moreover, we find that there was resistance both to the perceived domination of society by women and to the alleged stuffiness of formal behavior.[4] This criticism included allegations that leisure-class women were "commercialized" and "degenerate."[5] In the end, however, it was the commercialization of upper-class leisure and entertainment that effectively wrested control away from society women and usurped the role they had in providing carefully regulated spaces for social mingling and courtship.

For much of the period under review, women functioned as society's gate-keepers through regulating the access of newcomers. The increased formaliza-tion of social life—resulting as it did in the introduction of an increasingly elaborate code of etiquette and the ritualization of particular events in the social calendar—meant that women were entrusted with the task of placing new-comers. Accordingly, it was required of social aspirants that they go through a process of vetting that included being sponsored by someone from within the "inner circle." This was followed by introductions to members of society through a series of calls and, then, if the aspirants passed this stage, invitations to private and semipublic entertainments, such as dinners and subscription balls. The elaborate conventions devised to test the suitability of an applicant for membership in the charmed circle placed a considerable emphasis on the attrib-utes of gentility, such as knowledge of manners. At the same time, society matrons were responsible for inducting younger members of the social elite into the system. It was a mother's responsibility to promote the transmission of class onto her children by ensuring, for example, that they were well versed in social conventions. In this, more attention was paid to training daughters in the codes of gentility than sons, and one possible reason for this, but not the only one, was the importance given to women as social arbiters and the value that was thus placed on their knowledge of etiquette.[6] For most of the period in question, just like newcomers, male or female, the daughters of members of society had to go through a highly ritualized entrance into society to initiate them into its ways.

Débuts and weddings were female-centered rituals that marked important stages in the female life cycle. Using Arnold van Gennep's definition of "rites of passage," it is possible to identify these two rituals as marking the beginning and end of the coming-out process—the initiation of the young woman into adult-hood.[7] The début (that is, the rite of transition) constituted the first formal appearance in public of a young woman and denoted her sexual maturity and availability for marriage. It was followed by participation in a set pattern of social events over about three seasons, involving calling and leaving cards; attending receptions, dinners, and balls; and visiting the theater and opera. The débutante was guided through all of this by her mother (or substitute for her), the aim being to promote contact with men deemed eligible to be her consort so that one of them might be selected as her future husband. At the same time, of course, the young woman was initiated into her future role as a gatekeeper, learning the rules of social interaction.

The closing stage of the coming-out process was the wedding, a celebration of the successful negotiation of the marriage market and a reaffirmation of the social order through the reincorporation of the individual into the "tribe." As Barbara Myerhoff has argued, rites of passage "occur at moments of great anxi-ety" in an individual's life cycle and paradoxically announce separateness and individuality while simultaneously impressing upon the individual his/her membership in the group.[8] At the most fundamental level, then, débuts and weddings denoted a time of crisis in the life of an individual as she passed through one of the most significant stages of the female life cycle, going from girlhood to womanhood. This crisis was resolved by a daughter's marriage, which reaffirmed, furthermore, both the status of her family and its extended social circle through her incorporation into the larger group. As a period of crisis or anxiety, the coming-out process provided a focus for the relatives and friends of the débutante and was therefore a time when they became particularly aware of their shared interests and values as members of the social elite.

By examining both significant aspects of their life cycle as well as the everyday rituals of women's lives within the context of the economic transformation that took place between 1870 and 1920, we can see how women actively engaged in a effort to bring order to their social world. In what was effectively a class project, they built upon existing social structures and made use of the new methods of display and advertising that arose from the late-nineteenth-century culture of consumption. Women in the leisure class were—to borrow from Carroll Smith-Rosenberg's argument about bourgeois women generally—both "active participants in the dominant male class structure" and "male-constructed symbols of class distinctions."[9] As such, the display of class by women required thought, planning, exercise of judgment, work, and the use of resources and skills.[10] One way of understanding why women in the leisure class tacitly complied with the dominant male class structure, a class structure that heavily proscribed their participation in the public sphere, is to look at the compensations women received for their conformity.[11] This included both the access these women had to material resources as well as (for example) the pleasure they took in dressing in velvets, satins, silks, and brocades. Moreover, as Cécile Dauphin and her coauthors have pointed out, "the compensations received by women were not all of a passive nature. They also enjoyed *some power*" (my emphasis).[12] As Michelle Rosaldo has explained, women in the leisure class built a "public world of their own," one in which they were able to exercise influence and reap such rewards as fame, praise, and material success. They were able to do this by "elaborating on symbols and expectations associated with their cultural definition."[13] At work, then, was a fascinating and complex interplay of factors: women's power and influence, the symbolic representation of women, contradictions in women's responses to their situation, the negotiation of constraints upon women's sphere of action, and tensions and conflicts over power both between men and women as well as between parents and children. However, none of these factors erased the inequity of gender relations. On the contrary, despite the extent to which gender relations were redefined at the turn of the century, inequities remained. The question this raises, then, is why society women were unable to take advantage of their increased influence and enhanced public profile and transform these into real gains.

This chapter focuses on women's role in class formation and status maintenance and deals, in particular, with the initiation of daughters into their role in high society and with the ways that the vagaries of the marriage market were negotiated. Drawing upon etiquette manuals, society magazines, private correspondence, diaries, and memoirs, this chapter provides clues to the ways in which, at the turn of the century, elite women constructed and gave meaning to their lives.

Access Rituals

Female sociability was traditionally conducted within the home and involved the maintenance of networks of friends and kin. The home provided a place where the manners of newcomers could be put to the test, for it was manners rather than wealth that were regarded as the main marker of class. Few etiquette manuals were overt about class distinctions. Instead, they referred to the "lower class" euphemistically, as is illustrated by Mrs. Sherwood's warning to readers of the need for discrimination in the matter of introductions. As she pointed out, a lady should be "careful how she lets loose on society an undesirable or aggressive man . . . or a great bore, or a vulgar, irritating woman."[14] Likewise, in putting her case for the cultivation of elegant manners, Abby Longstreet implied the existence of connections between class and "correct behavior" by claiming that manners could "carry a stranger farther up the heights of social ambition than money, mental culture, or personal beauty."[15] Justifications for etiquette were frequently expressed in terms of "social harmony" and the smooth running of "machinery." At the same time, the metaphor of machinery can be found in combination with the notion of protection: "Etiquette is the machinery of society. It polishes and protects even while conducting its charge. . . . It is like a wall built up around us to protect us from disagreeable, underbred people, who refuse to take the trouble to be civil."[16] Underlying this rhetoric was the felt need to impose controls on social interaction. This need might have been expressed in terms of avoiding unpleasantness or embarrassment, but at heart it was about keeping people in their place.

At the same time, contrary to any who might agree that a system adopted from more rigidly stratified European societies was inappropriate in a democratic country, some etiquette writers affirmed the place of good manners in a democracy in egalitarian terms: "In no country in the world are general good manners so indispensable as in this democratic country. In Europe, where, in society as at the railway stations, different classes are recognized and kept apart by insurmountable barriers and vigilant guards, it is possible, if you happen to be among the high-bred 'firsts' or decent 'seconds,' to endure the existence of

the unruly 'thirds'." Without such barriers in the United States, good manners
were said to be "essential," otherwise "the refined" would go abroad and leave
Americans "to wallow in . . . brutality and foulness."[17] Writing over thirty years
later, Mrs. Kingsland puts a different spin on the need for good manners in a
democracy. For her, the openness of U.S. society, "where, untrammelled by
class restriction, all may make their way to eminence," meant that a knowledge
of manners should be available to all and not a barrier to those "entitled" to be
in "good society."[18]

Barrier or not, the first hurdle for social aspirants in seeking entrée into society was to persuade a sponsor to take them up so that they might be introduced
through a procedure of calls and card leaving. Some etiquette manuals regarded
the elaborate ritual accompanying this procedure as a consequence of the
expansion of society,[19] while others saw it as constituting the "basis" of society.[20] As one etiquette manual acknowledged as late as 1913, women played a
fundamental part in this access ritual: "The etiquette of card leaving is a privilege which society places in the hands of ladies to govern and determine their
acquaintanceships and intimacies, to regulate and decide whom they will, and
whom they will not visit."[21] By 1925, however, *Vogue's Book of Etiquette* noted
the passing of the custom of calling and leaving cards.[22] Between two women,
the procedure for calling went something like this. After meeting a newcomer
at someone's private residence and if further acquaintance was desired, the
superior of the two, that is, the woman who was in society in that particular
location, called upon the stranger. She sent in her own card and that of her husband, or father, and stayed no longer than fifteen minutes. The newcomer was
then obliged to return the call in person within a week if she wished to pursue
the acquaintance. Thereafter, hospitalities might follow with the initiative still
being taken by the woman of superior status. Should, however, "the new
acquaintance prove 'pushing,' or in any way obnoxious," card leaving ceased.[23]
Calls could not be made unless preceded by an introduction. According to Mrs.
Longstreet, New York etiquette followed the line that a woman sponsor should
leave her card along with the card of the lady to be introduced, writing in the
upper left-hand corner of her own card, for example, the words "Introducing
Mrs. Felix Grandcourt." The receiver was then supposed to call in person upon
Mrs. Grandcourt, or send a substitute for herself, and this call would have to be
returned within two or three days. If the acquaintance was to be taken up, then
the lady who had been approached by Mrs. Grandcourt's sponsor should offer
the first hospitality, such as an invitation to a reception or "at home" day. If not,
then the interaction was concluded after the newcomer's initial visit.[24]

Even before someone crossed the threshold, the card itself was treated as a
sign of someone's "social culture" and acquaintance with "good form."[25] A
card's "texture, style of engraving, and even the hour of leaving it, combine to
place the stranger whose name it bears in a pleasant or a disagreeable attitude,

even before his manners, conversation, and face have been able to explain his social position."[26] Numerous manuals referred to cards as representing the self, for example: "Cards are the sign manual of society. . . . The stress laid by society upon the correct usage of these magic bits of pasteboard will not seem unnecessary when it is remembered that the visiting card, socially defined, means, and is frequently made to take the place of, one's self."[27] The size of a card was said to be indicative of its owner's social pretensions and much space was given over to its dimensions. Margaret Watts Livingston advised that "a lady's card, bearing her name only, should never measure more than two and seven-eighths inches in length, by two and one-eighth inches in width; otherwise it will prove clumsy in handling." She went on to warn that a too small a card "appears childish and affected if carried by a woman over eighteen."[28]

The social citadel, guarded by these procedures and policed by women, encompassed not just the entitlement to participate in "fashion's passing show" but also gave access to what Leonore Davidoff has described with reference to London society as "a vast information network."[29] This was especially useful to businessmen in New York because they could gain access to information about high finance, stocks and shares, good investments, and strategies for keeping "ahead of the mob." In 1905 the *New York World*'s society page pointed to the phenomenon of businessmen doing deals in places of entertainment:

> In the foyer of the Metropolitan Opera House meet the men whose names are known in the money marts of the world, and sometimes they talk "shop." The other night Henry Clews was telling Darius Ogden Mills and some other prominent man that he was about to close a deal whereby he would exchange two lots on the north side of Thirty-fourth Street for $750,000. Somebody remarked that Thirty-fourth Street was destined to be the greatest business thoroughfare in the world for its length.[30]

Personal and easy access to leading figures in the world of finance, facilitated by social networking, was undoubtedly advantageous to all of those in society. Clearly, then, the two worlds of finance and society were intricately linked, but the side to this that is often ignored is the degree to which women were involved in the so-called male public sphere of business. Neither the nineteenth-century rhetoric of separate spheres—reproduced to some extent by twentieth-century historians—nor the trivialization of society as the facile playground of the rich does justice to the interconnections of Wall Street and Fifth Avenue, to the complementarity of women's socializing and men's economic ambitions, and to the significant contribution of women to class formation and status maintenance.

Another widely acknowledged aspect to the socializing and forging of social connections within the exclusive circles of New York society was the opportunity for cementing such connections through marriage. The bringing together of people in one place for formal entertainments where, through the implementation of an elaborate code of etiquette, there was close scrutiny of people's credentials afforded families opportunities for aligning themselves with other families of wealth and status and for promoting the prospects of the next generation. With respect to London society, Leonore Davidoff has argued that marriage was "one of the most essential points of access to high status group membership."[31] It must, however, be pointed out that in both London and New York, marriage was not the actual point of access. Rather, marriage was a confirmation of insider status for a newcomer who had successfully negotiated the vetting process. It was in this way that the access rituals for newcomers and those for introducing a daughter into society were interconnected. Because the marriage market was an important function of the season, therefore, access rituals helped to define the pool of eligible partners for marriage.

Débuts

In New York the début was a peculiarly female ritual. There was no equivalent occasion for sons. As Mrs. Longstreet indicated in her exposition on débuts, the celebration of coming of age underlined gender differences: "The young gentleman somehow slips into society without formality. . . . Certain it is that the young man finds his way into the charmed circle without much difficulty."[32] The underlying difference had to do, of course, with sexual reproduction and the perceived need to place daughters in marriage as early as possible upon maturing.

As regards the introduction of a daughter into society, in addition to the need to train her to take her place in society, protection was the note sounded most strongly in most etiquette manuals and magazine articles. The minor novelist Mrs. Burton Harrison, a self-appointed authority on New York etiquette, explained to readers of the *Ladies Home Journal*: "Until the age of 18 she's [the New York Society girl is] brought up in comparative seclusion from the world in which her mother takes conspicuous part; she is trained by experts in every detail of the accomplishments specified." Prior to making their formal entrance, moreover, New York débutantes attended weekly dancing classes, "controlled by a bevy of matrons," Mrs. Harrison explains, who "carefully select" those invited to join.[33] And according to one etiquette manual that catered to a well-to-do readership: "A début is a barrier between an immaturity of character and culture, and an admission of the completion of both." It was up to the parents, therefore, and especially the mother, to decide when this moment had arrived:

> The mamma determines the time when, by a proper celebration, her daughter shall be accepted by the world as a fully matured woman. . . . This ceremony

should convey the information to the world that the young lady has been graduated in all the accomplishments and knowledge necessary for her uses as a woman in society. In fact, it should mean that she has been instructed in all that deft wisdom which will be required by a *belle* of her circle and a queen of a household, for which she is, as all women are, a candidate.[34]

Daughters were given little opportunity to experience social autonomy. They were "fledglings," and their lack of a separate identity from their mother was symbolically represented by the fact that, in their first season, they did not have cards of their own; instead their name was added to their mother's card.[35] An 1888 manual advised readers:

> Very exclusive mammas . . . do not approve of the fashion of a separate card for a young girl, and while American etiquette does not forbid the use of such a card after she has been out a year, it does not, strictly speaking, permit her a separate visiting-card until that time has passed, and even after that it lends unqualified approval to the keeping of her name on her mother's card for all formal occasions, as has always been the custom where European etiquette prevails.[36]

The acquisition of a card was therefore a prerequisite for a young woman's participation in the specific rituals of female sociability, notably "calling," which were incorporated into the coming-out process. The first round of calls to be made by a débutante occurred as a preliminary to the issuing of invitations to an afternoon tea or reception. Accompanied by her mother, the débutante was taken round to call on or leave a card with all those who were to be invited to the début. Huybertie Pruyn Hamlin, an Albany woman who made her début in New York in 1891, has provided a lively account of the reasons as to why a daughter was not considered properly introduced until her mother had taken her to call on all the families on her mother's visiting list. Mrs. Hamlin recalled the business of making the first round of calls to announce her début as follows:

> It was slow work. . . . Mother had a book with the list and on some blocks we went to almost every house. Owen would climb off the box and take the cards and then we would watch like cats to see the door open and try to glean hope from the way the cards were taken. Often the maid would leave the door open and go on a search party for her mistress and from the noises we heard while waiting in the parlor—it seemed as if the poor woman had been routed out of bed and was slamming doors and drawers in her effort to get herself clothed. Louise [Huybertie's cousin] and I fumed at the delays and at the general misery of the afternoons and of having to smile sweetly as one after another would say—"Well how do you like being out?" . . . My diary says on Dec. 1st,—"This afternoon Mother took Louise and me on our stupid old visits—we made 14 and 10 were out—it is terrible—Louise and I sit and grin and say nothing."[37]

Edith Wharton too wrote of "the onerous and endless business of 'calling' [which] took up every spare hour."[38] While she was no rebel, Mrs. Hamlin's reminiscences show that she was disposed to balking at the emptiness and repetitiveness of this ceremonial routine, which appears to have lost much of its original meaning by this stage.[39] Her mother, however, was a stickler for form and went through the rituals of bringing out her two daughters in considerable style.

The interminable rounds of calls made to announce a daughter's début were, however, only one part of the preliminaries. Another centered around the clothes that were required for formal events. Once again, Mrs. Hamlin's reminiscences provide a rare and detailed insight into this part of the ritual. As the family lived in Albany, the shopping expedition for her "coming out" clothes involved an extended trip to New York, during which she and her mother stayed at the Cambridge Hotel on the corner of Fifth Avenue and Thirty-third Street. They visited the London-based couturiers, Kate Reilly's, in a brownstone one block to the south. Mrs. Hamlin recalled in loving detail the dresses that were purchased, especially the gown for her début at the Patriarchs' Ball in December 1891, which was made of

white chiffon over white satin and with the huge puffed sleeves of the period. From the left shoulder to the right side of the waist, there was a white velvet ribbon about three inches wide, ending in a knot at the shoulder. There was a bunch of white heather by the knot and some more around the skirt, about half way up. The skirt was down on the floor, was very full and had a small train, enough to have to be held up when dancing, and enough to make a modern dancer wild.[40]

With the help, or the insistence, of the mother, then, in being taken through the time-consuming activities of calling, leaving cards, and of making and shopping for clothes, the daughter was eased into her new role as an adult. As Barbara Myerhoff has pointed out, "the obsessive, formal, repetitive activity that rituals require" inhibit rather than encourage a questioning of the processes.[41] Huybertie Pruyn's experience testifies to her mother's determination to adhere rigidly to the formal routine and to brook no arguments from her reluctant younger daughter.

During the 1870s and 1880s the first formal appearance of a young New York woman was most likely to have taken place in her parents' home.[42] It usually consisted of a reception with a supper and dancing afterwards. The débutante customarily stood to the left of her mother as the guests entered so that she could be presented to the ladies and her elders. Gentlemen were presented *to* her. At supper, as manuals advised, it was the brother's duty to escort his sister to the table and to seat her on the left of their father. When the company proceeded to dance, the mother was expected to choose a dancing partner for her daughter from among close friends or relatives. Thereafter the débutante was to dance only once with any one partner.[43] By the late 1880s afternoon teas were the preferred form of entertainment for a début, as they were less ceremonious (and more economical) than either dinners or evening receptions. More important, however, they were highly recommended in manuals because of the increased likelihood of young men being able to attend. An 1888 manual noted: "The head of the family is absolved from attendance at such entertainments, and guests are not compelled to give more than a few minutes time to them. Perhaps the freedom thus gained wins favor for them with gentlemen, who yield more readily to the trammels of business than to the allurements of leisure or pleasure."[44] Mrs. Burton Kingsland noted even greater concessions to the routine of the male business world when, in 1906, she wrote of the popularity of Saturday afternoons for such festivities.[45] Not everyone was in favor of these afternoon teas; in the mid-1890s the Saunterer in *Town Topics* kept expressing the hope that such social functions would die out, "but each succeeding November, all the same, brings a larger number of these economical entertainments."[46]

For members of fashionable society, débutante receptions or teas at home were followed up by attendance at the Patriarchs' Ball or one of the other prominent series of subscription dances. Throughout the 1870s and 1880s during each season there were two or three Patriarchs' Balls, which were normally held at Delmonico's restaurant. Attendance was by invitation only, and the invitations were fastidiously vetted by the subscribers who hosted the ball. As such, the Patriarchs' Balls provided a formal and controlled social occasion for New York's marriage market at a large, public venue. Nevertheless, these balls were highly publicized, and on the day following such an event newspaper society columns contained long lists of those who had attended and details of what the women had worn. Huybertie Pruyn recounted that in 1891 she was "dragged" to New York for her first Patriarchs' Ball. She was "positively frightened by the idea," but her mother did not break the news to her until all the plans had been made and it was too late for anything to be done about it. Huybertie received "an enormous and gorgeous bouquet of flowers heavily wired" from the man who was to escort her into supper that night at Delmonico's, which led her to comment that she had never been "treated in this formal way before" and "did not know what to make of it." Her escort was "a second cousin and at least 55 years old." The hairdresser suggested that she wear her hair in a "Psyche knot," which was then very fashionable, but she obstinately refused to do so. At the ball, Huybertie was introduced to the famous collector of débutantes' portraits, Peter Marié: "I could feel instantly that I was far from measuring up to the necessary standards of being included in his museum—my plain hair was too out of date to give me the slightest chance." After going through the stately steps of the Lancers with her elderly cousin, Huybertie then promenaded with him, whereupon she encountered the Four Hundred's master of ceremonies, Ward McAllister. She commented: "My faithful diary states on my return to the nursery at Albany—'He is a F.O.O.L., we would not tolerate him here. I enjoyed it all as a sort of show circus but I would not care to go again.'"[47] Although Mrs. Hamlin did not consider her initiation into the theatricality of a Patriarchs' Ball a positive experience, she did later come to enjoy her social life in the metropolis.

A daughter's entrance into society was a liminal period fraught with anxieties both for the débutante as well as for her family and social circle. The desired outcome was marriage, as this would reaffirm the social order and traditional gender hierarchy as well as consolidate kinship networks and those of class and economic interests. To bring this about in a world that was becoming increasingly unpredictable and resistant to control, the formality of high society, through its various access rituals, served to screen out undesirables and to bring together in a controlled environment people of comparable social standing. To this end, women attempted to ensure that their offspring socialized with those most eligible for marriage.[48]

On the one hand, coming-out rituals necessitated display in order to draw attention to the young woman's change in status. This was coded visually. The requisite white gown, signifying her virginity in the traditional manner, marked the débutante out from the rest of the women present. The dress, often made of tulle or chiffon, symbolized her feminine delicateness.[49] Floral bouquets, heavy with scents signifying purity and innocence, added their symbolism to the coded sexuality and fragility of the feminine. At the same time, the outward appearance of the débutante emphasized women's subordination to men. It comes as no surprise to learn that many débutantes experienced a sense of painful shyness. Huybertie Pruyn had "a terribly shy fit and suddenly felt as if [she] must escape from the over-powering mass of flowers."[50] And Edith Wharton recalled that for her, "the evening was a long cold agony of shyness. All my brother's friends asked me to dance, but I was too much frightened to accept, and cowered beside my mother in speechless misery, unable even to exchange a word with the friendly young men." Wharton goes on to say, however, that when these same young men had dined at home with her family, she had regarded them as her "elder brothers." Significantly, it was the removal to a more formal and public setting and the fact that she was dressed in, or rather "put into," "a low-necked bodice of pale green brocade" with a white lacy skirt and had her hair piled on top of her head that distanciated the "friendly young men." From now on she would be regarded differently: She had been sexualized.[51]

On the other hand, with the display of so precious an asset, whose value depended upon virginity, the formality of social conventions carefully circumscribed heterosocial contact. Almost like museum pieces, débutantes could be viewed but not touched. With the move to more public venues for the celebration of débuts, which began early in the 1870s with the hiring of Delmonico's ballroom, the code of gentility was elaborated upon further to protect daughters from undue attention from strangers as well as from any hint of impropriety. Mrs. Burton Harrison warned:

> For the crucial test of her introduction into full-fledged society, the poor girl must needs equip herself in a shining armor of conventionality; must step neither to the right nor to the left of the line prescribed by custom; must, above all, repress her preferences in the matter of companionship, and mete out civility in equal share to all who are presented to her. What wonder that she often dreads, rather than welcomes, her great occasion? That it is an experience to be endured, even though her way be strewn, as it generally is, with flowers, must be admitted.[52]

A thin line had to be walked between attracting suitable men's attention and not earning the reputation of a flirt, an ordeal made increasingly problematic with the reluctance of young men to participate in formal entertainments.[53] This reluctance increased as the distractions of commercialized entertainment multiplied and offered more relaxed arenas for socializing and amusement. Moreover, the competition of informal nighttime entertainments undercut the insistence of society hostesses upon formal social events to promote heterosocial contact.

The extension of high society into public and commercialized spaces was full of ambiguities for women of the bourgeois elite. On the one hand, they had succeeded in augmenting their traditional sphere of operations and in laying claim to nightlife outside the home by making their concerns central to nighttime sociability. In doing so, ballrooms, theaters, and opera boxes were utilized by women both for self-display and for their own enjoyment. In such places, where domestic rules of decorum were applied to public space, women of the elite were attended by men of their own social class and thereby shielded from unsolicited encounters with strangers. At the same time, however, they were at risk—especially at night and in public places—of being misrecognized as courtesans, and so to reduce this risk they were hemmed in by all manner of restrictions in order to maintain the vital distinction between respectability and indecorum. Débutantes, in particular, were warned about the consequences of indecorous behavior or inappropriate dress, and rigid codes were invoked to protect them from the slightest smirch on their reputations.[54] In addition, the massive development of the print media and the machinery of publicity heightened the concern of those in fashionable society both about their own reputations and those of their daughters. Mrs. Harrison wrote of the inconveniences of newspaper publicity as the inevitable price that a "beauty" in American society had to pay, even though the horrors she described were potentially injurious to a woman's reputation:

The young woman advertised by the press in her first season as a budding belle, has often cause, before the end of it, to rue the hour her charms become newspaper property, to be hawked in weekly columns. A name thus established before the public, has the changes rung upon it with a persistence frequently without justification in fact. She finds herself announced as present at places where she has not dreamed of going, dressed in imaginary costumes startling in their eccentricity. She is called upon by urgent reporters to reveal her movements, opinions, plans, costumes; and, in the nervous effort to escape the snare, finds her words of excuse later misrepresented or twisted into published statements for which she blushes to find herself made responsible. . . . If she is seen more than once walking in the street with a man recognized by the chronicler, their names are liable to be recklessly bracketed and set adrift down the tide of gossip without defense to her from the annoyance.[55]

Not surprisingly, then, etiquette manuals abounded with advice on how a débutante should dress and behave in public, emphasizing at all times modesty and inconspicuousness. But nothing could absolutely protect young women, either from misrepresentation by reporters keen to publicize infractions and hold up transgressors to harsh censure or from exploitation by columnists anxious to get a scoop by announcing the engagement of an heiress without being meticulous about verifying their information.

Chaperonage and Courtship

For all the celebration of their adulthood, then, young women were hemmed in by constraints upon their behavior and mobility. Proper decorum demanded that a chaperon be present at all times when a débutante was in the company of men.[56] Accordingly, etiquette advisers defended and promoted chaperonage as a necessary protection. "It typifies," noted Mrs. Kingsland, "the sheltering care, the jealous protection, of something very precious. It sets a higher value upon the object by protecting and hedging it round in the eyes of others, and particularly in those of young men who are apt to sigh for the fruit that hangs highest."[57] Attempts to legitimize chaperonage were also underpinned by implicit notions of class distinction. As such, the argument for chaperonage echoed that for etiquette as a whole: the special regard in which women were held in a refined society and etiquette's utility as a protection for the respectable. The conceptualization of etiquette as a protective shield likewise conferred special value on "woman as object" and suggested "its" distinctiveness. Etiquette therefore functioned as a barrier, dividing people into two groups: the respectable and the not respectable.

The issue of chaperonage was a controversial one throughout the period. For some Americans it was a matter of national honor that a woman could travel unmolested, particularly prior to the time when more formalized codes of behavior were adopted in New York. In *Polite Society at Home and Abroad* (1891), for example, Annie White claimed: "In no country are women so highly respected, or treated so courteously as in America. A lady can travel anywhere, without an escort, and hear no disrespectful language, or sneers."[58] Whereas Annie White put her faith in a respectful American male population, the male author of an etiquette manual published in the same year emphasized the innate qualities of the American woman: "Her self-reliance is strong, her faith in herself abiding, her conscious innocence a stronger shield than ever duenna was against a breath of scandal."[59] Despite various disavowals that Americans did not subscribe to what were seen as European rules of chaperonage, most turn-of-the-century etiquette manuals contained advice on chaperonage.[60] One etiquette adviser looked back, in 1904, with nostalgia to the simpler days of the past:

> Little by little, in our great cities, chaperonage has become an accepted condition of our daily life. Our grandmothers knew nothing about it, but in their day everyone knew everyone else, and it was not considered a necessity to have some older woman in the company when there was an excursion, a picnic, or any party of pleasure. Mothers and fathers were busy about their own affairs, and they usually gave young people their head, and let them manage *their* own matters.[61]

It was with the growth of cities and the anonymity that such growth afforded that chaperonage became customary, especially in late-nineteenth-century New York, where the code of propriety was arguably more formal than in any other major American urban center.

It might well seem that the adoption of European-style chaperonage rules in the late 1880s to mid-1890s conflicts with evidence of a growing informality in social interactions and rituals. But the hardening of rules governing women's behavior, especially young unmarried women's behavior, both in public and in the presence of men, coincides with an intensification of the feeling in bourgeois circles that things were spinning out of control. In fact, the use of chaperons was an attempt to adapt to the new demands of modern life and greater mobility of young people. It was in some ways an obvious solution to the problem, but it was not done without reservations about some of its wider implications. Butterick's 1888 manual, for example, acknowledged that "innovations are difficult where opposing customs have taken deep root" and conceded that any "self-respecting young woman" might well question what society thinks of its members if it has to set a guard upon their actions.[62] Generally speaking, there was a tone of resignation as to the way things were. In his study of the transformation of American culture at the turn of the century, Jackson Lears has provided insights into the wider context of responses to the introduction of chaperonage. He points to abundant evidence of bourgeois concerns about the overcivilization of American society and the undermining of the republican tradition. "Throughout the last two decades of the nineteenth century," he argues, "critics warned against the effects of European luxury and fashion on national character" and advocated that Americans should be proud of their provincialism as an emblem of their freedom from aristocratic foppishness.[63] It is likely, therefore, that chaperonage may well have been viewed by some Americans as a retrograde step and as a sign of the deterioration of the republican social fabric. For others, it may simply have been regarded as an acceptance of European customs either by choice or default. And by the 1890s, much as Americans might have despised the need for such supervision and much as young unmarried women resented the curtailing of their liberty, the chaperon had become a mandatory agent of social control. The urban world of strangers—perceived as an unstable environment—seemed to demand it.

Rules of chaperonage were particularly strict for courting couples. Authors of manuals excelled in the delicacy with which they expressed their concerns, as the following example amply illustrates:

> A girl's natural protectors know by experience, if not by intuition, that her purity is her chief attraction to honourable manhood, that a certain coyness which hides the secrets of her nature, and a quiet dignity which reserves the charms which heaven has bequeathed her, for him upon whom she bestows the treasures of her heart, embody the allurements which men desire their wives to possess. They know that virginal freshness is a power respected by the most depraved, and that with true men the influence of such wives is almost omnipotent.[64]

Purity was power. It was both an allurement and a protection. For this reason young women were being asked to commit themselves to premarital celibacy at a time of heightened sexual interest and tension in their lives. They were being asked to believe that chaperonage enhanced the intrigues and maneuverings of courting couples, that it tantalized men. This was merely one of the tactics used by some etiquette writers to advocate the adoption of chaperonage, by appealing to its role in the game of "playing hard to get." The majority of writers, however, tended to stress that the late adoption of chaperonage reflected negatively upon the honor of American men and women.

Débutantes and engaged women were the particular concern of advocates of chaperonage. Safeguarding a young woman's reputation during the liminal phase preceding marriage was seen as paramount. At the same time, the unmarried woman occupied a marginal status and was therefore herself a potential threat to society. Unless carefully controlled, she might endanger her society and the high values it placed on monogamy and female chastity. This explains the ritualistic restrictions upon her mobility and public activities; they reduced the possibility of contact with ineligible, lower-class men and, therefore, of sexual impropriety, thereby strengthening the class boundaries of her group and its social definition.[65] As Mary Douglas has indicated: "The person who must pass from one [state] to another is himself in danger and emanates dangers to others." Moreover, if a person is marginal, then "all precaution against danger must come from others."[66] In American society, those "others" had traditionally been a young woman's parents or, at the very least, her community. There are, for example, numerous references in manuals to the mother as the "natural" chaperon.[67] But with increasing urbanization, especially in New York City, parental control became inadequate to the task of protection; new dangers posed themselves. Mothers were therefore forced to enlist the assistance of others: older married, or single, women and servants. At the same time, the rules of chaperonage became ever more elaborate, thus providing the etiquette-book industry with yet more excuses for constantly updating and revising their publications.

There was broad agreement that it was on formal occasions, especially at evening entertainments, that chaperons were necessary, something that tends to underscore the use of chaperons as a marker of class. But the spaces at issue here were public ones, after dark, where there was maximum opportunity for intraclass heterosociability. Daytime social functions were more likely to be attended predominantly by women unless, of course, they consisted of excursions, in which case "long-suffering" chaperons were again called for. In the 1880s, Florence Hall suggested strict supervision for the débutante who had just come out.[68] On the other hand, the "engaged girl" also required close attention:

> Nothing is more vulgar in the eyes of our modern society than for an engaged couple to travel together or go to the theatre unaccompanied, as was the primitive custom. This will, we know, shock many Americans, and be called a "foolish following of foreign fashions." But it is true; and, if it were only for the "look of the thing," it is more decent, more elegant, and more correct for the young couple to be accompanied by a chaperon until married.[69]

The correspondence of Elsie Clews, daughter of Wall Street financier Henry Clews, in the mid-1890s when she was a débutante clearly reveals the extent to which chaperonage was taken seriously in her circle.[70] In the summer of 1897, when Herbert Parsons was attempting to court Elsie, he arranged a party to go camping in the Adirondacks. He was completely taken aback when he was informed that Mrs. Clews had sent a cable forbidding Elsie to go, especially as Elsie had been on another camping trip earlier that summer with the Stanford Whites.[71] Stanford White's reputation regarding women, particularly his predilection for chorus girls, was known among his friends and acquaintances at this time. Herbert took it as an insult that Mrs. Clews found it possible to trust her daughter with Stanford White in the backwoods but not with him. He wrote to Elsie: "What will the world say if you do not go? That Mr. Clews will let his daughter go with the Whites but not with the Parsons. A pretty compliment for the Parsons."[72] He wrote to Mrs. Clews both to protest and to explain that the conventional proprieties would be more than adequately observed: "My brother-in-law is annoyingly careful. My sister has been married 11 years, has the four healthiest children in the country and was brought up a blue Presbyterian. What more of prudence and prudishness could you ask? Would the Whites offer as much?"[73] Mrs. Clews was unmoved.[74]

The career of the chaperon in the United States was, however, relatively short. Ironically, her appearance was rather a case of shutting the stable door after the horse had bolted. Definitions of acceptable behavior, particularly but not exclusively for elite women, became destabilized most notably from the mid-1890s on. Indeed, in the decades around the turn of the century a revolt took place against the constraints of Victorian gentility. Part of this revolt was related to the greater physical mobility of women, facilitated by the introduction of first the bicycle and then the car.[75] In addition, the proliferation of commercialized nighttime entertainments had created new spaces for informal heterosociability. But the public nature of such places meant that opportunities for reporters to snoop on the fashionable and wealthy were greatly enhanced, resulting in new methods of control and surveillance, ones that could be far more devastating in their effects.

One of the most ardent advocates of chaperonage was *Town Topics*'s the Saunterer. Starting in 1885, when the magazine was founded, up to 1920, he maintained that débutantes must be chaperoned in public. In the early 1890s he complained of the laxity of "the *fin de siècle* girl" who prided herself on her independence and had "come to regard the chaperon as superfluous and unnecessary." He continued:

> The result is that many a girl has not proved herself capable of safely guarding her honour, and has been guilty of the most serious infraction of the social conventionalities. . . .
>
> My remarks are based on personal observation. I see unmarried couples at the theater unattended, and after the theater I see them at Delmonico's drinking wine. After their wine I see them go forth and enter a closed cab, whereupon they take a midnight drive of perhaps a mile to the young lady's home uptown. Some of my readers not familiar with the facts will deny that such things occur among the members of the best society; yet my statements are true in every particular, as an investigation will prove.[76]

The Saunterer's power to monitor and publicize infractions of the social code gives some indication of the extent to which the gossip columnist was capable of effectively rendering the chaperon redundant.[77] Publicity for women in the public eye was clearly double-edged. Society columnists had the power to expose and censure, and as such were an extension of high society's capacity to police itself at a time when family and kinship networks were becoming inadequate to this task in a rapidly growing metropolis.

Weddings

Just as débuts became increasingly public events from the 1880s on, both because of where the social festivities took place and as a result of the newspaper publicity that heralded the new season's "buds," so too did society weddings develop as a public spectacle. Ideally, weddings represented both successful negotiation of the coming-out process and marriage market as well as the consolidation, or managed extension, of the social elite. The greater the success to be celebrated, therefore, the more public the wedding. From the floral displays to the gowns, from the social prominence of the guests to the wedding gifts on display, each detail was evaluated by participants, spectators, and journalists alike as a sign of the social and economic standing of the parties involved. Publicity was an important factor in the celebration of a marital alliance. A wedding ceremony was used as an opportunity to gather together not only family members but also an extensive peer group. The presence at such an event of distinguished politicians and diplomats or social leaders was intended to be read as testifying to the social position, power, and economic resources of the bride's family. According to Henry Collins Brown, the "vast publicity accorded these events" created an "insatiable" "public appetite for society news." Moreover, "the objects of this attention also suddenly changed their attitude of indifference and proceeded to install private secretaries galore." Brown attributes to these lavish weddings, especially those involving European titles, the origins of society journalists' reports, "in minute detail and profuseness," of the "doings" of the Four Hundred.[78] In late-nineteenth-century New York, elaborate rituals governed the final stages of the débutante's rite of passage. The announcement of an engagement, for example, might take place formally at a dinner for the affianced couple's families, followed by parties and dinners given by friends in honor of the couple.[79] And with the rise of society journalism from the 1880s on, the engagement of a socially prominent couple became a media event. Mrs. Sherwood, a well-known authority on etiquette, expressed concern regarding the harm wreaked by newspapers that reported engagements without formal notification.[80] Adele Sloane, a great-granddaughter of Commodore Vanderbilt, whose name appeared on the published list of McAllister's Four Hundred, read in the newspapers spurious reports of her name linked to various men. Even among friends speculation was rife, and at a party on 4 December 1894 at her grandmother's Fifth Avenue mansion, guests approached Adele asking if the occasion was intended for the announcement of her engagement. "What idiots people are!" she wrote in her diary. "I should think they would be busy enough with their own lives without looking after other people." In actual fact, her relationship with James (Jay) Burden Jr. was at a critical stage. They wrote to each other every day and were expressing their affection for one another, but Adele was unsure at this point in time "just how much" Jay loved her. On tenterhooks at this delicate period of her life, a week later Adele noted in her diary:

> Since I last wrote I feel as if I had crossed a wide boundary line and come out on the other side. It isn't theory or talk any more; J does love me, and I love him in a deep, serious, earnest way, and we are going to spend all our lives together.

She gave Jay her promise to marry him and they agreed to keep it to themselves for a week, but Adele did not think anyone would be surprised since their engagement "has been spoken about so much already and has even been dragged through the papers this last week." By Christmas most of the family had been informed, and on 14 January 1895 a public announcement was made. "No need for any more denying," Adele wrote with relief in her diary.[81] Adele's diary entries reveal, first, that she was already hardened to the ruthlessness of newspaper publicity and, second, that at the time of her engagement she exercised "some control" over the dissemination of information about her and her intentions. The engagement was publicly announced when *she* was ready, when *she* chose.

Parallel to the extensive purchasing of ball gowns, tea dresses, and winter suits for a débutante's first season was the acquisition of the wedding gown and accumulation of the trousseau. Huybertie Pruyn's wedding dress was ordered from Madame Lodaux's in Paris, where she had already been fitted for other dresses on European trips undertaken since she had come out. Her "going away suit was made at Dautricourts in New York and was of medium weight green serge."[82] Despite the difficulties involved in dressing in such formal garments and the constrictions of boned waist linings and high collars, she took a great deal of pleasure in the style and fabric of her clothes.[83] In fact, Huybertie enjoyed wearing fashionable clothes and reveled in the attention paid to her.[84] Etiquette manuals catering to those with more modest resources than the Pruyn family interpreted the preparation of the trousseau as an occasion for instilling wifely habits of thrift. "The average girl" of well-to-do parents, who married a young man "'with his way to make,' though he may be the son of a rich father," was still advised by Mrs. Burton Kingsland in her 1902 wedding manual on the necessity of thrift: "It is a mistake to buy too lavishly, for fashions change; new and tempting things, hitherto undreamed of, appear; added to which, there is pleasure in providing for recurrent wants." If this alone did not get the point across, then the next sentence reiterated the message: "The accumulation of great quantities of clothes is considered rather vulgar."[85]

Vulgarity, ostentatiousness, and extravagance were castigated in the pages of etiquette manuals. While lavish trousseaux were criticized, the display of wedding gifts to the public was also widely condemned. In 1887 Florence Howe felt such a display was in questionable taste; Mrs. Sherwood positively rebuked it. In Edith Wharton's novel *The Age of Innocence*, this shunning of ostentation is represented through the character of Mrs. Welland, the mother of the bride and an old New Yorker, who settles the family debate on the issue "with indignant tears" in her eyes, proclaiming: "'I should as soon turn the reporters loose in my house.'" The fictional construction of an 1870s wedding contained in this novel involves two well-established old New York families, and Wharton represents the attitudes to the press held by the modest, genteel older elite as being in stark contrast to those held by the publicity-conscious nouveaux riches. The effect is to antiquate old New York and to make the onset of mass-circulation newspapers mark both a temporal and cultural watershed. However, Wharton reworks the historical frame insofar as she accentuates the differences between the new and old elites when formulating Mrs. Welland's objection to the suggestion of dispensing with the awning "which extended from the church door to the curbstone" in order to protect the bride from "the mob of dressmakers and newspaper reporters who stood outside fighting to get near." At this point Mrs. Welland exclaims: "'Why, they might take a photograph of my child *and put it in the papers!*'" In the 1870s few pictures of any sort appeared in the press; it was not until the 1900s that photographs appeared.[86]

Weddings involving American women and titled Europeans seemed to raise the ante as far as standards of ostentation were concerned. When the number of such liaisons began to increase significantly during the 1890s, the criticism became strident. In 1895, after New Yorkers had been treated to two particularly lavish transatlantic weddings, the *Town Topics* society columnist, the Saunterer, commented: "They were both the most remarkable ceremonials of the kind ever held in New York, and in detail and in the lavish expenditure of money should be judged more as theatrical displays than as social events."[87] The presence of crowds jostling to catch a glimpse of the society folk as they entered and exited from the churches added to this theatricality.[88] At highly publicized weddings, policemen were posted to keep the crowd in order. This was certainly the case at the 1895 wedding of the duke of Marlborough and Consuelo Vanderbilt at St. Thomas's Church, New York City. After the fiasco that had occurred outside Grace Church when Cornelia Bradley-Martin, daughter of one of the most ambitious New York society matrons, married Lord Craven, the New York police authorities anticipated problems with both crowds and traffic jams at the Vanderbilt wedding. But the Saunterer showed no compunction about the invasion of the Vanderbilts' privacy, instead seeing it as the duty of the press to report on the activities of the very rich.[89] On the other hand, Consuelo Vanderbilt's memoirs of the occasion reveal the intrusiveness of both the press and crowds of onlookers from a very different perspective:

Every incident of my engagement had been publicised. Reporters called incessantly, anxious to secure every particle of news, from the cost of my trousseau to
our future plans. Since little news was given out, accounts were fabricated. I read
to my stupefaction that my garters had gold clasps studded with diamonds, and
wondered how I should live down such vulgarities.

Outside the church, "there were the usual crowds of curious sightseers on Fifth
Avenue," but, as they exited from St. Thomas's, "the crowd surged towards us
and women tried to snatch flowers from my bouquet."[90]

The international wedding of Anna Gould to the French marquis Boni de
Castellane in March 1895 also fascinated the American press and crowds of
onlookers. The fiancé was harassed by reporters from the moment he landed in
New York. During the week before the wedding sightseers hung around outside the Gould mansion, hoping to get a glimpse, before being moved on by
the police or private detectives, of the major actors in this Franco-American
pageant. The *New York Times* wrote its report as a fantasy piece: "Why not
make believe, then, that you and I have alighted from our cab at the awning
stretched from the massive front doors of the residence to the curb. . . . We pass
under this canopy, over the carpet, ascend the stairs, and stand at the doors.
They are thrown open. We enter. 'Your names, gentlemen,' says a man, courteously, as he looks over a typewritten list of names." And so it proceeds,
describing in detail the display of thirty-five thousand flowers, the jewels worn
by the women guests, the paintings on the walls of the Gould mansion, and
then, of course, the ceremony. Yet more detail is provided, however, of the
wedding breakfast, the bride's traveling gown, her trousseau, and the gifts.
Diamonds figured prominently among the latter. Anna's sister, Helen, gave her
an Esterhazy diamond, her aunt and uncle threw in a diamond collar, and
another relative contributed a "chain" of two hundred diamonds.[91]

New York society women had, with some degree of success, brought control
to the exceedingly fluid social situation of the post–Civil War period. They had
done so by supplementing existing structures that had their origin in private settings, thus enabling them to extend their domestic power and influence into
the semipublic realm. Their social rituals complemented male ambitions, and
because of this women were able to exercise "some power," even though it
was largely power over female-only activities and over other women, especially
daughters and social inferiors.[92] Nevertheless, women were able to extend the
family-based source of their responsibilities to legitimize their participation in
social affairs outside the home.

Women's use of formal etiquette in the late nineteenth century enabled
them to exclude undesirables, to colonize certain areas of public space, and to
make themselves objects of attention and courtesy. As a code governing behav-

ior and appearance, etiquette enabled women to deal with the scrutiny and sur-veillance they received from both onlookers and the press. However, etiquette did not resolve for women the contradictions arising from putting themselves in public circulation and of making themselves vulnerable to misrepresentation. Nor did it adequately deal with the realities of heterosocial contact and the move toward greater individual expressiveness. In this regard, then, etiquette both empowered and disempowered women. It disempowered them in the sense that the subordinate female role—which was embedded in etiquette, and which was based on notions of gentlemanly deference and female depen-dence—maintained beliefs in female fragility and vulnerability. Formality had served a useful purpose prior to the turn of the century but proved to be too inhibiting to the new generation growing up in an intensely commercialized culture and an anathema to businessmen, who required greater flexibility in both their business and social relations.[93]

3

Interiors and Façades

On his return to the United States in 1904, after a twenty-year absence, Henry James remonstrated that New York houses and clubs no longer had any interiors:

> The instinct is throughout, as we catch it at play, that of minimizing, for any "interior," the guilt or odium or responsibility, whatever these may appear, of its *being* an interior. The custom rages like a conspiracy for nipping the interior in the bud, for denying its right to exist, for ignoring and defeating it in every possible way, for wiping out successively each sign by which it may be known from an exterior. . . . Thus we have the law fulfilled that every part of every house shall be, as nearly as may be, visible, visitable, penetrable.[1]

Edith Wharton and the architect Ogden Codman Jr. were no more enamored of the modern trend toward open-plan interiors than was James, for privacy was a sacred element in their conception of civilized living. As they declared in their coauthored book *The Decoration of Houses,* halls were not to be treated as living rooms; they were a quasi-public thoroughfare, "crossed by the servant who opens the front door, and by any one admitted to the house."[2] In order to protect the privacy of the domestic interior, Wharton and Codman advocated the retention of the hall as a separate space from the vestibule and staircases. Indeed, Wharton herself included these features in the design of her own country house, The Mount: "The staircase in a private house is for the use of those who inhabit it; the vestibule or hall is necessarily used by persons in no way concerned with the private life of the inmates. If the stairs, the main artery of the house, be carried up through the vestibule, there is no security from intrusion."[3] At the turn of the century, Henry James endorsed this maintenance of the European tradition of having separate rooms for specific functions in his criticism of the pronounced tendency in the United States toward the type of informality that characterized architecture. Accordingly, he claimed that

> we see systematized the indefinite extension of all spaces and the definite merg-
> ing of all functions; the enlargement of every opening, the exaggeration of
> every passage, the substitution of gaping arches and far perspectives and re-
> sounding voids for enclosing walls, for practicable doors, for controllable win-
> dows, for all the rest of the essence of the room-character, that room-suggestion
> which is so indispensable not only to occupation and concentration, but to con-
> versation itself, to the play of the social relation at any other pitch than the pitch
> of a shriek or a shout.[4]

James had returned to New York at the time when the "organic style" of Frank Lloyd Wright was in full swing, when interior walls were swept away in order to increase the perception of interior space. Discarding the very func-tionalized mid-Victorian dwelling with its specialized rooms in favor of open-plan living, Wright sought to "make a unified space so that light, air, and vistas permeated the whole."[5] Wright's idea of making "the 'inside' becoming 'out-side'"[6] was no doubt anathema to James's preference for the privacy afforded by individual rooms. Wright's designs represented a reconceptualization of the relationship between the public and the private, a reconceptualization that James resisted fiercely. Private space was no longer so sacrosanct by the end of this period. Even electric lighting was blamed by Wharton and Codman for destroying privacy:

> Nothing has done more to vulgarize interior decoration than the general use of
> gas and of electricity in the living-rooms of modern houses. Electric light espe-
> cially, with its harsh white glare, which no expedients have as yet overcome, has
> taken from our drawing-rooms all air of privacy and distinction. . . . It would be
> difficult to account for the adoption of a mode of lighting which makes the *salon*
> look like a railway-station, the dining-room like a restaurant.[7]

And, as we have already seen, the insatiable greed of the press for details of inti-mate lives played its role in turning interiors inside out.[8] With advances in pho-tography, Sunday supplements and magazines published photographs not only of their quarry but also of the "public rooms" in the mansions of the rich and/or famous.[9]

In the years around the turn of the century, there was an interesting two-way flow between private and public spaces, a coextensive process whereby the pri-vate became publicized and the public privatized. On the one hand, a code of etiquette that had evolved from private settings was extended to include public areas in order to control the interaction of people of a different class and gender, and on the other, the private space of the home and family life were no longer impervious to publicity. Forms of sociability that had previously been largely confined to private dwellings were transferred to public arenas. These in themselves excited public interest and provided fodder for society columns. Knowledge of what went on in public areas whetted the appetite for what went on in the more exclusive private space of the home, and wealthy New Yorkers found themselves pressured to reveal more of themselves or else read leaked or fictionalized accounts of their private lives. Servants were a key source of information for prying journalists. The increased publicity given to private life broke down the barriers between what should remain intimate and personal and what could be divulged and shared with an increasingly inquisitive public.

The social life of old New York, as has been noted already, had revolved around the home much more than in the days of the Four Hundred or their immediate successors. This contrasted sharply with the fast pace of the fashionable set of the 1880s and 1890s, when it was common to have large dinners before the opera or a ball: "'Opera night' would not have been chosen," as Wharton pointed out, "for one of my mother's big dinners."[10] In the mid-nineteenth century, the home had been a significant center for maintaining social, business, and kinship networks. Dinners and calls were an important part of sustaining and strengthening such ties, whereas small dances and amateur theatricals were the kinds of domestic entertainments deemed suitable for intimate circles of kin and friends. The home was also, as we have seen, a place for celebrating family events, such as débuts and weddings. Little of this social life had found its way into the newspapers before 1870.

The move toward celebrating important life events, such as marriage or débuts, in more public places, along with the development of commercialized entertainment, had consequences for the design and function of the home in social life. The layout of domestic interiors tells us something about the trends both toward and away from formality as well as the social pretensions of their owners. The material culture of the homes of New York's social elite—furnishings, decorations, the use of space—was integrally connected to their "presentation of self." At the same time, the development from the 1890s on of fashionable restaurants and hotels catering to a wealthy clientele provided the kinds of rooms that mirrored, in their furnishings, the formal rooms of large mansions. Hotels and restaurants were a home away from home, providing domestic facilities without the inconvenience of personally administering a large household and domestic staff. They were a kind of public domestic space, flexible in response to the needs of their patrons, who could hire rooms for their exclusive use or share parlors and dining rooms with other patrons. Such spaces provided an extended stage for the genteel performances of the social elite, if not the central stage.

In this chapter, then, consideration is given to the private space of the home in the context of aggressive status competition among the wealthy in New York. This involves looking at how the home, particularly the city residences of elite families, was brought into service for the performance of gentility. The type of social life indulged in by the wealthy was dependent in large part on the employment of servants, and therefore, both front- and backstage are examined, "backstage" being the realm of domestic servants. Here, in carefully segregated rooms with their own separate access, servants worked to support the front-stage appearance of their employers. The facilities and the interior decoration of the back region of residences differed from those in the front region, and these differences denoted a social hierarchical arrangement within the household or public establishment. A picture emerges of the various dimensions that contributed to the elaborate staging of gentility.

The Decoration of Houses

The structure and decoration of houses provide important clues to social organization. As Norbert Elias pointed out long ago in his analysis of court society, rooms can be a key to understanding certain kinds of social relationships.[11] Spatial arrangements and room usage within private residences reveal the ordering of social relations both within the community of people who reside in them and with the outside world. The period 1870 to 1920 was perhaps one of the most opulent eras in the history of U.S. elites, when social pretensions were very graphically put in evidence with the building of enormous mansions in both New York City and its environs. Architects and their patrons drew heavily upon a European aristocratic heritage of French châteaux, Italian palazzi, and English country houses in respect to architecture, interior decoration, and gardens, in order to align the American bourgeois elite socially with the landed aristocracy of Europe. European art treasures, antiques, marbles, and so on were purchased wholesale and shipped back to the United States in vast quantities in the late nineteenth and early twentieth centuries. European structures and aristocratic accouterments harking back to courtly societies were thus imported and adapted to the needs of a powerful, wealthy business elite attempting to impose its leadership by *buying* history. It was one of the most extraordinary stages in U.S. social history, and there is something terribly ironic about its timing, as, in Edith Wharton's words, "a new class of world-compellers . . . [bound] themselves to slavish imitation of the superseded" and displayed a "prompt and reverent faith in the reality of the sham they had created."[12]

Henry James found the whole accent of Fifth Avenue in this phase both grating and superficial. He was not fooled by the attempt of New York's millionaires to buy history. At his most charitable, he saw "the elegant domiciliary" as an attempt by New York society to construct for itself "some coherent sense *of* itself, and literally putting forth interrogative feelers . . . into the ambient air." But, instead, it found a void. New York society did not have, like its European model, "a large, consummate economy, traditionally practised," with "old societies . . . arranged exactly to supply functions, forms, the whole element of custom and perpetuity." Rather, its beautiful houses, in both Manhattan and Newport, gave off an air of transience, of being conspicuous and wasteful "mistakes." Typifying for James this "interesting struggle in the void," this helpless "floundering" of "the upper social organism," were his impressions from a dinner party at a New York "palace." After dining in a magnificent setting with excellent service and beautifully arrayed women "in tiaras and a semblance of court-trains," the assembled company was left with nothing to do at eleven o'clock"—or for the ladies at least—but to scatter and go to bed." In London or Paris, as James explained, there would have been another social function to go on to.[13] It was common, in fact, for people in European cities to attend more than one function, even more than one ball, in a single evening. But in New York it was more usual to commit oneself to one social event, particularly if that event was a ball. To be fair, New Yorkers did have dinner parties prior to going to a ball or the opera. James's point, however, is that the women were not merely dressed for a formal dinner; instead their outfits suggested something more, which is why he felt only "a great court-function" would have "met the strain." But even if these women had gone on to a court function, they would, James surmised, have gone alone and had "proper partners" supplied there, for it was only the women who set "the material pitch" so high with their tiaras and trains in their palatial houses.[14] The men would have been out of place. It was the women who were the aristocrats.

The scene that James had witnessed could be said to have marked the ebbing tide of a formal social life in which the sexes were, as he puts it, socially out of step with each other.[15] Female modes of sociability—the daytime activities of calling, "at homes," and luncheon parties—helped to cement kinship networks as well as to nurture contacts initiated by men in the business sphere, and so they both complemented male interests and promoted those of the family. But female sociability alone was not enough to secure women's vision of order and harmony in society. Their class pretensions had to be mapped onto heterosocial activities, and to accomplish this, they required the compliance of men. Time and again, in newspaper columns, etiquette manuals, social commentaries, and autobiographies, complaints appear about the incompatibility of the sexes with regard to styles of socializing. Images abound of bored, dyspeptic businessmen with stiff, starched collars yawning over the endless courses of food, while the

women at their side, dressed to the nines, provided the only animation at elaborate, sumptuous dinners. Clearly, the kind of social life women of the *haute bourgeoisie* had in mind was very different from that favored by their menfolk. The
women required a formal space where strict codes of behavior were enforced
and where men deferred to women. This was provided in part by their own
homes, modeled on European palaces, which furnished a highly symbolic setting for the more public forms of private social life such as dinners and balls. The
formal entrances of their mansions, their reception rooms, and their ballrooms
all suggested active participation in a form of socializing reminiscent of European court society, even if they did not, in James's opinion, manage to pull it
off. But there was no court in New York, and by the turn of the century there
was no private home large enough to bring together all of the burgeoning social
elite in a visible show of class solidarity. Accordingly, social life had been forced
to move into public space, to semipublic venues provided by fashionable restaurants and hotels, and with this move went a code of etiquette that had been nur-
tured within the home. The rules of the private drawing room prevailed in the
opera box and public ballroom, thereby privatizing public space and making it a
respectable place for women of the social elite to be seen.

Integral to the performance of gentility, then, was the setting. The concern
about personal appearance and manners extended to interior décor and architecture; pretensions to elite status were mapped onto the design and furnishings
of homes. In this way, we can see how Wharton and Codman's 1897 publication *The Decoration of Houses* in many ways represents a resurfacing of the sentimental ideal insofar as it was predicated on the principles of simplicity and taste.
Just as the sentimental ideal tried to insist upon a consistency between the inner
and outer self, so too did Wharton and Codman argue for a consistency
between interiors and façades. More than this, the authors privileged their own
in-depth cultural knowledge of European architecture and interior design
while exposing the ignorance of those Americans who were appropriating
European culture without having an understanding of it. Karen Halttunen's
study of mid-Victorian society in the United States, concentrating as it does on
fashion, etiquette, and mourning rituals, develops the argument that sentimentalism was a response of middle-class Americans in the urban Northeast to what
they regarded as an increase in the use of artifice, that is to say the manipulation
of appearance and manner to beguile the unsuspecting. As an antidote to artifice or hypocrisy, antebellum Americans, she argues, strenuously promulgated
the ideal of sincerity through the production of conduct manuals. In develop-
ing "new rules of conduct," sentimentalism moved from the defense to the
offense and came to define middle-class status.[16] Rules of conduct and appearance were used to screen out undesirables whose dress and manners were
deemed not to match an inner refined self.

By attempting to make fashion, etiquette, and social rituals compatible with "the sincere ideal," sentimentalism opened the way for the "theatricality" of Victorian bourgeois culture. Apart from the heightening of social formalism, there was nothing to stop social pretenders from appropriating the sentimental code in their "confidence game" to gain access to polite society. But, according to Haltunnen, the theatricality of "parlor conduct" was vehemently denied by Victorian Americans, as manners were supposed to be "completely natural." By the 1850s, Halttunen argues, there was an acceptance of disguises and masks as integral to the implementation of social forms that ensured smooth social relations. This change in attitude is exemplified for her by the popularity of plays satirizing the pretensions of social climbers to gentility—as, for example, Anna C. Mowat's play *Fashion*—and by the popularity of private parlor theatricals, such as charades and *tableaux vivants*. Middle-class Americans thus reconciled themselves to the "theatrical performance of gentility" and its role in securing their social identity.[17]

Haltunnen's analysis can be applied to architecture and interior decoration and extended to the period immediately succeeding the focus of her work. Members of the old New York elite were appalled at the wholesale appropriation of European aristocratic material culture by the nouveaux riches as a way of laying claim to membership in the upper circles. This buying of history, as James put it, was a form of artifice, masking the shortcomings of a new class of worldly acquisitors, a view with which Wharton was in full agreement. Indeed, much of her New York fiction satirizes the pretensions of the plutocrats and exposes their superficiality. And if *The Decoration of Houses* is read in conjunction with her fiction, we can see how Wharton attempted to establish her authority on matters of taste vis-à-vis interior decoration and design and to claim it as her prerogative to be ruthlessly critical of the nouveaux riches. Many of the concepts of taste evident in her fiction can, in fact, be traced back to *The Decoration of Houses*.

Wharton's New York fiction is replete with detailed references to architecture and interior decoration. She deployed houses in her fiction as manifestations of psychical traits and social types. In *The House of Mirth*, the Greiner house on Fifth Avenue, which the Jewish financier Sim Rosedale buys, is described as having a façade like a "complete architectural meal"—an offense against "taste," it is the worst kind of nouveau riche monstrosity, a smorgasbord of architectural styles. On the other hand, the Brys's house is "thought to be" a copy of the Trianon and represents the next stage in the evolution of new money: "the desire to imply that one has been to Europe, and has a standard." The Trenors's Fifth Avenue mansion is the next step and has the saving grace of not looking like "a banqueting-hall turned inside out." The Fifth Avenue home of old New Yorker Mrs. Peniston does not compare favorably with the newer fashions—at least in her niece's eyes. The ugly and heavy black walnut furniture against a "charmless background" of "magenta 'flock' wall-paper, of a pattern dear to the early sixties" and the "large steel engravings of an anecdotic character" depresses Lily Bart to the extent that "each piece of the offending furniture seemed to thrust forth its most aggressive angle."[18] Likewise, old Mrs. Manson Mingott's midcentury Second Empire extravaganza "in an inaccessible wilderness near the Central Park" suffers a negative comparison:

> The house itself was already an historic document, though not, of course, as venerable as certain other old family houses in University Place and lower Fifth Avenue. Those were of the purest 1830, with a grim harmony of cabbage-rose-garlanded carpets, rosewood consoles, round-arched fireplaces with black marble mantels, and immense glazed book-cases of mahogany; whereas old Mrs. Mingott, who had built her house later, had bodily cast out the massive furniture of her prime, and mingled with the Mingott heirlooms the frivolous upholstery of the Second Empire.[19]

As for Wharton's fictional description of interiors, rooms are "refunctionalized" to denote the inability of the nouveaux riches to get it right—the yawning gap between the possession of wealth and the knowing how to spend it properly. The library at Bellomont, for example, which features in *The House of Mirth*, "was in fact never used for reading, though it had a certain popularity as a smoking-room or a quiet retreat for flirtation."[20] This disparity is reinforced both by the fact that the library, with its Dutch tiles and "classically-cased doors," is in the original part of an old Dutch manor that has been greatly extended by the Trenors and by the reference to the Trenors's lack of interest in adding to the collection of "pleasantly-shabby books" on the shelves. This can be contrasted with Newland Archer's library in his matrimonial house on East Thirty-ninth Street in *The Age of Innocence*. Set in the 1870s, this novel deals with the years just prior to the displacement of the old New York elite, and Archer, a member of a prominent clan, exemplifies the fastidious taste of the old elite in the personal arrangement of his library "with a dark embossed paper, Eastlake book-cases and 'sincere' arm-chairs and tables." This is the room to which Archer retreats for "solitary musings" but also the scene of "all the family confabulations." Important family events have occurred or been marked in this room: announcements of forthcoming births and engagements, a son's christening, and discussion of career moves. In all, it has provided a genuine "frame for domesticity" in Archer's life. In Newland's later years as a widower, his architect son has "done over" the room "with English mezzotints, Chippendale cabinets, bits of chosen blue-and-white and pleasantly shaded electric lamps," but Newland has symbolically clung to his "old Eastlake writing-table" as representative of "good in the old ways."[21]

Wharton decorated her fictional houses with an eye to detail, linking character traits to the accumulation and display of material objects. These objects evoke a multitude of meanings: taste, style, social status, cultural knowledge, and history. One of the prominent figures in her old New York fiction is the collector. Her collectors are invariably men and come from either old New York or the new invading class. Accumulation and display is a common trait among both "Aborigines" and "Invaders" in her fiction; what separates them is the extent of their cultural knowledge and their financial resources.

One story that exemplifies both Wharton's fictional representation of contrasting social types and her exploration of the collecting ethos is a neglected tale, "The Daunt Diana," which appeared in her collection of short stories *Tales of Men and Ghosts* (1909). In the story, a millionaire called Daunt, whose fortune comes from gold mines, goes bust and sells his collection of bronzes, marbles, and enamels to Humphrey Neave. Neave is a Harvard graduate, but little is revealed of his social background save that he comes from Mystic, Connecticut, and is a man of slender means. Neave's whole life is devoted to buying bric-a-brac, often broken or marred in some way, which he is able to afford on a small income earned "expounding the antiquities to cultured travelers" in Rome. As an expert, he is consulted by dealers and owners, and on a day prior to Daunt's bankruptcy Neave is asked by Daunt to give his opinion on a few items in his collection. It is on this occasion that Neave first sees the "Daunt Diana," a bronze that is the best piece in the collection and which wholly captivates him. Neave is known among his friends as someone who has a special way with handling art objects—his "long inquisitive fingers" seem "to acquire the very texture of the thing, and to draw out of it, by every fingertip, the essence it has secreted." After viewing the collection, Neave turns to his friend Finney, who has accompanied him, and says bitterly: "Good Lord! To think of that lumpy fool having those things to handle! Did you notice his stupid stumps of fingers? I suppose he blunted them gouging nuggets out of gold fields." Neave resents the fact that someone such as Daunt, a man who does not know the value of the things he has, should have such a great collection "drop" into his hands. Neave, on the other hand, has made himself into a "delicate register of perceptions and sensations" and has "romanticized the acquisitive instinct" in himself.[22]

However, when Neave unexpectedly inherits a fortune from an uncle just at the time Daunt's fortune crashes, he purchases the collection and houses it in a Roman palazzo, but within a year he sells the collection at a huge loss. This is because the dealers can attribute his desire to offload the collection only to its being disappointing and therefore become nervous about buying the pieces at auction. But, within a year, the dealers realize that there is nothing wrong with the pieces at all and their value shoots up. So why did Neave sell the collection? Finney finds out from Neave that he had taken no pleasure from acquiring the collection in one fell swoop, that he had not taken time to build up a relation to the pieces before purchasing them. As Neave explains,

"The transaction was a *mariage de convenance*—there's been no wooing, no winning. Each of my little old bits—the rubbish I chucked out to make room for Daunt's glories—had its own personal history, the drama of my relation to it, of the discovery, the struggle, the capture, the first divine moment of possession. There was a romantic secret between us."

Neave nevertheless still wants the Daunt collection, and so he sets about buying each of the pieces back, one by one, at a tremendous price, ruining himself in the process. When Finney sees him again in Rome six or seven years later after their last meeting, he finds Neave in a couple of cold rooms in a palace-turned-tenement house where the smells of his neighbors' cuisine penetrate. Neave has the complete collection once more "huddled on shelves, perched on chairs, crammed in corners." In the tiny room that serves as Neave's sleeping quarters—"a mere monastic cell"—at the foot of the bed stands the Daunt Diana: "She rules there at last, she shines and hovers there above him, and there at night, I doubt not, comes down from her cloud to give him the Latmian kiss."[23]

In this tale, Wharton offers a stark and overt parallel between the collection of inanimate objects and the collection of women, a parallel that is present in more subtle ways in her other fiction. One very fine moment in the story is when she links the acquisitiveness of the collecting ethos to the capitalist ethos by making the source of Neave's multimillion-dollar fortune a corset factory. His uncle was "the creator of the Mystic Superstraight": "One had fancied that the corset was a personal, a highly specialized garment, more or less shaped on the form it was to modify; but, after all, the Tanagras[24] were all made from two or three molds—and so, I suppose, are the ladies who wear the Mystic Super-straight."[25] Remy Saisselin makes a similar connection between women and the bibelot in the nineteenth century when he claims that "the work of art functions as an object within an intimate interior space inseparable from woman herself. . . . Woman herself turns into a most expensive bibelot and yet is, at the same time, a voracious consumer of luxury and accumulator of bibelots."[26] Like *objets d'art,* men—and in particular capitalists—liked to display beautiful women elaborately arrayed, Saisselin argues, but made a firm distinction between the women they "bought" and the woman they married. The wife "was out of the market, so to speak; just as the objet d'art in a museum was beyond it, so the wife."[27]

If women were *objets d'art* in their palaces-cum-museums, they were also curators.[28] In the mid- to late nineteenth century they filled their homes with clutter. Delia Ralston's drawing room in Wharton's novella "The Old Maid" contains two "rosewood what-nots" filled with "tropical shells, feld-spar vases, an alabaster model of the Leaning Tower of Pisa, a pair of obelisks made of scraps of porphyry and serpentine picked up by the young couple in the Roman Forum, a bust of Clytie in chalk-white biscuit de Sèvres, and four old-fashioned figures of the Seasons in Chelsea ware."[29] Meanwhile, on West Twenty-eighth Street, Mrs. Archer and her daughter, Janey, occupy their days cultivating ferns in Wardian cases, making macramé lace, and embroidering linen, presumably to adorn their cramped quarters.[30] In her fiction Wharton played on the actual and well-documented propensity of mid-Victorian American women to indulge their sewing skills and surround themselves with decorative homemade objects alongside their collections of souvenirs from various trips to Europe. Her own views on this décor were made abundantly clear in *The Decoration of Houses.* Commercial knickknacks, cheap reproductions of works of art, were anathema to her, and little was to be gained from an "indiscriminate amassing of 'ornaments.'" On the other hand:

> Good objects of art give to a room its crowning touch of distinction. Their intrinsic beauty is hardly more valuable than their suggestion of a mellower civilization—of days when collecting beautiful objects was one of the obligations of a noble leisure. The qualities implied in the ownership of such bibelots are the mark of their unattainableness. The man who wishes to possess objects of art must have not only the means to acquire them, but the skill to choose them—a skill made up of cultivation and judgment, combined with that feeling for beauty that no amount of study can give, but that study alone can quicken and render profitable.[31]

Noticeably, it is men who are ascribed the potential to collect *objets d'art*. As Saisselin has explained, in both Europe and the United States the "bibelotization of the interior came to be regarded as a particularly feminine trait to be distinguished from the more manly enterprise of collecting works of art."[32] While Wharton's fiction does, to a large extent, follow these gender lines at least as far as Americans are concerned, she nevertheless defers to the taste of the European aristocracy, male and female. In *The Age of Innocence* the only woman who is credited with taste in the art of interior decoration is the Europeanized countess Ellen Olenska, who by "the skilful use of a few properties" has transformed her unpromising aunt's New York drawing room "into something intimate, 'foreign,'" while May Welland is destined to follow in her mother's footsteps and decorate her drawing room with "purple satin and yellow tuftings" and "sham Buhl tables and gilt vitrines full of modern Saxe."[33] Even old New Yorkers could be limited in their tastes.

Family Sociability

Comfort was the key note in Wharton's conceptualization of domestic space, and in no other room was this so important for Wharton than the family drawing room. Clutter in the form of "trashy 'ornaments,'" she and Codman strenuously argued, detracted from comfort.[34] Comfort was also the note struck by magazine writers in advising their readers on parlor furnishings. In the *Ladies Home Journal*, F. Schuyler Matthews recommended that the modern parlor should be "the most sociable, as well as the most comfortable room in the house," suggesting mahogany furniture, Japanese vases, Oriental rugs, and embroidered pillows for the divan.[35] The following month, James Thomson, in his article on parlor furnishings, derided the parlor of the past in "the dark age of decorative effort," which "one never entered without a chill, nor departed with delight."[36]

In her fiction, Wharton makes ample reference to nouveau riche types and their inability to convey a genuine domesticity in their household arrangements: the Wellington Brys's "recently-built house, whatever it might lack as a frame for domesticity, was almost as well designed for the display of a festal assemblage as one of those airy pleasure-halls which the Italian architects improvised to set off the hospitality of princes."[37] Similarly, Undine Spragg Marvell's drawing room in *The Custom of the Country* has been furnished by her with "cushions, bric-à-brac and flowers—since one must make one's setting 'home-like,' however little one's habits happened to correspond with that particular effect."[38]

One of the predominant trends in parlor decoration in the 1890s that formed part of the move toward informality was the creation of the "cozy corner." As Karen Halttunen has adroitly detailed in her article on the development of the Victorian parlor into a living room, this particular trend constituted a late Victorian reaction to the "moral parlor" of the mid-nineteenth century and its rather rigid arrangement of furniture around the walls. The cozy corner disrupted these uniform lines by placing a divan across one of the corners in the parlor, while the furnishings that were used were designed to create an informal space for intimate conversation. Cushions, with their suggestion of comfort, abounded, forming a stark contrast to the rigid-backed parlor chairs. "Baghdad curtains" were artistically hung across the corner, parallel to the divan, and Oriental bric-a-brac and Persian rugs added to the exotic effect.[39] As is well known, this was a time when Oriental furnishings and objects of art were popular. Jackson Lears has suggested that, with regard to late Victorian interiors, "exoticism and theatrical display intensified" in the 1880s and 1890s, and the interior functioned as "a stage set for private fantasy."[40] This trend in interior decoration for bourgeois parlors is also, however, reminiscent or at least suggestive of artists' studios in the second half of the nineteenth century.[41] Cozy corners could, however, only amplify the effects of the cluttered parlor. A regular writer for the *Ladies Home Journal*, Maria Parloa, warned of the danger of making cozy corners "stuffy corners." Overornamentation and excessive furnishings detracted from the original notion of the cozy corner as "a snug, comfortable place to rest and chat." The three goals to aim at, Parloa told readers, were "partial privacy, snugness and comfort."[42]

Along with cozy corners went cozy teas. Mrs. Burton Kingsland, writer of etiquette manuals and a regular contributor to the *Ladies Home Journal*, advocated teas as a form of "real sociability" among regular friends, with chairs drawn up to the fire "in cozy nearness to each other" and divans "made most alluring by a 'riot of downy pillows.'" She claimed that the tea was a descendant of the salon, and as such was an informal, mixed social gathering, with men "dropping in" between five and six o'clock.[43] It seems that accompanying a reaction against clutter there was also a reaction against "crushes" with "the cry of the time for few friends and good ones."[44] The Pruyn family of Albany, New York, were inveterate tea givers. Mrs. Pruyn inducted her daughters into the convention of a regular tea for friends. When staying in Paris in 1885–86 on an extended visit, Mrs. Pruyn invited the daughters of the Hampden Robbs every Sunday afternoon to take tea with her two daughters, Harriet and Huybertie. On each occasion they would "cook" over an open fire, making hot chocolate and molasses candy, and serve cakes from the Pâtisserie Anglaise on the rue de Rivoli.[45] In fact, teas were a regular feature of the Pruyns's social life, both formal and informal.[46] Among the family papers is a photograph of the family at tea. Given the technical difficulties with interior exposures, it is interesting that it was this family sociability that the Pruyns wished to memorialize in the form of a photograph. In her memoirs Huybertie explained that

> in those days, a photograph of an interior took long time exposures, and it would be impossible for anyone to sit still long enough to be in a picture. So, the problem of the picture of all at tea was solved in a roundabout way. First the room was photographed. . . . Then each of us was photographed out on the piazza, sitting in the chair in which we would appear. . . . After that, we were each cut out of our picture and pasted on the picture of the room, and, when that was done, the picture was taken over again so as not to show the pasting.

Her father is shown sitting "in a large mahogany and leather chair" that he used to use in the state senate, while her mother is "sitting at her tea table by the fireplace." For Huybertie, the image of her mother in the library at afternoon teatime was the one she most often remembered. For the Pruyns, the library was the heart of intimate family sociability.[47] It also held fond memories for Mrs. Pruyn of her married life. In her deep grief for the loss of her husband, she reminisced in her diary: "What lovely hours my dear Bean & I had sitting up late at night in his Library."[48]

Informal dances with relatives and close friends were also a feature of family sociability for the Pruyns. Harriet noted in her diary for February 1887, for example, that in their Albany home they had an informal *thé dansant* in their back parlor and dining room, while a band played in the front parlor. The women danced in their bonnets, and refreshments were served in the "china room."[49] Her use of the term "informal" clearly did not denote "unplanned" or "spontaneous" but referred instead to the style of dress. Even while living at the Hotel Bristol on the place Vendôme during an extended stay in Paris, Mrs. Pruyn entertained friends by having them for dinner in her private apartments at the hotel. On the evening of New Year's Day, for example, she rented a piano so that the invited company, which included the Richard Morris Hunts, could dance after dinner in the parlor.[50] This was the Christmas just prior to Harriet's eighteenth birthday and début in Paris, and such forms of socializing were probably intended to help Harriet prepare for more formal occasions. Even so, Harriet preferred informal entertainments, as did her sister, Huybertie, and there is a sense from both of the sisters' diaries that social interactions on such occasions were more meaningful and less artificial. They were able to relax and enjoy themselves, as opposed to feeling that they were on show and there-fore subject to scrutiny.

Formal Sociability in the Home

Among the very wealthy, such as the likes of Mrs. Astor, formal sociability in the home was integral to the social rituals that helped to define the boundaries of the elite. Dinners and balls as well as receptions in private homes were used to consolidate relationships within the inner circle. In the mansions of New York and Newport gala apartments were designed to provide the appropriate setting for such heightened formality.

In the homes of the wealthy the drawing room was a "ceremonial apart-ment" and used for formal rites of social observance.[51] It therefore contained the most impressive furnishings of the house, those designed to impress upon visitors the wealth and social standing of its owners. Wharton and Codman's advice was to make the company parlor gay. Walls "should be brilliantly deco-rated, without needless elaboration of detail," furniture should be movable so that groups could be spontaneously formed, and there should be no profusion of either small furniture or objects, so that movement should be unimpeded. In their scheme of things, electric lighting was, of course, proscribed. Wharton and Codman were scathing about any attempt by Americans to make the draw-ing room "uninhabitable" in order to qualify as the "best room" in the house and thereby sacrifice the comfort of the family. They also cast aspersions on the pretentiousness of the custom of spending most thought and money "on the one room in the house used by no one, or occupied at most for an hour after a 'company' dinner." In an effort to correct this tendency they evoked practices in "the grandest houses of Europe" where "the spectacle of a dozen people languishing after dinner in the gilded wilderness of a state saloon is practically unknown."[52]

The drawing room played an important role in the access rituals of the New York elite. Impression management came to the fore in the way in which guests were received on formal visits, whether these consisted of calls of ceremony or invitations to dinners or receptions. Even though, as has already been indicated, calling was one of the most common forms of social activity, it was never conducted casually. A particular time of day was set aside for visits and advertised to friends and acquaintances, a specific room was set aside for the reception of visitors, the hostess wore reception gowns designed specifically for these occasions, and an elaborate code of etiquette governed interpersonal relations and behavior. Little was left to chance.[53] Everything from setting to appearance was designed to convey certain impressions about the family who resided in the household being visited, which helps to explain the degree of control that was exercised over the rituals of calling. At a time of heightened social mobility and competition, ceremonial calls helped to reaffirm the shared values of the elite. The emphasis on politeness and knowledge of form shaped the interaction between visitors and hostess, and it tested the suitability of newcomers as potential members of the inner circle. This was combined with the material setting that gave off signs to be read by the visitor as to the sociocultural standing of the hostess. Acknowledgment of the value of the setting could convey the degree of cultural knowledge of the caller, an act that had to be carefully balanced between declaring one's knowledge without conveying a naive fascination for, or overfamiliarity with, the objects in question.

Dinners and other formal social entertainments that took place in the home were also governed by the principles of impression management. Dinners could be an arduous test for newcomers, as one etiquette manual warned: "The etiquette of dinner-giving is oppressive, when you are new to it, and inexorable always."[54] Parodying the intricacies of dining etiquette and the formality of dinner gowns, Francis Crowninshield (of *Vanity Fair*) advised in his mock manual: "When a lady beside you is so generously avoirdupoised or embonpointed that it is a physical impossibility for her to see the food upon her plate, it is sometimes an act of kindness to inform her as to the nature of the bird or beast so hopelessly removed from her vision. This saves her the trouble of lifting it above the horizon in order to discover its exact species."[55]

In *The Custom of the Country*, a finely tuned tragedy of manners, Wharton uses the scene of a formal dinner to trace the social nuances in the clash of manners between the "Invaders" and "indigenous" New Yorkers. The novel opens with a dinner invitation being extended by an old established New York family to a young nouveau riche woman, Undine Spragg. It is to be a small dinner of family and close friends at a Washington Square address, a location that seems to Undine hopelessly beyond the realm of high fashion. It is, moreover, Undine's first real test in her attempt to break into society. Thanks to newspaper descriptions of the "smart small and exclusive" dinners of her hostess, Undine has high expectations, but her evening proves to be an exercise in disillusionment. To Undine's eyes, "the house . . . was small and rather shabby. There was no gilding, no lavish diffusion of lights: the room they sat in after dinner, with its green-shaded lamps making faint pools of brightness."[56] As her hostess discovers, Undine's range of reading is limited to novels such as *When the Kissing Had to Stop*, as well as to the society columns in *Town Talk* and the *Radiator*. Undine's dinner party experience is presented as an evening in which she misreads "genuine" politeness and taste as insults or condescension and dowdiness. Undine does not hold the newspapers to account for embellishing on Mrs. Henley Fairford's dinners. Indeed, she blames Mrs. Fairford for failing to live up to her public image. It is therefore Mrs. Fairford who is at fault rather than the newspapers. Undine is singularly disappointed by the interior décor, the meal, and the company:

She had expected to view the company through a bower of orchids and eat pretty-coloured *entrées* in ruffled papers. Instead, there was only a low centre-dish of ferns, and plain roasted and broiled meat that one could recognize—as if they'd been dyspeptics on a diet! With all the hints in the Sunday papers, she thought it dull of Mrs. Fairford not to have picked up something newer.[57]

Wharton writes directly counter to newspaper discourse and infers a glaring disparity between the journalistic construction of a Washington Square dinner and her own fictional account, which is presented as authentic. More often than not, she represents private dinners as family or tribal rituals, which illustrates John Kasson's conclusion that dinners and dinner etiquette constitute "a great effort to maintain social order, hierarchy, and individuation." Moreover, "Victorian table manners . . . checked any sort of deviation from the paths of social propriety, whether they led in the direction of individual assertion or communal transformation."[58] Undine's misrecognition of the situation can therefore be read as a direct critique of the journalistic misrepresentation of the social elite and the failure of journalists to appreciate the deeper meanings of social interaction within the elite.

Although dinners were the most private of all formal social entertainments, they nevertheless received publicity from the columnists. Information about the dates of dinners and guest lists were supplied to the press both officially and unofficially. Mrs. Astor's dinners received the most kudos in New York and were represented as being supplementary to her other main social event of the winter season, the Astor ball. The emphasis in newspaper reports was on guest lists, the menu, and the decorations—details of which were meant to impress readers with their luxury and lavishness. Columnists rarely went further unless information came to light of some untoward incident at a dinner. The Saunterer, for example, cataloged a small list of "informalities" that had occurred at private entertainments "concerning which the guests have been requested to observe discreet silence. But tongues itch to wag." These included the sister of a millionaire on Fifth Avenue dancing at a dinner party a tarantella almost as well as a professional (an obvious slur).[59]

Private after-dinner entertainments took on a new dimension at the turn of the century with the onset of the vaudeville craze. Mrs. Stuyvesant Fish was described in *Town Topics* as a "feminine Moses" for attempting to lead New York out of boredom in the dull season of 1899–1900.[60] She organized three Saturday nights in January 1900 at her new home at 25 East Seventy-eighth Street. In its Sunday society page the *New York Times* carried a description (without comment) of the second of these, according to which a plantation scene was constructed on the stage of Mrs. Fish's private theater, with the storyline about a "young 'dud' darky" who had just returned from New York and who relates his experiences of fashionable life in New York. The entertainment revolved around mimicking well-known people in New York society (who were guests at the party), including Mrs. Herman Oelrichs, Mrs. Ogden Mills, the George Goulds, and Stanford White.[61] *Town Topics* did not hold back in declaring the entertainment to be one and a half hours of "drivelling idiocy."[62] Mrs. Fish's attempts at satirizing "the fashionable struggle for gentility" were clearly not appreciated.[63] One reason for this was that they laid bare the theatricality, pretentiousness, and hypocrisy of formal social life, and came close to bringing society into disrepute. Five years later, in 1905, Mrs. Fish was evidently still out of favor with the Saunterer, who derided another of her dinner parties that included theatrical entertainment. Information about the 1905 entertainment appeared in the journal over a period of three weeks. The issue prior to the event divulged that she had hired the Casino Company to come and perform parts from *Lady Teazle* for her dinner guests, and the issue after the event complained that there was so much tobacco smoke that her drawing room was like an "Eighth Avenue backroom" and that Mrs. Fish had managed to engage only the chorus girls from the show, although it still cost her $2,500. Further information was divulged—probably from a servant—saying that in her effort to turn her salon into a German beer garden, Mrs. Fish had used artificial flowers and grass, but that the grass had to be ripped up for the dancers, with the result that green dye had penetrated the hardwood floor.[64] However, by the time of her death in 1915, Mrs. Fish's reputation had been rehabilitated in the pages of *Town Topics*; she was now described as having been a woman of infinite variety and originality, even though she had frequently been misunderstood.[65]

Mrs. Astor's reaction to Mrs. Stuyvesant Fish's sending up the social formality of the Four Hundred with her eccentric entertainments was to suggest that they would have been better located "under a circus tent rather than in a gentlewoman's house."[66] Certainly not all hostesses followed Mrs. Fish's line in trying to enliven dinner parties with private theatricals or by holding mock formal dinners for monkeys and dogs, but her break with convention did signal a revolt against the kind of formality exemplified by Mrs. Astor. By this time, that is to say in the first decade of the twentieth century, New York society had broken up into competing sets. Mrs. Fish, Mrs. O. H. P. (Alva) Belmont, and Mrs. Herman ("Tessie") Oelrichs, backed by their husband's vast fortunes, entertained lavishly, if unconventionally, and always with an eye to publicity. The Stuyvesant Fish mansion on Seventy-eighth Street was designed by society architect Stanford White, who figured in Mrs. Fish's social circle. It was a thirty-five-room Venetian-style mansion containing a white marble hall and one of the largest ballrooms, if not the largest, in a private dwelling in New York.[67]

For those with the means to give general entertainments, town or country houses on a grand scale were necessary. The "gala rooms" of a house consisted of a *salon de compagnie*, a drawing room used for formal dinners and large entertainments, a ballroom, a music room, and a gallery. Wharton and Codman pronounced that gala rooms, as rooms for entertaining, should be entirely separate from family apartments, preferably by being located on a different floor. Once again, their concern was with defining the boundary between public and private. As rooms intended for general entertainments, they were supposed to be "large, very high-studded, and not overcrowded with furniture." In fact, "a gala room is never meant to be seen except when crowded: the crowd takes the place of furniture."[68] One of Wharton's best fictional descriptions of gala rooms appears in *The Age of Innocence*. The Beauforts's mansion

> had been boldly planned with a ball-room, so that, instead of squeezing through a narrow passage to get to it (as at the Chiverses') one marched solemnly down a vista of enfiladed drawing-rooms (the sea-green, the crimson and the *bouton d'or*), seeing from afar the many-candled lustres reflected in the polished parquetry, and beyond that the depths of a conservatory where camellias and tree-ferns arched their costly foliage over seats of black and gold bamboo.[69]

In *The House of Mirth*, set some thirty years later than *The Age of Innocence*, hostesses vie with each other over the size of their ballrooms. Judy Trenor is said to be "rankled" by the dimensions of the ballroom in the new mansion of the social climbers, the Wellington Brys, and has grandiose schemes to "build out" a new ballroom from her Fifth Avenue mansion, having purchased the house behind.[70] Ballrooms were indispensable parts of the equipment of society queens both in Wharton's fiction and according to the society columns in the press. The giving of general entertainments in one's home enabled an established hostess to determine who was in society, or at least in her set. Invitations conferred or reaffirmed social membership. General entertainments were meant to include all those who were "in." While the inner circle of New York society was still small enough, Mrs. Astor had been able to fulfill this requirement, but by 1890 or so it was impossible to hold such entertainments in private homes without giving offense, and so public ballrooms were used. Mrs. Ogden Mills, however, gave what was nominally a "small dance" in the third week of January despite constant adverse comments in the society columns about her exclusiveness in limiting invitations to two hundred.[71] As Florence Howe pointed out in her 1887 etiquette manual, the problem with small dances in private houses was that it made enemies, caused offense, and excluded mothers.[72] Private dances came back into vogue after 1900 with the fragmentation of New York society into smaller social sets.

In *The House of Mirth* the Wellington Brys, social aspirants, take advantage of a dull season and falling prices in Wall Street to launch their attack on the social citadel by giving a "general entertainment." In a daring move they decide to circumvent the slow, drawn-out process of calling and leaving cards and instead attack society "collectively." Their social guide and sponsor, Mrs. Fisher, "had decided that *tableaux vivants* and expensive music were the two baits most likely to attract the desired prey" and arm-twists "a dozen fashionable women to exhibit themselves in a series of pictures" to be arranged by the society portrait painter Paul Morpeth. Society succumbs and, "in obedience to the decorative instinct which calls for fine clothes in fine surroundings," assembles in Mrs. Bry's ballroom, presenting "a surface of rich tissues and jewelled shoulders in harmony with the festooned and gilded walls, and the flushed splendours of the Venetian ceiling." The *tableaux* are taken from "old pictures" by Goya, Titian, Vandyke, Kauffmann, Veronese, and Watteau. Behind the "layers of gauze," society women pose, allowing "magic glimpses of the boundary world between fact and imagination." The illusion is carefully orchestrated by Morpeth so that "the pictures succeeded each other with the rhythmic march of some splendid frieze, in which the fugitive curves of living flesh and the wandering light of young eyes have been subdued to plastic harmony without losing the charm of life." Indeed, one participant, Miss Smedden of Brooklyn, "showed to perfection the sumptuous curves of Titian's Daughter." The warmest appreciation of the audience is, however, saved for an even more daring revelation of curves when the curtain parts on Lily Bart's *tableau*. Lily has chosen Reynolds's *Mrs. Lloyd,* which enables her to dispense with "distracting accessories of dress or surroundings" and allows the men in the audience "an exceptional opportunity for the study of the female outline."[73] Lily is an expensive *objet d'art*, a "moment's ornament" who provides aesthetic pleasure for a brief thirty seconds while the curtain is raised on her *tableau*.[74]

The House of Mirth can be read as Wharton's "backward glance" to an era of sentimentalism, something that is all the more pronounced in an age when protections of privacy were being steadily dismantled and when the display of wealth was so conspicuous. In both *The Decoration of Houses* and *The House of Mirth*, Wharton sees New York society as self-deluded about the important things in life. In the earlier book, she condemns empty show—such as, for example, the placement of *objets d'art* in halls where their only function is to give a fleeting impression to guests passing through. In her novel, she represents a society that has become obsessively theatrical: The actors are so caught up in it that they have lost sight of the purpose of society. As Lawrence Selden says to Lily,

> The queer thing about society is that the people who regard it as an end are those who are in it, and not the critics on the fence. It's just the other way with most shows—the audience may be under the illusion, but the actors know that real life is on the other side of the footlights. The people who take society as an escape from work are putting it to its proper use; but when it becomes the thing worked for it distorts all the relations of life.[75]

Wharton went against the grain of her own times in arguing that people were self-deluded in thinking that openness and informality denoted a greater honesty and personal freedom, especially as far as women were concerned. As a young unmarried woman with certain desires and foibles, Lily Bart is, in fact, shown to be extremely vulnerable in the kind of society that Wharton criticizes. It is a society in which mass-circulation daily newspapers are plugged into private networks so that they amplify not only the desired effects society stages for public consumption but also its scandals and its *faux pas*. At the same time, Wharton reveals an ambivalence about old New York, as represented in part by Selden, whose understanding of Lily is limited to seeing her mission as a decorative one. As with *The Decoration of Houses*, *The House of Mirth* can be seen as involving a resurfacing of the sentimental ideal, insofar as it attacks the hypocrisy of high society.

Backstage

Formal sociability in the various forms discussed in the last section took place in the gala rooms, the "front stage" for genteel performances.[76] But, as Erving Goffman pointed out in *The Presentation of Self in Everyday Life*, "when a performance is given it is usually given in a highly bounded region, to which boundaries with respect to time are often added."[77] In accordance with nineteenth-century etiquette, it was tacitly understood that guests were not supposed to wander into the private rooms or kitchen area of houses, into what Goffman calls the "back region." This would undoubtedly have drawn attention to the appearance of the front region and to the behavior of those in it as something contrived simply by the sheer contrast in décor and furniture and by the presence of those elements that went into staging the front region performance (for example, food preparation, processes relating to the laundering and maintenance of clothes, facial cosmetics). Guests might also come across those servants who were confined to the back region and not as well attired as those who serviced the gala rooms. Goffman's analysis of the role teams play in staging a performance is also pertinent here, and indeed, he gives as an example of a team a hostess and her servants.[78] As he points out, a member of the team can disrupt the team performance "by inappropriate conduct," which highlights the dependency that each team member has on the others for maintaining the performance. "When members of a team have different formal statuses and rank in a social establishment, as is often the case, then we can see that the mutual dependence created by membership in the team is likely to cut across structural or social cleavages to the establishment and thus provide a source of cohesion for the establishment."[79] But in such a situation involving society women and their household staff (which typically numbered between twelve and fourteen),[80] there was no guarantee of cohesion, especially as there was such a high turnover of servants in New York City, where there was also a shortage of well-trained servants.[81] Anna Pruyn was not the only society woman to engage staff in Europe and transport them back to New York. It was a common perception that Europeans were better suited to domestic service than Americans, and if experienced servants with good references could be hired in Europe, it was considered an investment.

The "servant problem" had generated considerable debate in the United States throughout the nineteenth century and had been a bone of contention particularly between the British and the Americans, as British visitors, such as Mrs. Trollope, had often been critical of the poor standards of service in the United States. Americans were therefore sensitive about the quality of service, especially when attempting to maintain the kind of lifestyle that depended on high standards of service and was exceedingly demanding of servants in terms of their conditions of employment. In fact, a wide range of issues came to the surface in a series of interviews with society women about domestic service that appeared weekly over a two-month period in the *New York Times*. Some of the comments are very revealing about the attitudes of society women.

The articles had been prompted, in part, by a woman reader's asking why it was that men took their friends to dinner at their clubs and why so many people were having private dinner parties in restaurants instead of at home. One of the reasons this woman had given was that servants were incompetent. Of course —and this was the pattern of rhetoric for all of the society women who participated in the *New York Times* debate—she herself had little trouble with her own servants. Mrs. Russell Sage, of Troy and New York, blamed mistresses for the poor service and rapid turnover of servants in New York. She felt that servants were paid too much and that if they did not have enough to do they became quarrelsome. She recommended that three house servants and two for the stables were more than adequate; if she herself had any more, she would not be able to devote herself to the "important outside work" she undertook. Mrs. Sage attributed her success in retaining her servants to the fact that she herself had been properly trained by her mother: "I gained my experience by mother's side and I was capable of taking charge of a house when I was 18." The philanthropist Grace Dodge agreed with Mrs. Sage that it was the mistress who was to blame because women did not seem to know how to treat their servants. Mrs. Charles Parkhurst, wife of a famous Fifth Avenue clergyman, echoed these sentiments and thought mistresses should show interest in the welfare of their servants and allow them time off.[82]

In her comments, Mrs. W. H. Schieffelin indicated that she did allow her servants time off, sometimes to go to the theater, provided that there were always at least two servants in the house at any one time.[83] Her servants had their own rooms and she advocated allocating servants a room in which to sit after work. She herself gave her servants a large front room in the basement, which was carpeted and furnished, had a supply of "good books," and was a space in which they could receive friends and do their ironing. "They cannot," she said, after all, "lead lives of deadly dullness."[84] Mrs. Spencer Trask, the wife of the railroad magnate, who lived in Saratoga Springs and New York, also advocated giving books and pictures to servants and not treating servants like machines—a phrase echoed by Mrs. Delafield. The Trasks had established a home for domestics in Saratoga, one that trained young women for domestic service, and Mrs. Trask spoke with some fervor about the need both to inculcate in servants respect for their position and for employers not to treat servants as "a class apart": "Here is this great mass of people brought, as individuals, into the closest possible contact with our lives, who feed us, who take care of us, who see more of our children than many of us do ourselves, and yet they are spoken of and treated as though they were either machines or a class so far below us that they have no touch or sympathy or part with us in any way."[85] Mrs. Schieffelin agreed entirely with this view. She claimed that she felt indebted to her servants, especially at times of sickness and sorrow in her family: "They have been so kind and sympathetic that I have felt that they were friends." She also revealed her interest in educating her servants: "I like to talk with them and try to elevate their ideas." She had found in the previous year that her "up-stairs girls" were interested in women's suffrage.

Mrs. Walter Lester Carr took a stricter view of the servant-employer relationship. She said that she never let her servants off for an afternoon during the week, only on Sundays, but that they could go out in the evenings after their work was completed as long as they returned by eleven o'clock. Houses, she advocated, should be run "on a strictly business basis." Mrs. Carr asserted that she hired only servants who had served in "the old country" because they knew their place better. Her ethnic preference was for the Irish even though she was aware that Swedish servants were often favored. As far as she was concerned, Swedes had "no heart." In a statement replete with racist epithets, she advocated against the hiring of African Americans: "I have had a great deal of experience with colored servants, but I know and love them too well to employ them. They are not strong, and more of them are needed to accomplish the required work. They do their work in a slow, lazy manner."[86] The ethnicization of the discussion of servants in America was not uncommon. In a chapter entitled "The Servant Question," Mrs. Sherwood wrote of the "shoals" of immigrants who were arriving daily in New York and who made "poor domestic servants." She referred specifically to Italians. In her hierarchy of ethnic preferences, she listed French cooks as the best and French butlers, waiters, and footmen as "excellent" but "expensive." French maids were "dishonest." She favored Irish women as nurses but not as cooks. The Swedes she thought "eccentric" and the Germans unwilling. She painted a dismal picture of the management problems facing a fashionable woman in New York and claimed her life was "apt to be slavery."[87]

Analogies to slavery appeared on both sides of the mistress-servant relationship. A few weeks after the series of articles in the *New York Times*, the paper carried a letter purportedly from an "Irish girl" in which she spoke of domestic service as a "mild form of slavery." "It seems," the letter said, "to be an understood thing that the servant must be kept down." Given Mrs. Carr's sentiments, the analogy with slavery is not surprising. Moreover, Mrs. Carr would not have been an exception within the employer class. In a 1902 manual dealing with the rights and duties of domestic servants, the vast majority of the discussion is given over to "duties." In outlining the duties of a lady's maid, the author, Mrs. Seely, insisted that these should be performed in a "cheerful, kindly" manner, showing respect at all times. There were potential rewards for "deference, obedience, industry, and strict honesty"—the mistress would be more likely to be a "friend." In a list of "Don'ts for Servants," Mrs. Seely advised:

> Don't be always standing on your dignity as to what is and is not "your place"—
> if you cannot get along go away, but while you are in a house be pleasant. . . .

Don't think your mistress is unbearable because she may sometimes be a little
short in her manner,—ladies often have worries and responsibilities of which
servants have no idea. . . .

Don't spy on your masters and mistresses—the fact that their bread is in your
mouth should be a reason for keeping it shut.

The "Don'ts for Employer" constituted for the most part principles of good
household management, that is, consistency, fairness, acknowledgment of good
service, and so on. However, the list also contained the following points:
"Don't discuss servants in general, or those of any particular nationality, while
you are being waited on at table." Why specifically does Mrs. Seely stipulate
while being waited on at table? Was the employer more at risk then of getting a
bowl of soup in her lap? The clue is embedded in the chapter on "Dinners and
Dinner-Giving": "Dining-room servants should be so trained that they serve
the dinner in silence, not even the sound of a footfall should be heard."[88]
Discussing servants at a dinner party would have drawn the guests' attention to
the presence of servants, whereas they were supposed to be unseen and
unheard. While the rules for servants serving dinner were supposed to make
their employer unconscious of their presence, the rules for the mistress acted to
make her conscious of what she said and when. There is an interesting paradox
here with the requirement to be simultaneously unconscious and conscious,
something which comes up again in other matters of etiquette governing
women's behavior.

To return to the "Irish girl's" letter in the *New York Times*, one further point
of interest is made in its criticism of the employer class:

Another source of annoyance to our mistresses is our aping their dress and manners. I wonder if it ever did occur to them that they are setting the example
when they ape the manners and customs of their English friends. . . . Why can't
great, free, independent America afford to be original, have manners and customs exclusively their own?[89]

This raises the issue of national identity and proposes a concept of manners as
being preferably national and extending to all classes. This would have appealed
to the sympathies of those Americans whose concept of national identity was
strongly rooted in the revolutionary heritage and the casting off of the British
aristocratic system. It can also be read as attempting to show that European
immigrants' image of America reinforced that heritage, and that they identified
more strongly with their new home rather than with the country they had left.
With regard to the matter of class and manners in her study of domestic service
in nineteenth-century America, Faye Dudden comments that servants "could
not help but buttress or sabotage their employers' status claims" and resented

the way they were used by employers in "status competition."[90] It is not surprising that European immigrants working as domestic servants should have had a heightened consciousness regarding the contradictions between U.S. political traditions and the deepening class divisions in the late nineteenth and early twentieth centuries.

The employer-servant relationship in the households of New York's elite—an uneasy one at the best of times—came under even greater pressure with the publication of society gossip in newspapers and magazines, sometimes as a result of the bribing of servants by reporters.[91] As has been shown, this relationship depended on a great deal of trust in servants maintaining and sustaining the "team performance" of gentility, and by the same token it also required a great deal of tact from employers. The development of the public social life of fashionable society and the commercialization of the catering industry also had an impact on domestic service insofar as it reduced some of the pressures for elaborate formal entertainments at home. The increase in mobility and seasonal migration further complicated matters, especially with regard to the retention of servants. Many servants were, in fact, hired on short-term contracts. The decline in immigration during the war years was the straw that broke the camel's back, so that there was no return to the elaborate kinds of private sociability that had dominated high society in the late nineteenth century. In 1918 an article in the *Ladies Home Journal* spoke of the "famine of servants in the Eastern cities" largely because of the decline of immigration.[92] As a result of this, the author envisioned a new way of living that would involve more and more people using restaurants and living in apartments. *Vogue's Book of Etiquette*, published in 1925, confirmed this view:

> Housekeeping, on any large scale, is certainly becoming rarer in modern cities than it used to be. Comparatively few big, roomy dwellings are left to ordinary citizens. Mammoth apartment buildings are springing up on all sides, and more and more families are giving up the struggle to keep the old easy space about them and the old easy service.[93]

In this chapter we have explored the transformation of leisure in private spaces and considered the impact of commercialization on the home and domestic service. Even though the home was gradually displaced by commercial venues in providing the "stage" for leisure-class social life, the home itself came under greater public scrutiny, with illustrated magazine articles about the homes of the rich and famous and the public fascination with the private lives of the wealthy. Drawing upon Goffman's analytical framework, we have considered the ways in which architecture, interior decoration, and furnishings as well as patterns of sociability and the deployment of servants all contributed to a managed presentation of self on the part of the leisure class. Evidence of this has been gleaned from personal accounts of leisure-class life as well as from etiquette and household manuals. Additional evidence, of a critical nature, has been drawn from the fiction and nonfiction writings of Henry James and Edith Wharton.

4

Women Abroad

It is worthy of remark that, during the past decade, both in America and in England, sudden and violent changes have somewhat ruffled the placid waters of society. These new conditions of life have naturally necessitated new methods of social procedure. The telephone, coeducation, wireless telegraphy, motor cars, millionaires, bridge whist, women's rights, Sherry's, cocktails, four-day liners, pianolas, steam heat, *directoire* gowns, dirigible balloons, and talking machines have all contributed to an astonishing social metamorphosis.

Curiously enough no book of etiquette has taken account of these violent changes.[1]

Women of all classes were encouraged by the forces of consumer capitalism to venture beyond the home for both leisure and other social activities, yet there was nevertheless a great deal of ambivalence in social attitudes toward the presence of respectable women in public. Clergymen, among others, attributed the decline of domesticity to women's spending more time outside the home. On the other hand, etiquette authorities adapted rules of decorum to enable women to go out in public and retain their "respectability" and, spanning the entire period from 1870 to 1920, chapters on etiquette "in the street" or "in public places" routinely appeared in manuals. Women were assured by these manuals that if they dressed inconspicuously and walked quietly through the streets, they would be "sacred from insult or injury, even by the rudest."[2] In 1881, for example, John Ruth asserted: "No gentleman will stand in the doors of hotels, nor on the corners of the street, gazing impertinently at the ladies as they pass. That is such an unmistakable sign of a loafer, that one can hardly imagine a well-bred man doing such a thing."[3] However, well-bred men most certainly did do such things, according to the Saunterer, who regaled readers with details of a purportedly common occurrence on the piazza of the Reading Room, Newport's fashionable men's club:

> One of the many nuisances that the Reading Room will never stamp out is the many unpleasant persons who loaf on the piazza. Some modulate their voices when they are commenting on women obliged to pass the place, but not the chief offender, and hardly a woman passes but comes in for some sort of remark that can be heard all the way across Bellevue avenue. "Damned fine. Eh? What?" "Getting a little far now, but all right, all right." "Dress a little short, eh? Pretty trim ankle though!" and so on until women shudder when they approach the most exclusive club in America.[4]

It was in 1915 that these alleged remarks by members of Newport's Reading Room were said to have been overheard. They were the kind of remarks to which women in general were said to be at risk throughout the period in question merely by virtue of being in public. Public space was so fraught with risks for respectable women that they had to pay special attention to their demeanor. Women did not belong, it seems, in public space: It was alien territory, and they could not count on traversing it unmolested.[5] The presence of women automatically sexualized the context for men, as is evident from the alleged remarks of the Newport clubmen. Despite the long established code of gentlemanly conduct that decried such behavior, it was still anticipated that men would transgress that code. And, it was argued, men were most likely to transgress it in the face of female provocation, so that etiquette manuals concentrated on encouraging women to exercise bodily control to avoid drawing attention to themselves.[6] The double standard of morality pervaded etiquette discourse. Nevertheless, despite the constraints upon behavior that manuals advocated and despite their harking back to old, established traditions of social interaction, rooted in European aristocratic society, etiquette manuals contributed to the modernizing world. They enabled women to negotiate new areas of public space within the parameters of patriarchal gender relations. While this argument would appear to situate etiquette manuals as a progressive influence upon gender relations, it depends on whether modernization itself is seen as progressive. On the one hand, modernization seemed to promise certain social freedoms and release from some of the more stifling traditions of a gender-segregated society, whereas what we also see is that modernization led to a reinscription of patriarchal values in modern society.

Women nevertheless responded positively in the late nineteenth century to the extended access they began to enjoy to public space and the resources it offered for socializing and leisure. New urban facilities met the growing demand of women shoppers for ways of sustaining their presence downtown. Women's clubs, for example, offered women in town a respectable place to stay or simply to rest and freshen up. Women also took advantage of new means of mobility that freed them both from the paraphernalia of traveling by private carriage and from the social preclusions on traveling alone on public transport. In the mid-1890s the bicycle was taken up with initial enthusiasm, although mostly as a recreational form of leisure rather than as transport. It was not until the advent of the automobile that women's mobility took a more decided turn in favor of independence.

In the period 1870 to 1920, the cartography of public and private space was aggressively contested by New Yorkers and by urban dwellers in general. It was contested, in part, in terms of female sexuality with regard to the boundaries between respectable and promiscuous behavior, as can be seen in a wide range of text types, such as sermons, newspapers, etiquette manuals, and fiction. At the beginning of the period women's access to public space was temporally and spatially zoned in heavily restrictive ways. By the 1910s, however, the world outside the home had opened up considerably to the freer traffic of women, in cars or on foot. Nevertheless, women's access to and mobility within public space remained subject to forms of control, even though it was less hampered by the formalities of social decorum. We see this particularly with regard to society women, for even though women of the New York social elite found themselves with greater access to public space, they also found that the public had greater access to them. And there abounded voices of convention to insist upon the maintenance of behavioral codes, from clergymen to gossip columnists. As Judith Walkowitz has written of London in the 1880s:

> As the end of the century approached, this "dreadfully delightful city" became a contested terrain, where new commercial spaces, new journalistic practices, and a range of public spectacles and reform activities inspired a different set of social actors to assert their own claims to self-creation in the public domain.[7]

Clearly, there are parallels with what was happening in New York at this time. While etiquette encouraged a self-consciousness about dress and decorum, the rise of society journalism brought to bear an external form of monitoring, one that drew upon codes of etiquette in order to justify its comments and claim authority on social matters. Etiquette manuals prescribed behavior, but society columns purported to describe actual behavior. Both functioned as agents of social control.

Etiquette manuals and society columns performed yet another function. They remapped urban space for members of the "respectable" classes by providing city guides, both literally and figuratively, to the ever-changing topography of New York and indicating places of danger.[8] In effect, gender, class, and racial grids were superimposed upon the metropolis. And with the growing accessibility of urban space to bourgeois women in the late nineteenth century, concerns were expressed with regard to the ambiguity of gender and class boundaries, especially with reference to the sexual dangers that city streets posed to the bourgeoisie. As Mary Ryan has persuasively argued, these concerns bespoke an anxiety with the close proximity within nineteenth-century urban spaces of "diverse occupants" and an attempt to impose a moral order and social hierarchy on the perceived social chaos.[9]

In this chapter, I focus upon the representation of society women in etiquette, journalistic, and fictional discourses with specific reference to the ways in which women pursued new leisure activities, such as shopping, cycling, camping, motoring, and touring. While etiquette manuals provided women with guidelines on how to behave in new public spaces to enable them to negotiate the dangers of public space, society journalism, particularly in the form adopted by *Town Topics*, was much more blatantly part of a "repressive system for the reproduction of the status quo."[10] It upheld a certain ideal of high society and measured the activities of members of the social elite against it. Furthermore, in reporting and commenting upon the lives of the rich and famous, it sustained a moral order by reporting their deviancies and exposing them to public scrutiny. As such, the society journalist claimed power over metropolitan space and social relations within it by calling to account people of considerable material power. On the other hand, in her fiction Edith Wharton explores and exposes the pitfalls and contradictions of life in New York at a time of rapid change. In particular, she draws attention to the vulnerability of society women to the competing demands of propriety and publicity.

Women about Town

In the 1870s and 1880s, the "man-about-town" was a particular social type in New York, familiar to journalists and onlookers of the social scene. He was a clubman, a *bon vivant*, who could frequent a variety of theaters, hotels, and clubs all within a stone's throw of each other. He was a man of social position and wealth, but not an idler because not only did he enjoy the various resources of the city at this time, but he also served on planning and reform committees. He was apparently at his height when social life centered around the lower half of Fifth Avenue and Broadway, around Madison Square, and was said to have disappeared by the turn of the century. The death blow allegedly was dealt when Delmonico's moved, in 1897, from Twenty-sixth to Forty-second Street, a move that signaled that the center of fashionable high life had shifted further uptown, to the vicinity of Times Square.[11]

There was no female equivalent to the man-about-town as such. The social type he represented was clearly confined to one gender—to the one that had the freedom of the city both by day and by night. He could go where he pleased, alone or in company. Of all the streets in New York, it was Broadway that typified the temporal and spatial zoning that characterized social relations in the this period. During daytime it saw "the endless procession of well-dressed, handsome women" out shopping at the various department and specialty stores that lined it on either side. At night, the Great White Way became "a spinal column of midnight pleasureland," brilliantly illuminated by the electric street lamps and blazing shop windows and cafés. After dark, the midnight throng was said to consist of respectable and responsible men who had worked hard downtown and who were now in search of relaxation.[12]

The section of Broadway that attracted "respectable" women during the day in this period was known as Ladies' Mile. It was a shopper's paradise: "The fashionable stores of New York are to be found principally on Broadway, Fifth and Sixth avenues, and Fourteenth and Twenty-third streets. They embrace dry-goods, millinery, jewelry, fur, clothing, shoe, and other stores, and their customers consist almost entirely of ladies."[13] Amongst the most notable stores of this period was the first successful department store in the United States, A.T. Stewart and Co., a Venetian cast-iron shopping palace on Ninth Street, just north of Grace Church.[14] Another Venetian palace with a cast-iron façade was Tiffany and Co., the jeweler on Union Square. Arnold Constable and Co. stood on the corner of Nineteenth Street and was patronized by the rich and famous, including multimillionaires Cornelius Vanderbilt and John D. Rockefeller and the actresses Lillie Langtry and Ethel Barrymore, while Lord and Taylor occupied the corner one block to the north at 901 Broadway.[15] One of the few etiquette manuals to include shopping etiquette was Daphne Dale's *Our Manners and Social Customs* (1891), in which it was claimed that women had established certain rules "designed to preserve the proprieties and to maintain the rights of others."[16] One such rule was that it was "unladylike to enter a store unless you have a real errand." This, however, is not suggestive of the kind of retail capitalism prevalent in the 1890s, which encouraged impulse buying. Ladies were also told not to waste the clerk's time by not knowing what it was that they wished to purchase, or by chatting with a friend and keeping a clerk waiting. This appears to have been a problem that crossed national boundaries, because it was parodied by Zola in *Au Bonheur des dames,* his novel based in part on Le Bon Marché, the first great department store in Paris.[17] And, when purchases had been made, readers were advised to arrange for the goods to be sent home, because "a lady loaded down like a packhorse is not the most graceful object in the world, and in a public conveyance she is little less than a nuisance."[18] Shopping etiquette clearly lagged behind changes in the retail sector intended to stimulate purchasing and encourage browsing. It certainly conflicts with journalist James D. McCabe's portrait of fashionable shopping in 1880s New York as somewhere where "no one is urged to buy, but all the goods are readily shown to those who desire to examine them. Articles purchased are promptly forwarded to the residences of buyers, and every effort is made to render the task of shopping pleasant."[19] The leisurely enjoyment of browsing and handling goods without purchasing them was, however, closely scrutinized, according to McCabe. The liberalization of shopping practices was accompanied by the surveillance of store detectives.

The enticement of women out of their homes during the day into commercial, public space opened up possibilities for those in the catering trade, especially as numerous restaurants were located in the same vicinity as the shopping district. And if women were to be kept in the retail district as long as possible to maximize sales, then department stores also needed to look to the nutritional needs of their customers.[20] Women were able to partake of casual lunches in stores and restaurants with their friends and relatives.

Lunchtime, in the season, was claimed as a social affair, and ladies' luncheons became very fashionable in the 1890s. These generally took place in private homes, although restaurants often catered for them. Hotels specialized in offering afternoon teas, and tearooms became very popular around the turn of the century—so popular and fashionable, in fact, that it was not unknown for society women who had fallen upon hard times to start up their own business by opening tearooms.[21] Mrs. John A. Lowery, for example, drew the attention of *Town Topics* in 1896 when she opened a "tea-room," modeled on Parisian tearooms, at 291 Fifth Avenue. The Saunterer expressed surprise that "hard times" had "forced her to follow the prevailing fashion and go into trade."[22] This comment was relatively mild in contrast to the Saunterer's diatribe against the kind of men who frequented tearooms in order to prey upon susceptible society women:

> Of the many kind of petticoat trailers that infest New York there is none more objectionable and pernicious than the one who infests with his noisome presence the corridors of our big hotels, and persistently ogles and insults women who happen to be depending on the security of houses of the first class for protection.

The particular man the Saunterer had in mind here was someone who had failed to get into society, who haunted "all the tea-rooms and other gathering places of women . . . leering and laughing through his sandy mustache."[23] Sherry's, the popular society restaurant, was apparently prone to such "petticoat trailers." Worse still, in the Saunterer's eyes, were those men who also preyed upon young society men naive about the ways of the world. Once again, an unwelcome trend was regarded as European:

This gorgeous collection of limp lilies . . . these picturesque, if undesirable, adjuncts to modern civilization, are common in Europe, and we, active in the assimilation of old world vices have accepted them among other imported necessary evils.[24]

In the 1880s and 1890s, women who had closed their homes for the summer sought accommodation in hotels when they came up to town to do shopping and run errands. Out-of-towners, such as Mrs. Pruyn of Albany, always stayed at hotels in the city. Even for short visits, as her daughter Huybertie recalled, a great deal of luggage was necessary: "We each had a dressing or toilet bag and these were often quite heavy as they were fitted with English silver topped glass bottles—ivory brushes—a portfolio—ink-well—a hand glass and generally a pair of travelling candlesticks in a round silver case. If there was any space for a nightgown and sponge, you were lucky." In the 1880s Mrs. Pruyn favored the Brevoort House on the corner of Fifth Avenue and Eighth Street. There facilities were fairly basic. Mrs. Hamlin remembered that they had a tin bathtub that was tucked away in a cupboard off their first-floor sitting room, and open coal fires in every room because furnace heat was not available in every room. At that time most of their friends lived in the vicinity of the Brevoort House, mostly in Washington Square.[25] When the Brevoort became "very far down town," the Pruyns stayed at what Huybertie called "that old fire-trap, the Brunswick, on Fifth Avenue." Without much success they had tried the Cambridge Hotel, on the corner of Fifth Avenue and Thirty-third Street, but found the plumbing "ancient and probably unsafe." In 1892 Holland House opened at the corner of Fifth Avenue and Thirtieth Street, and the Pruyns patronized this hotel for some years, as it offered modern plumbing and "an excellent table." Mrs. Pruyn preferred the suite on the fourth floor overlooking the Collegiate Church, because it was sunny and relatively quiet. The suite contained "a small hall with a coat closet, a sitting room, two bedrooms with baths" and cost $17.50 per day, which "was considered a very high price indeed." Mrs. Hamlin tells the amusing story of her mother's negotiation of a piece of new hotel technology, the "teleseme." This was "a large disc set in the wall" with a "finder" that one set according to one's order, anything from ice water to the doctor, before pressing a red button.

One morning, Mother had an engagement with Mrs. John Erving who was to come to see her at eleven o'clock. It was a warm spring day and she asked for a glass of water. Mother went confidently to the "Teleseme" and pointed the finder at ice water—or so she thought—pushed the red button and the buzzer buzzed. The two friends spent a few minutes marvelling over modern inventions and then settled down to a pleasant talk. Mother suddenly realized that a long time had passed but no water had appeared so she tackled the "Teleseme"

again; then she heard talking in the hall, then a knock and in came a waiter carrying a table, followed by another waiter carrying a large pail of ice, with a bottle neck sticking out. It seemed that mother had set the finder at champagne and
a quart bottle on ice was the result of the modern time-saving invention for
these two ultra Victorian ladies in the middle of the morning.[26]

At the turn of the century, the new women's clubs competed with the hotels
for female clientele. In an item on women's clubs in New York in 1902, the
New York World said there were three flourishing: the Town and Country Club,
the Woman's University Club, and the Woman's Club. The Woman's Club
was the most recent addition, having opened in November 1901 at 9 East
Forty-sixth Street.[27] According to the woman behind the club, Mrs. S. Everett
Oakes, the intention was to provide accommodation for women from out of
town who did not wish to go to a hotel or impose on friends, to provide "some
nice place to which a woman could go and feel perfectly at home without
being under obligation or having to pay an expensive hotel bill." The club
occupied two brownstones and offered as facilities to members Turkish baths
and a pool (in the basement), dressing rooms, clothes lockers, "lounging parlors," and dining and luncheon rooms, as well as manicuring, hairdressing, and
chiropody services. Single or twin bedrooms were available at $1 and $2 per
night, respectively. The article included a list of ways in which women could
make use of the club:

> They can run in after shopping to have their hair fixed.
> They can take an afternoon nap in the lounging room.
> They can hire a chaperon.
> They can buy theatre tickets, call a carriage or use the telephone.
> They can "put up" for the night and have breakfast served in their rooms.
> They can leave their "things" in the lockers to be kept till called for.
> They can have goods sent there from the dry goods stores for their inspection.

Reminiscent of a subscription ball, membership was decided by "social leaders"
who were invited to act as patronesses and to send a list of those women eligible to be members. Application for membership could only come through a
patroness. Alternatively, two existing members could propose a new member.[28]

In July 1895 the *New York Times* had carried an article revealing extraordinary antagonism toward the idea of mixed clubs. The Metropolitan Club had
provided an annex for mixed gatherings, such as dinners, dances, and receptions, and very occasionally held a "Ladies' Day" when women were admitted
to the main rooms of the club. Otherwise men's clubs were male sanctuaries.[29]
The idea of mixed clubs struck at the core of gender-segregated sociability and
current conceptualizations of masculinity and femininity. Walter S. Logan of

Yale was quoted in the article as saying that there was nothing in men's clubs to attract women. He continued: "Club life largely signifies a place for feasting. Men have an appropriately heavy way of satisfying grosser appetites. Women have corresponding appetites and ways of daintiness. . . . A man enjoys a 'small hot bird and a large cold bottle' at midnight in his club! At that hour a woman is apt to want to do up her hair in her dressing room—to make us happy the next day." If mixed clubs took off, Logan thought, this would result in "more shadowy corners than ever yet were known to exist in the architectural possibilities of today" and full calendars in the divorce courts. The editor of *Harper's Weekly*, Henry Loomis Nelson, quoted in the same article, also presaged the image of society falling apart: "It would be like admitting two or three women into large bachelor apartments. Clubs are decidedly bachelor institutions. They are for the indulgences of lapses into bachelor life." Like Logan, he also indicated that sex could not be separated from good fellowship with women and suggested that it was important for men and women to have the opportunity to get away from each other "once in a while." Besides which, if women were admitted to club membership, the cost of membership would soar, as club entertainments would undoubtedly become more elaborate.[30]

One of the most outspoken opponents of what was seen as a trend in the mid-1890s of women attempting to do everything that men did was the Reverend Charles Parkhurst. In his first article in a series for the *Ladies Home Journal*, he pointed to an "element in the feminine world" that he called "Andromania," which he defined as a "passionate aping of everything that is mannish." He further elaborated: "It is an attempt on the part of those affected with the disease to minimize distinctions by which manhood and womanhood are differentiated, whether as regards their culture, their interests or their activities."[31] Edward Bok, the *Journal's* editor, echoed these sentiments in his editorial in the following issue with his criticism of the "New Woman" and the movement "which seeks to disassociate women from the home."[32]

Bourgeois women made their presence felt downtown in a wide variety of ways during the day. Women's participation in the world of department stores and specialty shops contributed to their role in displaying the wealth of their husbands and personifying their own leisure. Women of the social elite also engaged in charitable and philanthropic work, which enhanced this role. At the same time, they did things for themselves: They established clubs as separate, safe spaces for women in the city, they willingly colonized retail areas, and they benefited from their consumer power.

After Dark

Ladies do not call upon a bachelor, in his rooms, after attending a dinner given by him—except in Mrs. Wharton's novels.[33]

Women were more successful at establishing a claim over public space during the day, but at night they were still especially vulnerable to harassment from men. There was little mercy for women who might find the need to be in public space alone at night: "Ladies who venture out alone at night must not expect to escape notice, nor must they be surprised if they become the victims of rudeness and the subject of severe criticism."[34] The dominant view was that there was only one category of women who were in public at night unaccompanied by an escort or chaperon: women who were sexually available.[35]

In all of her New York society fiction, Wharton explores the distinction between moral and immoral women, a distinction that, as I have argued, became increasingly problematic as women became more mobile and had greater access to public space. This ambiguity concerning the boundaries between respectability and promiscuity is a significant theme in *The House of Mirth*. Lily Bart, the female protagonist, finds herself in a series of compromising situations: being caught coming out of a bachelor's apartment during the day and lying about her reason for being there; getting entangled in a relationship with Gus Trenor, a married man who gives her money that she thinks is her own; being manipulated by a married woman friend as a decoy for that woman's own adulterous affair; being used by a lawyer to launch a western divorcée into society and being offered money to bring off the divorcée's marriage to a man in Lily's former social set. All of these situations, apart from the first, involve Lily's own misrecognition of what is occurring; but it is the first incident, the one that sets in motion the other events, that involves Lily being "misrecognized" by a third party. As she exits The Benedick, a building of bachelor apartments, after paying a quick visit to her friend, Lawrence Selden, Lily is seen by the Jewish financier Sim Rosedale. She compounds the situation by saying she has come to town to see her dressmaker and by snubbing his offer of a lift to the railway station. Rosedale, who owns The Benedick, draws from her discomfiture and obvious lie the conclusion that she is covering up a sexual liaison with one of the residents.[36] Through Rosedale, then, Lily enters into the circulation of male gossip as a sexually promiscuous woman, because he imparts what he has seen to other men in her social circle. This male construction of her character comes back to Lily in the form of a taunt issued by Gus Trenor, a married man who is besotted with her. He complains to her that she is leading him on while "letting a lot of other fellows make up" to her: "Gad, you go to men's houses fast enough in broad daylight—strikes me you're not always so deuced careful of appearances." In a flash she makes the connection with Rosedale: "This was the way men talked of her."[37]

Lily finds herself in another compromising situation when she is lured to the Trenors' Fifth Avenue mansion by Gus one night when his wife is out of town. This situation is, however, much more threatening. First of all, she is in danger of being raped by Trenor. Second, she has to make her exit at night onto Fifth Avenue, where she is likely to be seen by members of her social circle; because of this, "an insistent voice warned her that she must leave the house openly." Despite her superhuman effort to maintain the appearance of respectability by getting Trenor to ask his servant to call her a cab and then insisting that Trenor escort her to the cab, Lily still cannot control the assumptions made by two witnesses to her exit. Selden and Lily's cousin, Ned Van Alstyne, just happen to be walking along Fifth Avenue at that precise moment and both know that Trenor is alone in his townhouse. Van Alstyne is privy to the current male gossip about Lily's promiscuous activities. Earlier that evening he had commented in mixed company with reference to her that "there is no provision as yet for the young woman who claims the privileges of marriage without assuming its obligations." He nevertheless asks for Selden's discretion. Instead of reading the situation in the most charitable terms, Van Alstyne assumes the worst and yet tries to make the case for thinking otherwise by pointing to the inadequate lighting on the avenue.[38] There is a nice irony here. Inadequate lighting leaves room for doubt, but broad daylight or the glare of electric light leave no such room, and yet Selden is the one who is complicit in Lily's first exit from his apartment and showed no sign of scruples then. This time, seeing Lily exit from Trenor's at night, he too assumes the worst, showing himself to be hidebound by convention and a complete hypocrite. This is the man who dallies with married women under their husband's noses and thinks nothing of it, but who casts the first stone when he thinks he sees an unmarried woman having an affair with a married man.

As a modern woman in the 1900s, Lily Bart pushes the boundaries of acceptable behavior, such as smoking, gambling, flirting with married men, and traveling without a chaperon. In doing so, she puts herself precariously outside the dominant norms of her society. As an unmarried woman and orphan of limited means without an extensive family prepared to support her, she finds that she cannot transgress boundaries as easily as her married companions. Indeed, her vulnerability is repeatedly marked in the text when she is portrayed in particular situations that allow certain male characters to read her behavior as promiscuous.

The degree of Lily's fall from grace grows increasingly severe as the narrative progresses. She starts out being constructed as a *demimondaine*, the alleged mistress of first a bachelor (Selden) and then of two rich married men (Trenor and Dorset). Ejected from the charmed circle of the fashionable, she becomes the (unwitting) associate of a pimp (Mr. Stancy), and then, when she no longer has a private income, she becomes a working girl employed in a milliner's. The latter is heavily laden with symbolic significance because hat shops were notorious as fronts for brothels. She hits rock bottom at the end when she is misrecognized as a streetwalker. She sits down on a park bench, exhausted from walking, and remains there till after dark illuminated by a "white circle of electric light"—again this holds symbolic significance in the code of prostitution, with streetwalkers standing beneath street lamps. In Wharton's own code of interior decoration, electric light is irretrievably vulgar. For the first and only time, Lily is *unconscious* of her setting and her appearance.[39]

The great irony here is that at no time does Lily sell her body—not even in marriage, which was supposedly the respectable thing to do. She sells only her skills and labor. But these do not make her financially independent; instead, she remains dependent upon her family and friends. Wharton paints a grim picture of a society woman who falls on hard times.

Women Outdoors

The concern that women should be inconspicuous in public space meant that women were advised to avoid attracting any attention whatsoever either by "an extreme peculiarity of dress, manner or gait."[40] "Quiet colors" were uniformly recommended. There was a strong sense of dressing appropriately for the occasion, so that for shopping or visiting the business district, "showy costumes and brilliant colors" were deemed in bad taste and lacking in refinement. "For walking or paying visits on Fifth Avenue in New York," on the other hand, Florence Howe advised that "it is allowable to dress more handsomely."[41] Back in 1860 Florence Hartley had recommended in very practical tones that, for shopping, dresses "should be of such material as will bear the crush of a crowded store without injury, and neither lace nor delicate fabrics should ever be worn."[42] Even window-shopping was cause for concern in one manual: "A lady should always walk in an easy, unassuming manner, neither looking to the right or to the left. If anything in a store window attracts her notice she can stop and examine it with propriety, and then resume her walk."[43] The attention paid to street dress was extended to all kinds of dress for women in the nineteenth century. Advice was fairly conservative with regard to the variety of costumes that might be worn in public space. It is little wonder, then, that when women began to participate in sports and recreation, which required considerable modification of their usual daytime clothes, questions of propriety were raised. The mobility that was necessary for undertaking some of the new sports and pastimes meant that women had to abandon the sometimes crippling immobility of their daily dress, especially corsets and skirts that trailed on the ground. Indeed, involvement in sport was another means by which women laid claim to public space, and it was one that provoked considerable controversy.

In the 1890s the New York social elite embraced the outdoors and took up with enthusiasm a wide range of leisure activities from swimming and golf to cycling and camping. Nevertheless, fashionable society constituted a capricious set of people who indulged in fads, which they abandoned when the mood took them, and the leisure trade suffered from their fickleness. Skating and cycling clubs for the elite came and went; even golf clubs could not reckon on their future if dependent upon the patronage of the fashionable.

Among the enduring traditions of leisure in public was driving around town or in Central Park in a private carriage.[44] There was a "fashionable" hour when the wealthy, mostly women, would drive out to Central Park in their carriages—a custom that linked them to the elites of European cities. The most popular hour of the day for this was between 4:00 and 5:00 P.M.[45] The spring and early summer months constituted the coaching season. In June 1906 the *New York Times*'s society page noted that despite the new popularity of the automobile as a fashionable mode of transport for the wealthy, equipages in Central Park had shown little falling off from earlier in the spring.[46] The prominent bachelor and socialite John Henry Smith caught the attention of *Town Topics* in that same season with his alleged tendency to gather around him women who attracted attention because of their beauty or clothes. His companion on the day of the annual parade of the New York Coaching Club was Nathalie Schenck Collins, who was described by the Saunterer as "the most daringly attired woman in the show. Her toilette was exceedingly conspicuous."[47] Huybertie Pruyn Hamlin recalled spring days in New York when

> the four-in-hands started from the Brunswick for their daily trips to Pelham Bay, New Rochelle or Yonkers. Colonel DeLancey Kane, Colonel William Jay and Mr. Frederick Bronson were the usual drivers and it was a pretty sight as they were beautifully turned out and the lady on the box seat was an object of deep envy as she sat with her flounced parasol tipped on one side.[48]

Kane was a well-known driver of carriages and a leading member of the New York Coaching Club. Mrs. Hamlin also recalled one of her favorite sights in New York during the winter months when there was heavy snow on the ground: the sleighs on Fifth Avenue on a fine afternoon:

> Some of the turn-outs were very fine, particularly with Russian sleighs. . . . The coachmen and footmen wore beautiful capes and collars and generally fur caps and the fur robes matched this fur or else were a complete contrast. There were cutters too and an invitation to go in one and be driven out beyond Central park where there was mild racing, was really coveted. The streets were badly lighted, that is, according to modern ideas, but they were bright enough to make the sleighs look very gay and almost a stage scene as they returned from their decorous tours of the park, often stopping to watch the skating on the park lake.

By 1906 women's driving had become acceptable and the Ladies' Four-in-Hand Driving Club had its own annual parade in May. According to *Town Topics*, one of the first women to learn how to drive was Mrs. Tommy

Hitchcock (née Eustis) who had first driven "a four" in the Bois de Boulogne fifteen years before, when it was then regarded in New York as a "disreputable" activity for a lady. Mrs. Hitchcock was supposed to have introduced the fashion to New York; she was also credited with "the introduction of the fashion of riding astride among society women."[49]

In their study of Central Park, Rosenzweig and Blackmar suggest that the Park's carriage drives were more democratic in their accessibility to new wealth than were the city's clubs or the boxes of the Academy of Music. In the Park social aspirants could drive in their carriages alongside those who were firmly positioned within the charmed circle of the elite. In this indiscriminate mix of people, it was crucial to be able to recognize who was, and who was not, in society, a task that was becoming increasingly difficult, as the economic resources of the aspirants sometimes outstripped those of the "ins." At the same time, the barriers between respectable women and those of dubious reputation were threatened by the presence of Madame Restell, an abortionist, and Josie Woods, an uptown brothel keeper, brilliantly arrayed in their splendid equipages.[50] Back in 1888, the Saunterer had complained of "Parisianization" with regard to "the turnouts of the *déclassés* and 'professionals'" who were "fast out-doing in quiet elegance the equipages of the irreproachables." The latter, he claimed, had been dubbed "Ladies of the Lake," and he wondered what names would be given to "the Phrynes of our Park."[51]

Driving, rather than walking, in Central Park was considered more respectable for women because carriages enabled them to keep their distance from the public. Also, they could wear silk dresses and be on display; it was yet another opportunity to see and be seen. In the winter of 1905 it was a matter for comment that society women were going for morning walks. *Town Topics* announced that the "walking mania has a stout grip on fashionable women" and mentioned Mrs. Perry Belmont and Mrs. Egerton Webb as two exponents of this form of exercise.[52] At this time, horse riding in Central Park was still popular as a form of recreation. The Saunterer noted that the early morning was favored by businessmen, late morning was the time for children, and in the afternoons everyone thronged the bridle path. He complained about the dress and style of some of the equestrians. One fifth of "the grown up girls" were riding astride and there appeared to be a "wide difference" in the way they were dressed, while the men were even more remiss in their apparel, with only a few wearing breeches with boots or leggings.[53]

In 1905 skating was revived with the establishment of the St. Nicholas Skating Club on Sixty-sixth Street and Columbus Avenue. The *New York Times* devoted a page to the revived fad, commenting: "First the wheel drove it out. Then it was winter tennis, then winter golf, then badminton. Then along came the auto, and no snow or mud was a bar to the enthusiasts. But one by one the fads have had their little innings, and even the auto is getting to be no novelty and the day must be propitious and the going good before the society girl will venture out." Like other clubs, membership was carefully vetted, thus providing a space for the elite to skate "aloof from public gaze," as nonmembers were barred. Members were said to include the J. J. Astors, the Cornelius Vanderbilts, the J. R. Drexels, Mrs. Vanderbilt, the W. K. Vanderbilts Jr., the Bayard Cuttings, and Jean Reid and her close friend Gladys Vanderbilt. Between ten o'clock in the morning and eleven o'clock at night there were three sessions, with the ice being renewed during the intermissions. The club colonized the west balcony, which was described as being exquisitely carpeted and furnished with "dainty chairs and lounges." A home away from home, the club provided the society woman with "all the comforts of her own boudoir": "A great wood fire burns in the marble fireplace. Easy chairs and settees invite rest and relaxation. Vases filled with roses stand in every conceivable place; candelabra shed a soft light over the cozy room when the daylight is gone." Every thought was given to the skaters' comforts: maids, card tables for bridge players, supper for those who came to the evening session, and, for men, locker rooms with leather chairs and a bar service.[54]

Ice skating was perhaps the least contentious as well as the oldest of pastimes. Roller skating attracted slightly more attention from critics because of the opportunities for instructors to take advantage of young women learners. But it was cycling that excited the most controversy when, in the summer of 1894, society women "took up the wheel." This was a short-lived fad but it received more publicity, particularly of an adverse nature, than any other. It may have had something to do with the mobility it gave to women in public space, particularly in the city. Women's recreational cycling in the countryside seems to have been more acceptable because there women's appearance on a bicycle could be associated with the benefits of physical exercise. Of all the features of bicycle riding, however, it was the manner of dress that caused most consternation and debate. For safety reasons, it was preferable for a woman to wear bloomers or a divided, or "short," skirt. All of these options aroused antipathy. In addition to dress, the mere fact of women riding astride on a bicycle suggested mannish behavior, which perhaps explains the association of women's cycling with the "New Woman" of the mid-1890s. Within high society, cycling appealed across the board to women of different political persuasions and differing attitudes toward modern life. Mrs. Henry Clews, who was best known for wearing the latest fashions, and who, according to newspaper accounts, conformed to the standard conventions of women's behavior in the leisure class, was an avid cyclist. Meanwhile, her unconventional daughter, Elsie, was also a keen wheelwoman. Alva Vanderbilt, one of the most famous society leaders and an ardent suffragist, took up cycling at the height of her fame as a society hostess. She was said to ride eight miles a day in Newport and was reported as having been seen riding along Ocean Drive wearing a "thick dark veil."[55]

As with other recreational activities, society cyclists soon formed an exclusive club and established an arena for learning to cycle in private. The Michaux Club was formed in December 1894 on Broadway near Fifty-third Street. Its key organizer was a British aristocrat, Mr. C. Wyndham-Quin, the cousin of Lord Dunraven, and the management committee included Elisha Dyer Jr., better known as a cotillion leader. During the previous summer in Newport, James Van Alen was said to have been instrumental in encouraging cycling and had organized a noted event, a lantern ride. Those who did not have bicycles or could not ride had, at that event, followed the cyclists in "broughams, traps and phaetons, with the necessary accessories of coachmen and footmen."[56] Society women too had been involved in the initial phases of the "bicycle craze," as it was depicted. Miss Gammell and Miss Hunter had organized a club in Newport in the early part of the summer of 1894 and were said to have been supported in this venture by Mrs. Henry Clews and Mrs. Stuyvesant Fish.[57] The latter two's appearance on bicycles in New York City had excited attention from the newspapers. Under the headline "Pretty Girls on Wheels—Leading Society Women Have At Last Taken up the Cycle as a Fashionable Fad," the *New York Herald* stirred curiosity by suggesting that at twilight "mysterious forms creep out" on West End Avenue: "Just for a moment you are startled by an apparent chance resemblance. You recognize a neck, for instance, that you have seen swathed in tulle or lace."[58] From the very early days of society women's cycling, their appearance in the streets was called into question. The way they were dressed and the fact that they rode bicycles astride was a matter for comment, and such comments had the effect of sexualizing them. In the mid-1890s, then, the society columns of newspapers and society magazines disclosed an anxiety with the latest of women's fads. Above all, the fear was that women were adopting masculine behavior.

Advertisements in the newspapers for women's bicycling costumes gave expression to such fear. In selling such a controversial product, retailers were at pains to reassure all readers of the suitability of such a mode of dress. An advertisement for "The Luey" bicycle costume that included an illustration of a suit consisting of a jacket, a short divided skirt and leggings was accompanied by a description that ran:

Nothing about "The Luey" costume suggests masculine attire. It is essentially effeminate in appearance, and yet has none of the disadvantages of a long skirt, which must be hooked or strung up, and which is always in danger of catching in the wheel.

The skirt permits ease of movement, and at the same time hangs gracefully, and is always stylish. . . .

No lady cyclist can look other than bewitching in a "Luey" costume.

The costume, furthermore, had multiple uses; the advertisement suggested that it was also ideal for the mountains, golf, and tennis.[59] The accentuated features of the costume were its femininity, its safety, its mobility, and its grace. And despite its practical design, it was still something attractive to men.

Society women were apparently reluctant to adopt the popular Parisian costume for cycling—bloomers. Newspapers reported that most women usually wore cycling skirts, which were shorter than their usual street dress. In the second summer season of the bicycling craze, the *New York Times* reported that only one woman was courageous enough to appear in bloomers in Newport and then only under the cover of darkness. Other Newport women chose to ride in long black skirts with silk waists.[60] Mrs. J. C. Minor, winner of the Michaux Club tournament in January 1895, wore a "suit of black cloth bloomers" that was described as presenting "a graceful and fetching appearance as she wheels around the big hall to the enlivening strains of the orchestra."[61] Huybertie Pruyn purchased a bicycle suit in Paris at the Magasin du Louvre:

> It was tailor made and had a quite short coat and a skirt to the tops of my shoes and bloomers of the same dark brownish cloth underneath. The hat was a very small brown felt. It looked trig and made for business and the skirt escaped catching in the wheel which often was a cause for bad accidents. It went down acceptably in Paris—nobody noticed it but later in Albany it was a sensation.

The sensation that she referred to included newspaper publicity while "several older women" told her that they hoped she would "discard such a costume."[62]

In the summer of 1895 a male cycling outfitter made a strong case for bloomers as the preferable costume for women cyclists because they combined safety, or the practical elements of the design, with that of its modest appearance. As a result, a *New York Times* reporter was dispatched to check out the outfitter's establishment and gather details on the bloomer costume. The outfitter had copied the prevailing Parisian costume of trousers with pockets that were free at the knees like a young boy's knickerbockers. In making his case, the tailor said that if women had costumes for riding, bathing, and the ballroom, why not for cycling? After all, the bloomer suit was more modest that either a bathing outfit or an opera dress. He blamed "the lower element" for bringing the bloomer costume into disrepute "by going to extremes and showing vulgarity," something that he claimed was in any case true in all kinds of dress. For those who persisted in wearing skirts, he had the following advice to prevent the skirt from blowing up: "They should ride with their knees close together—almost rubbing in fact." One interesting feature that the tailor revealed in his interview was the tendency of women to ask for pistol pockets to be made in their bicycle bloomers. He claimed that a large number of women wanted to carry a revolver, explaining further:

The liking for night riding has grown rapidly, and even one or two instances that have been published of women being molested by tramps or others are not the only ones that have happened.

Two or three of my customers have told me of attempts to halt them by men, which they frustrated by riding swiftly on, but they added that if it were not for the pistol in their pocket, which they had for use in extremity, they would have been too much frightened to ride fast. It is from the very best class of my customers that I get these stories, and they are practically the only ones who acknowledge carrying revolvers.

It was, moreover, society women, according to the tailor, who knew how to shoot. Women's access to public space was not trouble-free. This comment provides yet another small window on the sexual harassment of women in public space.[63] The comments that women elicited from people in the street as they rode were doubtlessly as personal as the Newport clubman's on women passing the Reading Room.

One of the ways in which women could protect themselves against unsolicited attention was to ride with chaperons. Chaperons were, in any case, expected if bicycling parties were mixed. Combining the requirements of sociability with the demands of etiquette could be trying. Elsie Clews Parsons's correspondence in the mid-1890s contains numerous letters from friends who were cycling enthusiasts, thus providing insight into the arrangements that were necessary for cycling outings. Cycling out to the suburbs of New York City for tea or dinner seems to have been a popular thing to do. Two letters from Henry G. Barbey indicate the logistical problems involved in getting people together on a fine day. In the first of these, dated 18 April 1898, he suggested to Elsie that he try to organize a bicycling party "to take dinner at Washington Heights":

> In way of chaperonage I have Mrs. Newbold Morris née Helen Kingsland; I do not know whether you know her and whether you think she would do, her husband is very interesting, but energetic young bicycling couples are scarce as you know and it is a question whether they are better than none at all. I leave this also to your good judgement.
>
> Is party of six or eight the better?
>
> Please suggest another lady or two with appropriate "young men."

Neither of the two dates he suggested seems to have been convenient, so he tried tentatively again ten days later to set things up, asking: "Are you sure a ride of 9 miles before dinner and 9 miles after is not too much. Apart from its distance the inn and Washington Heights I believe is good." If the weather was bad, he had contingency plans for a dinner and play in town. In an embarrassed postscript, he added: "Please excuse my troubling you so often but I do not yet feel sufficiently confident to struggle alone. All I want from you are names."[64] Fred Crosby was another of Elsie's male cycling friends; he apparently balked at the idea of chaperoned rides:

> Here I am again and ready for another night bicycle ride if you feel like giving me the treat. I wish it were all right for you to go out for a run with "Uncle" alone. Don't you think your Mother would allow it? To such an end I will let you *call* me "Uncle" all the evening.
>
> If you fix on any evening, please give me time to get a wheel, and may I have it sent to your house. If you have to send up for your wheel, perhaps you would let your man get one for me at the same,—but this time *I* pay, See?[65]

A letter from the architect Tom Hastings, a close friend of Elsie's and of Stanford White's, hints at a problem Elsie may have had with a male cycling companion. He demanded to know all about the "great row" in the Park and the "bicycle ride to the sea" and the name of the man in question. He chided her: "After all this my feelings will be greatly hurt if you ever refuse to ride with me in a plain hansom cab! In Harlem New York or any where else."[66]

Elsie's women cycling companions in New York and Newport included Helen Ripley Benedict and Dolly Potter, daughter of Bishop Potter. All of Helen's letters regarding plans for cycling mention chaperons. One letter refers to a cycling party that included the famous illustrator Charles Dana Gibson and his wife, Irene. They were to meet at the Fifty-ninth Street entrance of the park at 4:30 P.M. and cycle to a German restaurant. And in 1894 Helen sent a message to Elsie canceling their arrangement to ride in the Park on the following Saturday as she was going to a football game: "If you want to ride alone I will send a good man with a machine to meet you anywhere at any time you say (this Saturday)."

By the summer of 1897 Helen's enthusiasm for cycling had begun to wane even though she had just purchased a new Columbia bicycle and had written to Elsie telling her she was bringing it with her, in the hope of riding it more often there than she had been able to in Indian Harbor, Connecticut: "Whether it has been the dust or the swims or the golf I cant say but I have been unable to get up any enthusiasm about bicycles."[67]

Cycling was, in fact, part of the general move to life outdoors that society men and women took up at the turn of the century. More of their recreational activities were conducted out of doors and, for that matter, in the country. At the end of the century, camping became very popular and families or groups transported themselves to the Adirondacks in upstate New York for trips of varying degrees of roughing it. Some families owned summer houses in and around the popular tourist resorts of the Adirondacks, others stayed in clubs or hotels, and the hardiest went out on "rough camp," camping out in the woods.

The Adirondacks held a particular place in the affection of Huybertie Pruyn as a young woman. One of her cousins had a camp near Newcomb, Essex County, north of Saratoga, to which she was invited on four separate occasions. Looking back from the 1930s, when sports clothes were much more an accepted part of a woman's wardrobe and when the range was considerably more extensive, she marveled at how she and her female relatives and friends had managed in the 1890s with their "almost-long skirts, our high collars, ruffled shirt waists, and pointed shoes." Sweaters were heavy and uncomfortable, she recalled, and their leggings were "very hot for walking." In the 1890s the journey to the camp took ten hours. From North Creek, where they stayed overnight at a "primitive hotel," they had a drive of thirty-five miles over very rough roads in a wagon. On her first visit, she and her friends were amazed to find the camp so well equipped: "The outside was not yet finished, but inside we had every luxury, even a piano." There were even five bathtubs. The camp consisted of five cabins, as sleeping quarters, and a main house linked to them by a "wide covered piazza." In the evenings the party amused themselves singing popular songs either in the big living room or around a campfire outside or by playing games and indulging in amateur theatricals. During the day there were opportunities for long walks, boating, and fishing.[68]

In the summer of 1896 the Pruyns had a holiday at the Pearl Island camp on Upper St. Regis Lake. A number of their friends and acquaintances were nearby either renting camps or staying at their own summer camps. Their Corning relatives rented a camp on Spitfire Lake, and the New York State governor Levi P. Morton and his family stayed at the Twombly camp. A small section of Albany society had thus reconstituted itself in the Adirondacks that summer, with the addition of the Whitelaw Reids, who had a summer lodge on Upper St. Regis Lake.[69] The Pruyns's camp consisted of tents with wooden platform floors and a main house with a living room, dining room, kitchen, and pantry. They reached the camp by taking the train to Lake Clear, then drove on buckboards from the station to the lake, and from there rowed over to the camp. The Mortons's camp, as Huybertie recalled, was somewhat more luxurious and like a country house, while the Reids's summer lodge re-created the comfort zone in sumptuous style, described by Huybertie as follows:

> When we went to the Rogers' island or the Reids' camp, we were welcomed by a footman in full uniform who helped us out of the boat as it docked. Mother and I dined with the Reids and he [Whitelaw Reid] told us of his pleasure in "roughing it" for a few weeks. Our "rough" dinner consisted of five courses with champagne and other wines, with a butler and two footmen to serve us.[70]

Two years earlier Huybertie's mother had made her first trip to the Adirondacks in the company of Bishop Doane of Albany, who had been visiting the outlying parts of his diocese. Mrs. Pruyn was not what might be called the "outdoors type" and made few concessions to the terrain in the way she dressed: she wore black silk dresses "with a slight train" and "leg-o-mutton sleeves" and high, tight collars. Her only concession, in fact, was to wear a black straw hat. On one occasion when they were walking between lakes, Mrs. Pruyn and the bishop were drenched to the skin by a thunderstorm. Then, as her daughter noted: "When they reached the shack, Mother said to the man in charge that she would like hot water and a bath. The man pointed at the stove and said, 'There's the kittle. Take that!'" When they arrived at the train station, Huybertie commented: "I never saw anyone more relieved than Mother when she got on the Pullman and had the morning papers and after-noon tea."[71]

One of Huybertie Pruyn's contemporaries, Elsie Clews (they were born within a year of each other), was, like Huybertie, enamored of the outdoors life.[72] Her mother, moreover, was more interested in the outdoors life than Huybertie's, who was more likely to spend time at health spas and who became very friendly—almost inevitably—with one of her neighbors at Newport, Dr. Silas Weir Mitchell, the famous "rest cure" physician. Instead, Mrs. Clews was an avid cyclist, while Elsie herself cycled, swam, played golf and tennis, walked, and went camping in the Adirondacks.[73] One of Herbert Parsons's early letters to Elsie invited her to stay at his family's summer home, Stonover Farm, at Lenox, listing the offerings of Lenox: "If you will come prepared for the horse-back ride we missed in Newport, for cycling, walking, driving, rowing, tennis playing, golfing, Latining, botanizing, in fact almost anything but swimming—which in Lenox is only a male's pastime—you will fit in with the entertainment which I may provide for myself."[74] Elsie was apparently less enthusiastic about motorized transport, which was Herbert's passion, than bicycles or horses.[75]

Chaperons and proper dress regulated women's involvement in the outdoor life but did not prevent it. Little by little, women were contesting restrictions on movement and challenging their confinement to safe domestic hobbies and occupations. Active participation in the outdoor life was very quickly becoming an accepted way for women to signify wealth and leisure.

The Female Tourist

American Women Abroad.—The one essential thing for every American girl and woman who travels abroad to remember is that men in Europe, generally speaking, have a different attitude of mind toward women than that of men in America. They inevitably associate the freedom from accepted European conventions which marks the independence of the American woman as license. Especially where the young girl is concerned, their more exactly observed etiquette in all matters relating to chaperonage, moving about unattended in public, etc., is apt to lead them to erroneous conclusion. In Europe only the _grande dame_ and the _demi-mondaine_—in other words the two social extremes—can afford to ignore the accepted conventions. Therefore, lest her character be misunderstood, the American woman travelling in Europe, especially if she is travelling alone, cannot be too circumspect in her conduct in public and in private.[76]

The advent of transatlantic steamers made travel for leisure far more feasible for women, and the years after the Civil War witnessed an exodus of wealthy female tourists, traveling mostly in family groups. The European tour became almost a standard excursion for wealthy New Yorkers, and as contacts proliferated between the social elites of New York and European cities, the European world of private social life opened up to Americans, enabling them to participate in activities of sociability and networking similar to those at home. When they did not have entrée into the high society of European cities, they might have, instead, the community of American expatriate colonies. Europe augmented their social and leisure activities and provided a reconstitution of life at home with shopping, the opera, theater, private dinners, and semipublic balls, but in a different setting and with different people.[77] In effect, the more travel New Yorkers were prepared to undertake, the more social seasons they could fit into a single year and the more opportunities they would have to enhance status and make new contacts.

The Pruyn women were keen travelers and strong Anglophiles. Mrs. Pruyn ensured that her daughters, like herself, were given part of their education in accomplishments in Europe and presented at the British court. And both Harriet and Huybertie, like their mother, had their honeymoons in Europe. Mrs. Pruyn actually accompanied Huybertie and her husband for much of their wedding tour. The diaries of all three women reveal a remarkable energy for travel and sightseeing. They covered an inordinate amount of ground on their various European tours, more than enough to exhaust the modern-day tourist, notwithstanding modern transportation and clothes. Such trips involved considerable organization and planning, as well as the support and labor of servants, and because of this, such tours were not undertaken "lightly," to evoke an expression used by novelist Frances Hodgson Burnett.[78] For the Pruyns such a journey abroad usually lasted several months, if not a year. They would rent houses or apartments for extended periods when staying in London or Paris; otherwise they stayed in hotels. Couriers were employed to assist them with arrangements for traveling and settling in, and personal servants would be engaged. On at least one occasion, Mrs. Pruyn used her European trip to hire British servants, whom she then took back to Albany to work for her at her Elk Street home. In London, the Pruyns often rented the homes of people they knew in the British aristocracy, complete with domestic servants and carriages with liveried coachmen and valets. In Paris, they were frequent guests at the Hotel Bristol and were personally welcomed by the proprietor. Mrs. Pruyn favored private hotel suites "au premier" in consideration of her health and declining mobility. When her health worsened she would go to fashionable German spas.[79] Sightseeing and shopping constituted the main staple of their daily lives while abroad in Europe. Anna gave her daughters an informal cultural education, with visits to museums, art galleries, artists' studios, churches, and historic buildings. Harriet's diaries are full of architectural and historical details of the buildings she visited and of her impressions of the art she saw. Anna also took her two daughters on touring holidays around the Scottish and Italian lakes, to Venice and the French Riviera. On these occasions, they invariably stayed at hotels and ate at the *table d'hôte*, something they did not do at the Bristol. Harriet was in raptures about the beauty of the lakes, oppressed by the mountains, and appalled by the existence of a casino in the midst of natural beauty at Monte Carlo. She wrote in strong terms in her travel diary about the vice of gambling:

> An unattractive place to my mind in every way—it seemed wicked even to be there as a sightseer. Women seemed to predominate over men, and their faces were intent and intense, as they bent over the table, for roulette or trente et quarante, as the case may be. . . . I was glad to go, and didn't want to go there again. . . .
>
> This is our last evening on the Riviera. To me, Cannes offers the most attractions. This pretty, rocky point of Monaco and Monte Carlo is completely saddened in its beauty to me by the presence of the gambling house and the strange people it brings. It is true that away from the Casino the place seems like an English country town, so quiet is it, but nevertheless I cannot forget that such a building is near, in which, from noon till $^1/_4$ to 11 P.M. every day, the sad vice is being practiced.[80]

Edith Wharton relished travel. She was one of the earliest owners of a motor car, purchasing a Panhard-Levassor in 1904, and was driven around England and the Continent by her chauffeur, Charles Cook. Her first experience of driving in a car was in 1903, when she was offered a lift in the motor of the American ambassador to Italy, George Meyer, in order to visit the Villa Caprarola, a round trip of a hundred miles. She described the car as "a sort of high-perched phaeton without hood or screen, or any protection from the wind." It was "blissful," she wrote in her memoirs, "not to have to worry about tired horses or inconvenient trains" and swore to buy herself a motor as soon as she had made enough money. She particularly enjoyed the mobility afforded by an automobile and the ability to explore the countryside, notwith-standing poor roads, getting stuck in ruts, and suffering "the jeers of horse-drawn travellers."[81] She wrote Moreton Fullerton: "I love the long days in the motor, & the great adventurous flights over unknown roads."[82] Anything that made travel easier and more independent of railroad schedules and routes appealed to Wharton, who had from an early age been taken to Europe for extended visits. She continued the custom, whenever possible, of getting away to the European continent in the summers while she was still domiciled in the United States, that is, until 1913, when she took up permanent residence in France. She had grown up in the new age of steamship travel and made sixty or so transatlantic crossings in her lifetime.[83] For Wharton, traveling had to be accomplished in some degree of comfort; she was not a devotee of "roughing it." But she did like adventure and did not restrict herself to the well-trodden paths of tourists.

In 1917, during the First World War, Wharton leaped at the opportunity to visit Morocco at the invitation of the resident-general, Hubert Lyautey, whom she had met in Paris. The object of the invitation was to visit the general's annual industrial exhibition, which was being held in Rabat that year, but the trip was also to include a three-week motor tour through Morocco, descriptions of which appeared in *Scribner's* in 1919 and were then collected into a book, *In Morocco* (1920). "The brief enchantment of this journey through a country still completely untouched by foreign travel, and almost destitute of roads and hotels," Wharton wrote in her memoirs, "was like a burst of sunlight between storm-clouds." Wharton had been engrossed in war work in Paris, including running a workroom in her *arrondissement* for out-of-work seam-stresses and *lingères*, setting up American hostels for refugees and fund-raising. She had been on a motor trip in North Africa once before, in 1914, with Percy Lubbock and Gaillard Lapsley, being chauffeured by her own driver in her Mercedes from Algiers to Tunis and from Gabès to Médénine. In her memoirs, Wharton was reticent in giving any details about this trip, claiming it would tire the reader, especially as the kind of journey she had taken then had now become, in the 1930s, "a commonplace of North African travel."[84] At the time, she wrote to Moreton Fullerton fulsome descriptions of the places she visited and imagined that such a letter "would do very well in a memoir"—no doubt because it was not a love letter.[85]

In her descriptions of both trips to North Africa, Wharton was fascinated by the absence of European traces, by which she meant none of the modern alter-ations to the landscape to mark the intrusion of the present upon the past. She liked to think she was seeing things just how they were thousands of years ago.[86] In her preface to *In Morocco*, she justified her travel sketches as offering glimpses of Morocco "when its aspect and its customs were still almost unaffected by European influences." Tangiers had been despoiled by markers of the European presence: Western clothes and signs in European languages, and it belonged, in her view, like Algiers, to "the familiar dog-eared world of travel."[87] Ironically, Wharton was writing a travel book, one that might encourage North African tourism, and yet she distanced herself from the tourist hordes, from the indelible marks they left on the landscape, and their destruction of the mystery she claimed to find in regions untouched by Europeans, especially by those who lacked taste and discretion and who imposed their own culture unthinkingly. She privileged her gaze as that of someone who was seeing Morocco before it would be destroyed through its new accessibility to tourism and yet complimented French imperialism for facilitating this access through the construction of roads. In effect, she repressed her own complicity in this process. Her gaze was not to be repeated by others, but then it was not harmful like that of the tourist hordes, who would inevitably follow her once the war was over. Here, in 1917, she was seeing the forbidden, treading on sacred ground where few Europeans had been allowed to go before, and yet *she* was not an intruder.

She was also intrigued by the people of North Africa and wrote Fullerton that she did not see how she could ever go back to Europe and "look at ugly monkeys in comic clothes after such perpetual manifestations of human beauty." But her gaze romanticized and exoticized North Africans, mediated as it was by her reading of *The Arabian Nights*. In a letter to her sister-in-law she called Morocco "a fairy world,"[88] and to her close friend Bernard Berenson, the art historian, she spoke of being in a "fairy tale."[89] Indeed, it was Berenson she told that she felt she was in "an unexpurgated page of the Arabian Nights!"[90] In Algiers, she wrote, "the beauty & nobility of the native types makes the whole scene poetic—here, with equal picturesqueness & variety, it's all effeminacy, obesity, obscenity or black savageness."[91] The imaginative meanings that Wharton gave to Morocco bear all of the marks of an imperialist discourse, deriving from French travel books, European literary representations, and historical constructions of the Orient. Despite the "picturesqueness" of the people she saw, it is clear that she regarded Occidental civilization as superior to Oriental civilization. Above all, she praised her French host, General Lyautey, and his efforts to repair ancient Moroccan edifices—left to crumble by the Moroccans—and to keep Europeans from erecting their own tasteless buildings in the old cities of Morocco. The French, for Wharton, provided a beneficent influence by helping "the mysterious North African civilization," ravaged by contradictions, such as the coexistence of "barbarous customs and sensuous refinements," and "the patient and exquisite workmanship and the immediate neglect and degradation of the thing once made," to find "political stability" so that the "higher qualities" of its people may reach "fruition."[92] In describing it thus, Wharton legitimized the French imperialist presence in Morocco.

Despite her construction of Morocco as mysterious and romantic, Wharton did not edit out the disturbing features of Moroccan life, neither the "sexual improprieties" nor the "savagery." Instead, she took advantage of her gender to gain entry to the harems of various sultans and to give an account of the things she saw. Still, her descriptions of those aspects of Moroccan life of which she disapproved are shot through with adjectives that position her as a civilized Occidental. The ritual dance of the Hamadchas in Moulay Idriss, which involved self-mutilation, is described as a "bestial horror"; a sultan is described as a "fat tyrannical man, bloated with good living and authority, himself almost as inert and sedentary as his women, and accustomed to impose his whims on them"; and life in "the rich and leisure class" is said to be conducted from a very early age "in an atmosphere of sensuality without seduction."[93]

Wharton's picture of the "pale women" leading "colourless eventless lives" in a "mouldering prison" in a harem in Fez, women entrapped "in a conception of sexual and domestic life based on slave-service and incessant espionage," stands as an interesting parallel to the world of women in old New York portrayed in the novel she began publishing in serial form in the same year that *In Morocco* came out in book form, that is, *The Age of Innocence*.[94] But while her travel sketches enable the reader to follow Wharton down the dark, damp, winding passages to the inner recesses of the harem, the reader has no such access to the inner female sanctum in *The Age of Innocence*.[95] The female characters conspire offstage, behind the scenes; the reader is presented only with the consequences of their machinations. Indeed, Cynthia Griffin Wolff has suggested that *The Age of Innocence* is "unmistakably influenced by the Moroccan adventure" in terms of its references to "barbarism, taboos, and ritual sacrifice,"[96] "the primitive" that lies just below the surface of New York's refined society, which took life "without the effusion of blood."[97]

There is no doubt that Wharton enjoyed the freedom and mobility of traveling by car, but it was this very freedom that was challenged by those who saw the automobile as presenting opportunities for promiscuity. Even her motor trips around the Berkshires did not escape the eagle eye, let alone acerbic tongue, of the Saunterer, especially as they took place around the time of the breakup of her marriage. In one of his "blind" paragraphs, the Saunterer obliquely refers to Wharton as a "literary personage" living in Lenox, where she has been seen driving "her Washington admirer" around the area without her coachman. The admirer is identified, for those in the know, as being "as ripe in years and as rosy of cheek as his name suggests," in other words, Walter Berry—an American lawyer and long-term companion of Wharton's. Wharton's husband is said to "look with indulgent eyes on this flirtation" and to plan trips away from home when the "admirer" visits his wife. At the same time, the source of the gossip appears to have come from Lenox residents, as the piece ends with the suggestion that Wharton's "fashionable neighbors" pan her because she holds herself to be superior to them.[98] This is a fine example of *Town Topics* getting things hopelessly wrong. Ironically, Wharton had at this time recently returned from Paris, where she had come close to consummating her affair with Moreton Fullerton. By this stage in her life, Walter Berry was a close friend but certainly not her lover.[99] We may guess at Wharton's response to seeing or hearing of the scurrilous article in "Saunterings"; while still in Paris she had written to Fullerton: "Something gave me the impression the other day that we are watched in this house . . . commented on. . . . How degraded I feel by other people's degrading thoughts."[100] Clearly, the surveillance of servants and that of society journalists detracted from her freedom of action. The Saunterer's tone about declining standards became quite menacing about women driving in cars with men. In 1915, when one would have thought that regulations governing chaperonage had eased a little, the Saunterer referred to a young débutante who had been seen driving out to a roadhouse on the Old Boston Post Road in the company of a professional dancer, where the two tried out the latest steps. At first the Saunterer advised the mother "to inquire more closely into the manner in which her daughter passes her Saturday afternoons," but, at the end he threatened to print the daughter's name on the next occasion of her "clandestine junketing."[101] The infraction committed by the débutante through driving alone with a man was compounded further by the fact that he was a professional dancer, a man considered to be of doubtful reputation and otherwise known as a "gigolo" or "tango pirate." In any case, he was a man of lower social status. Second, they were dancing—in public—the latest dances that had come in for severe censure in "Saunterings" only the month before:

> The dancing craze . . . has been responsible . . . for a whole lot of scandals that might never have happened were it not for the promiscuity of the thé dansants, supper dances and other affairs . . . open to the public. . . . The old skating rink, denounced by the pulpit and press, was a veritable kindergarten in the éducation sentimentale compared with the present-day temples of the dance, for there was neither occasion nor opportunity for surreptitious embraces by handsome instructors, nor was there the incentive inspired by the sensuous music and the voluptuous rhythm of two bodies moving in unison over the smooth floor.[102]

As far as the Saunterer was concerned, the threats to young débutantes' reputations seemed to be multiplying out of control. With every new technological innovation, such as the bicycle or the automobile, and with every new fad, especially if it required instruction, the potential for scandalous behavior was increased. The Saunterer's comments about dancing instructors echo his concerns about the bicycling craze among society women in the 1895 season.

Cycling instructors were also deft, it appears, at slipping their arms around a young lady's waist, not to mention pedaling off out of reach of her chaperon. Indeed, forms of instruction involving bodily contact provoked comments about the vulnerability of upper-class women to lower-class men. It was in this context that the Saunterer reported that

> colored men . . . are favored by more prudent women, not only from their skill
> in instruction, but because, as one lady recently remarked, "They seem to know
> their place better," and I have myself noticed that they are not so inclined to dis-
> card the use of a belt in teaching an attractive woman to ride the wheel as
> quickly as their white brothers, and do not grasp her around the waist at every
> possible opportunity, nor lift her on or off her wheel.[103]

The Saunterer, however, was not out of touch with conventional etiquette. A 1913 manual advised that young (unmarried) ladies could drive alone on public roads in the afternoon and in the Park, but that it would be "unconventional were a lady to drive along with a gentleman in his motor car, unless he were nearly related to her, or unless she were engaged to be married to him."[104] Ten years later, manuals were still advising mothers to take particular care in vetting their daughter's automobile companions:

> Every careful mother will know when, where and with whom her young
> daughter motors. She will see to it that all her motoring is done in accordance
> with the established laws of chaperonage and good breeding. . . . She will not
> allow her daughter to be exposed to the free and easy intimacies of the auto
> "petting party" in a high-school boy's roadster, so easily calculated to destroy
> modesty and respect for self in the young girl.[105]

Women's presence in public space in the late nineteenth century was highly contested. Access to public space for women of the *haute bourgeoisie* was circumscribed in order to reduce the risks involved in their mingling with anonymous men and women of a lower social class, people who were represented as being a potential threat to the well-being or peace of mind of genteel women. The dangers of unsolicited attention from unknown men or of being mistaken for a prostitute were held over young women to keep their appearance and behavior in public in check. Both the danger of losing one's reputation by being in the wrong place at the wrong time and that of losing one's dignity in public shaped and determined women's access to the world beyond the home.

Women's pursuit of new leisure and recreational activities and their experience of new forms of mobility and speed also brought with it the threat of harassment and greater possibilities for surveillance by journalists. Yet despite the fact that new leisure activities presented opportunities for displaying class and leisure and challenged formality in social relations, the rules of propriety were extended to cover them and curb any movement toward autonomy. Journalistic practices reinforced self-discipline. They held leisure-class femininity up to close scrutiny and adjudged society women's behavior with a view to controlling the wider female community.

"Fifth Avenue," William Thomas Smedley, *Life and Character: Drawings by W. T. Smedley* (New York: Harper and Bros., 1899), p. 44.

EVERYMAN TO HIS TASTE

"Everyman to his taste," Charles Dana Gibson, *Gibson's New Cartoons: A Book of Charles Dana Gibson's Latest Drawings* (New York: Charles Scribner's Sons, 1916), n.p.

Costumes in tableaux vivants, *Vogue*, 12 February 1910, p. 10. Courtesy of The Winterthur Library: Printed Book and Periodical Collection.

"Is a caddy always neces-
sary?" Charles Dana
Gibson, *The Best of Charles
Dana Gibson,* edited with a
biography and introduc-
tion by Woody Gelman
(New York: Bounty
Books, 1969), p. 9.

"Wireless Telegraphy," Charles Dana Gibson, *The Best of
Charles Dana Gibson,* edited with a biography and introduction by Woody Gelman (New York: Bounty Books, 1969),
p. 69.

"Aunt Jane,"
Charles Dana
Gibson, *Gibson's
New Cartoons: A
Book of Charles
Dana Gibson's
Latest Drawings*
(New York:
Charles Scribner's
Sons, 1916), n.p.

HOUSEHOLD DECORATION
Mantel ornaments for domestic cheer.

"Household Decoration," Charles Dana Gibson, *Gibson's New Cartoons: A Book of Charles Dana Gibson's Latest Drawings* (New York: Charles Scribner's Sons, 1916), n.p.

"Le Matin après le Bal," A. A. Anderson, *Vogue*, 5 December 1907, n.p. Courtesy of The Winterthur Library: Printed Book and Periodical Collection.

"New York's Latest Fad—The Michaux Cycle Club," drawing by T. de Thulstrup,
Harper's Weekly, 19 January 1895, p., 65.

"The Announcement of Her Engagement," Charles Dana Gibson, *Gibson's New Cartoons:
A Book of Charles Dana Gibson's Latest Drawings* (New York: Charles Scribner's Sons,
1916), n.p.

Automobile Apparel

FOR

Spring and Summer

THE SCANDINAVIAN FUR AND LEATHER COMPANY is the only house in this country dealing *exclusively* in motoring, boating, driving and pedestrian apparel.

Attention is directed to our latest importations from Paris, London and Copenhagen, especially to examples by Paquin, Doeullet, and Max.

In selecting garments for the coming season, the greatest variety is afforded in linen, pongee, silk-rubber, silk, cloth, mohair and leather.

These garments may be had ready-made or tailored to order.

STYLE FRIQUET

Ladies' Silk=Rubber Coat

A smart, loose-fitting garment made of the highest grade silk-rubber. Designed with a Watteau back, is double-breasted, has an upstanding, inlaid collar and trimmed cuffs.

Catalogue showing Spring and Summer Styles upon request

Scandinavian
Fur and Leather Co.

16 WEST 33d STREET

(Opp. Waldorf-Astoria) NEW YORK

Advertisement for Scandinavian Fur and Leather Co., *Vogue*, 12 October 1905, p. 413. Courtesy of The Winterthur Library: Printed Books and Periodical Collection.

"Leap Year," Charles Dana Gibson, *Gibson's New Cartoons: A Book of Charles Dana Gibson's Latest Drawings* (New York: Charles Scribner's Sons, 1916), n.p.

Cover, *Town Topics*, 6 August 1903. Courtesy of Henry Francis Du Pont Winterthur Museum.

5

"Optical Excursions"

For, more assiduously than anything else in this world, we, the wealthy, seek the praise and admiration of the crowd.[1]

At the turn of the century display and spectatorship operated within gendered paradigms. Society women signified with their bodily presence and appearance high social class and respectability, which in turn reflected on their male provider's monetary wealth. What represented their "other" in terms of respectability and class were the women from whom they were strictly segregated in a society that indulged the male double standard—that is to say, *demimondaines* or high-class prostitutes, women without class and beyond the pale of respectability who nevertheless also signified male wealth. By appearing in public and displaying luxury, particularly in places of nighttime entertainment where conspicuous dress was allowed, the society woman took on the role of the courtesan in exhibiting herself as the possession of one man and evoking the envy of others. As Juliet Blair has put it, "A woman who can be observed in public, or by men who are not related to her by ties of kinship or marriage, is considered in many cultures to be provoking attention to her sexuality."[2]

While display was concentrated on the sexualized body of the woman, spectatorship was a predominantly male activity. As Nicholas Green argues in his study of Paris during the Second Empire—and I deliberately infer parallels here between these two great metropolitan centers—"the differential power relations inscribed in gendered spectatorship . . . position[ed] the metropolitan gaze primarily in relation to the priorities and pleasure of men."[3] This argument recalls John Berger's claim: "Men look at women. Women watch themselves being looked at. This determines not only most relations between men and women but also the relation of women to themselves. The surveyor of woman in herself is male: the surveyed female. Thus she turns herself into an object."[4]

For the double standard of morality to operate with reasonable ease, wives and mistresses were kept in different worlds. But the access of respectable women to new places of nighttime entertainment from the mid-1890s on created new challenges to traditional lines of segregation. More discretion was required, for one. Restaurateurs colluded with society men in their participation in the *demimonde*, providing them with private dining rooms. This was seen as a French custom, and in the late 1880s it was alleged that the best uptown restaurants in New York, in contrast to Paris, provided rooms only for parties of at least four.[5] At the same time, the New York restaurant business demonstrated a keen understanding of the dynamics at play in the public social life of the leisure class. It also catered to the needs of society men and women by providing fairly exclusive venues for both the display of the sexualized body of society women and male spectatorship. Theaters had already become more class-segregated after 1850 in an effort to carve out a market for respectable theatrical entertainment. Those theaters that aimed at a more refined patronage "cleaned up" their premises, starting with the third tier.[6] Just because theaters were cleaned up to accommodate women of the respectable classes did not mean that women of the *demimonde* had surrendered their access to such places. Even in such respectable institutions as the Metropolitan Opera House or the Academy of Music, the demarcation of space was vulnerable to violation, for, as Timothy Gilfoyle has explained, these two venerable auditoriums were, at different times, the venue for the "French Ball," "an annual erotically charged masquerade" attended by a large range of people from Wall Street businessmen to prostitutes. On one occasion a "leading" madam sat in the box usually occupied by Mrs. Astor while over two hundred men passed by, paying her homage.[7] Prostitutes in brothels or streetwalkers might, from time to time, be harassed by the city authorities and temporarily removed from certain areas, but this did not guarantee the segregation of respectable women from the *demimonde*. The mistresses of wealthy men, in their elaborate gowns, jewelery, and carriages, were able to mingle with respectable society at the theater, in the Park, or on Ladies' Mile. Such "passing" fueled masculine anxieties about the potential exposure of men's illicit activities. In addition, it made it more difficult to distinguish between courtesans and women of the respectable classes.

This crossing of boundaries could also give rise to much mirth. In 1903 the Saunterer reported with glee in *Town Topics* an incident that had occurred at the Newport polo grounds:

Early in the afternoon two closed cabs drove up to the grounds. From them alighted four painted and perfumed beauties, the notorious denizens of a house known by repute—or ill repute—to every Newporter. The quartet, a bit subdued at first by their strange surroundings, made their way to the club-house veranda, where they were soon joined by their leader and a fifth satellite, while two men, unknown to the dwellers on Bellevue avenue and the Cliffs, hovered nearby. The regular habitués of the club-house began to arrive, and a glance at the group on the veranda was enough. Escorts were despatched into the very midst of the contaminating group, whence chairs were abstracted and placed on the lawn. I suspected the motive of some shrewd matrons in thus recklessly sending their cavaliers to such a perilous spot, and their attitude justified my suspicions. They watched the men narrowly for some sign of recognition, but these heroes came and went with stolid, expressionless faces. It was a superb vindication of Newport's moral tone. Not one of these men, it was obvious, had ever before laid eyes on any of the painted ladies, and the innocence of some of them was so entire that they appeared not even to guess the character of the unwelcome guests on the veranda. Such ignorance argues a purity almost too great for this world, and I trust the more worldly-wise women gently enlightened their unsuspecting husbands and brothers.

The "veranda group" grew more at ease and made themselves "more and more conspicuous," first by ordering "highballs and cocktails" and then by their voices becoming "louder and hoarser." Just as Mrs. Stuyvesant Fish, Mrs. Ogden Mills, and two others were leaving the premises, the "noisy band" also made for the exit, and one of the "girls" trampled on Mrs. Mills's gown as she "pushed roughly forward." Looks of "intense disgust" were said to have followed these "brazen creatures" out, but peace of mind was quickly restored and there was a general "scramble for the veranda."[8]

This story offers an interesting juxtaposition of society women and prostitutes. Physically the two groups of women keep their distance, the prostitutes taking up their position on the veranda while the society women sit on the lawn. The prostitutes occupy the preferred seating in the shade, doubly emphasizing their encroachment of the space of polite society. The pollution metaphor of contamination helps to stress the invasive nature of their presence, and the conspicuousness and noisiness of the party adds to the "pollution." The discomfort of the society women is described largely at their expense: "Townie Burden strolled up the veranda, stared, gasped and beat a hurried retreat," and Miss Elsie Whelen was "mortified." On the other hand, we are told, Mrs. Fish and Mrs. Oelrichs, leaders of the fast or fashionable set, considered the whole thing a "great joke." All the society women are said to recognize immediately these women as prostitutes; they read the situation and categorize the intruders at a glance. The men, on the other hand, are portrayed as being innocent of the distinction. Rhetorically the Saunterer makes a clear distinction between the two groups of women: The society women are all named—adding, no doubt, to their discomfort—while the prostitutes are designated collectively as "painted ladies" or "sirens" or "brazen creatures." There are, in fact, two dramas taking place in this interesting triangle of society women, society men, and the prostitutes (the male companions of the last do not have a speaking part here). On the one hand, there is the effrontery experienced by the society women with the appearance of the prostitutes on their territory, and on the other, there is the curiosity to know if their menfolk know these women. The men survive the test but are "too nervous to drink their tea" and heave "sighs of relief" at the departure of the "noisy band." Their discomfort, too, is a source of mirth for the Saunterer. In this particular issue, the story is constructed so as to make fun of the apparent discomfort of society; there is even a hint that society has brought this upon itself. On other occasions, the Saunterer took up a much more blatant stance in opposition to the presence of prostitutes in public places frequented by respectable society.[9]

By 1903, of course, the staid society of old New York had long disappeared and some attitudes toward extramarital sexuality and divorce had become much more relaxed.[10] Certainly in the 1890s and 1900s the boundaries between the *monde* and the *demimonde* were becoming much more fluid as women became more mobile and began to push against the constraints upon their activities in public space. In fact, the spaces of the two worlds were becoming increasingly coextensive. The development of commercialized nightlife aimed at the rich also attracted prostitution. As Timothy Gilfoyle has noted: "Houses just off Broadway, and others adjacent to such enterprises as Daly's Theater, the Metropolitan Opera House, Wallack's Theater, Carnegie Hall, and the Waldorf-Astoria, were the most valuable bordellos in New York City."[11] The situation was exacerbated when society women went "slumming" in restaurants or cabarets regarded as risqué.[12] However, there was never the same degree of complacency about the coexistence of the two worlds in New York as in Paris, partly because of the concerted challenge from bourgeois women to the double standard of morality and partly because of the Protestant tradition, which still exerted a strong influence over attitudes toward laxity and self-indulgence. Nevertheless, certain commercial developments affected both New York and Paris in similar ways, developments that linked society women problematically with new methods of display.

The problem for society women was that the notion of a woman displaying herself was firmly associated with the world of prostitution. The *demimondaine* made herself into an object of desire and of luxury in order to appeal to a high-class male clientele, appearing like an actress in the marketplace and, as Saisselin has explained, "exhibiting herself to advantage" in the same way that commodities were "shown to advantage in the boutiques."[13] How then, did society women step out onto the public stage—into the fashionable streets, the Park and the opera—and exhibit themselves *without* running the risk of being misrecognized? It was one thing to display oneself within a closed society of kin, friends, and acquaintances, but quite another to do so in the public realm, where there was no reciprocity of vision. There were "sinister eyes" out there in the promiscuous crowd.[14] With the rise of society journalism, moreover, there was a new vicarious visual dialectics, which extended the audience for the new performances of display. Reporters were recording their observations and "reverberating" them to those who could not be present to see for themselves. This dramatically changed the dynamics of seeing and being seen in the late nineteenth century: Those who were looked at did not necessarily see those who were doing the looking. And it required self-discipline to put oneself on display and thereby exercise some control over what was seen and how it should be seen. Nevertheless, the society reporter's gaze could register transgressions and unintended slip-ups in the performance as well as excesses.

The general culture of display that became increasingly evident at the turn of the century in New York City is related to the development of a public social life by the leisure class. The processes at large intensifying display had important ramifications for society women, and this can be seen with particular reference to one example of public space for leisure-class nightlife, the opera house. In this connection, the prescriptive advice given in the form of etiquette discourse to women on how to behave at the opera is indicative of the ways in which bourgeois women colonized public space. The opera was central to high society right through the period 1870 to 1920, and opera etiquette was a regular feature in etiquette manuals. In her fictional representation of women's participation in commercialized nightlife, Edith Wharton provides an interesting interpretation of the class and sexual dynamics of heterosocial nightlife. She sounds a very critical note in her representation of women's participation in "the society of the spectacle,"[15] a note finely attuned to the sociohistorical changes taking place. Developments in consumer culture in metropolitan New York had serious implications for how society women negotiated public space. Not only the boundaries between the *monde* and the *demimonde* were brought into question, but also those dividing the world of theater and the world of high society.

The Culture of Display

Never had so much been on show in the cities as in the second half of the century. There were exhibitions everywhere.[16]

William Leach has provided us with a fascinating interpretation of how a commercial aesthetic developed in the United States at the turn of the century. With regard to the retail industry, he points to the development of a commercial aesthetic, with the expansive use of color and lighting in the display of goods in shop windows and inside department stores.[17] Displays became more daring in their bid to evoke desire as early manifestations of advertising and display shifted the focus away from the commodity itself and toward feelings and fantasies associated with its possession. Commodities, Leach writes, were made to evoke "glamour, stardom, luxury, sensuality and leisure activities." As he argues:

> The evolution of display and decorative strategies helped . . . forge a new commercial aesthetic that would henceforth dominate the visual space of urban Americans. . . . This commercial aesthetic carved out a wide terrain of desire and longing and contained elements of a new secular carnivalesque, one that played at the margins of unacceptable thought and behavior. It celebrated metamorphosis, the violation of boundaries, and the blurring of lines between categories— luxury and necessity, artificial and natural, night and day, male and female, the expression of desire and its repression, the primitive and the civilized.[18]

This display culture was evident in public social life in New York: in theaters, restaurants, hotels, places of amusement, museums, and expositions.[19] What was on display was not simply an array of objects but also lifestyle and social status. Wealthy New Yorkers advertised their wealth and performed "class acts" in laying claim to high social status. Putting themselves on display and into circulation was an essential part of asserting and maintaining this claim, as was explicitly acknowledged in *Town Topics*:

> The 400 are in the social business. . . . They do not spare pains, expense or advertising for the sake of maintaining a brilliant and refined series of continuous social performances.
>
> They are the actors, the rest of us are the spectators; but there is this difference between their show and all other shows, that they not only give the performance, but they do not charge anything for the privilege of looking at it.[20]

This, of course, came from a magazine that was making a handsome profit from the free peep show. Moreover, the above-quoted formulation disguises the social relations caught up in this display and the ramifications of a spectatorship that was far from passive: The Four Hundred was "sustained" by the "looks of envy."[21] Through publicity, glamor was commodified by society magazines and sold to those who envied the rich. Retailers similarly commodified glamor through evoking that same envy for the lifestyle of the rich in advertising their merchandise. The display strategies of department stores turned shop windows into stages upon which dummies reenacted scenes from daily life, defamiliarizing them in the process and presenting the goods that they advertised as objects of desire. The strategy was to get onlookers to identify with the contexts in which such goods might be used and to project themselves imaginatively into the idealized scenes of domestic felicity. One shop-window display in 1894 depicted in its plate-glass gallery a scene from a high-society dinner party:

> Brilliantly dressed dinner parties at perfectly appointed dinner tables in the foreground of shop windows apparently discuss the Horse Show, or the new Carmen, indifferent alike to the curious crowd on the pavement side of the glass or to the paucity of edibles at the sham feast; ladies at protracted "at homes" in Paris gowns, serve tea and eternal wax smiles as sincere as their social counterparts.[22]

By looking in shop windows, then, crowds could vicariously consume a fictitious representation of intimate society life. Retailers used society as a selling ploy in other ways, for example, by getting a "personality" to endorse a product. However, window displays of society drawing rooms were obviously a far less expensive way of encouraging potential consumers to identify with the fashionable lifestyle of the people they read about on the society page. One Broadway store went so far as to construct a mock *tableau vivant*, complete with dummy and the "reproduction of some unknown old master." The model displayed "the exquisite fit of a brand of hygienic underwear."[23] The window displays in New York therefore provided their own street theater, with gaping crowds and "daily devotees." New rules of display and spectatorship developed in metropolitan centers, rules that were closely connected with the "new marketing technologies" predominant in the world of commerce and of which mass-circulation daily newspapers were an integral part. The advertisement and performance of class intersected, then, with the emergent form of consumer culture, and we find here complex interconnections among high society, fashion, publicity, consumption, leisure, gendered display, and spectatorship.

Tactics other than inanimate window displays were used to evoke society. When ultrafashionable New Yorkers attended the opening night at the opera, newpaper reporters seized the opportunity to "broadcast" this gala occasion to a wide readership. Society columns abounded in minute details of the gowns worn by female opera-goers. Occasionally a society columnist might step outside this perfunctory requirement and reflect upon the significance of the event. At the start of the 1904–05 winter season, for example, the *New York World*'s society page described the first night of the opera season at the Metropolitan Opera House as "the most gorgeous and brilliant spectacle known to the local world of fashion. Foreigners admit that the splendid gowns and the regal jewels worn in 'parterre row' made an elaborate and scintillating display the like of which is not seen even at Covent Garden or at the Paris Opera House." As if the favorable comparison with London or Paris were not enough, the article went on to say that the Metropolitan had all the advantages over the recent horse show at Madison Square Garden. That "saturnalia of gowns and gossip" had been conducted in a "stifling atmosphere" with a noisy and bustling crowd, who had mostly come to view the society folk in the arena boxes—the horses were incidental.[24] In contrast, the Metropolitan offered an optimal setting that was well lit and well ventilated. By 1904 the Horse Show and the first night at the opera had become the two time-honored rituals that announced the opening of the winter season, but they were two very different kinds of "spectator events." In the first, society folk put themselves on display for the general public. With regard to the Horse Show, the *World* asked what it was that attracted the crowds:

> Is it not that renowned eagerness of curious New Yorkers for spectacles? . . . New Yorkers in general are a harmless body of inquisitive people, with a thirst for knowledge. They are always sightseeing and exhibiting an eagerness to obtain information, a disposition to investigate causes and an attempt to discover everything by searching curiosity. . . . There is an exhibition in the arena boxes of all those who have won fame, fortune and position in the social and business world. Sometimes they, too, parade. It is in the society people that a large percentage of the Garden visitors are particularly interested.

The difference between these two events is captured neatly by the *World*'s journalist: "At Madison Square Garden society is on view for the benefit of the crowd; at the Metropolitan it is on view for itself."[25] In constructing this social spectacle as part of a regular newspaper discourse, journalists provided their readers with markers by which to negotiate the constantly changing metropolitan space of fashionable theaters, restaurants, and luxury stores; they provided a window onto the luxurious lifestyle of the wealthy, a lifestyle that could be emulated, at least in part, in the fast-expanding entertainment and retail sectors aimed at those of more modest incomes.

The success of any major social entertainment, commercial or otherwise, involving society women came to depend largely upon opportunities for display. The Metropolitan Opera House is a case in point. The arrangements of its *parterre* were integral to its commercial success. The importance of display not only to high society but also to commercial institutions can be further illustrated by reference to a newspaper account of an opening night that was proclaimed a flop. In December 1901 the Metropolitan, instead of putting on its usual production of *Faust,* chose *Tristan and Isolde,* which that apparently had too many long periods of "semi-darkness" and too few intermissions. The *New York World* commented: "Certainly the audience—both the box-holders who went to see each other and the feminine portion of them to study each other's gowns, and those in the stalls—was listless and apathetic to a marked degree."[26] And from the Horseshoe to the Horse Show, this display principle remained paramount. In the various venues of the elite's public social life, boxes were the conventional seating arrangement. They created a frame around their occupants, drawing attention to their social status. As has been noted earlier, they also marked the boundaries of propriety.

Newport, although limited in its opportunities for public display by virtue of its nature as an exclusive summer resort for the wealthy, nevertheless had locations and times for society to show itself off to itself. As one "old cottager" expressed it for the *New York Times* in 1905: "The great charm of spectacular life there is to be in the public eye." The Newport Casino, to which society flocked just before noon to listen to the band or to watch the tennis, pandered to this desire:

> It is Newport en revue. It is more intimate than the Madison Square Garden Horse Show and much more satisfactory than the Opera—for the person who cares for that kind of thing. Newport society—the most representative in America—is more at its ease and seemingly less on exhibition, presumably unconscious but happy in the possession of an admiring crowd.

When, according to this newspaper item, there was an attempt to move this noonday gathering to the Country Club, where "the other half" could not see the fashionable world, the exercise proved a complete failure because of the absence of spectators.[27] Time and time again, in the pages of the society columns, the connection was made between display and spectatorship.

In August 1902 the British artist Sir Philip Burne-Jones made a trip to the United States. He was interviewed by a *World* reporter and made particular reference to the display of society women's clothes: "Luxury has never elsewhere risen to such a pitch. Display was never elsewhere so organized and perfected. . . . It is like the pageant of some splendid barbaric dream." Interestingly, he found the effect of so much wealth "oppressive": "It rather numbs one—produces in a man of moderate means a feeling of abject poverty, begets a feeling quite as if one were trailing about in rags, you know. . . . It is a tremendous spectacle; it is a colossally sumptuous picture." Burne-Jones also explained that in Newport he had found that the spectacle of so much wealth was at the expense of "human interest." He could not imagine that people who spent their lives "so artificially" could have much individuality: "Their clothes are so overpowering, so aggressive and insistent a—a phenomenon. Their souls are way down somewhere, wrapped up, hid away, buried, probably, but one doesn't easily catch sight of them. It is difficult to get at their real selves because of their clothes—their gorgeous clothes."[28]

By the late nineteenth century, then, women's clothes had certainly become a major dimension in the enactment of class and leisure. Hundreds of dollars were expended on gowns, dozens of hours were spent trying on clothes at couturiers, and immense labor went into the making and the laundering of expensive gowns, which had only a short life in the wear and tear of a winter season. Society women themselves were "active" consumers who gazed at each other and took pleasure in their knowledge of *haute couture* and the enactment of class privilege.[29] The business of high fashion was a very lucrative one and it is little wonder that so much space was given to advertising its products both in the society column of daily newspaper and in the advertisements that appeared on other pages.

Disciplining the Gaze

The expansion of public venues for display increased women's access to public space and therefore had ramifications for the ways in which social relations were organized around men and their needs. After the Civil War, the entry of fashionable women into public space, especially after dark, meant that social activities became much more stratified, partly to preclude such women from intermingling with men from a lower social class, partly to segregate such women from women of the *demimonde*, and in part to enhance the social pretensions of the upwardly mobile by introducing a dimension of exclusivity to their social and leisure activities. To support this stratification, etiquette was called into service to preserve class barriers. In this connection, we can point to the way in which numerous authors of etiquette manuals constructed etiquette as a protective device. For example, in 1878 Mrs. Longstreet represented etiquette as "a wall built up around us to protect us from disagreeable, underbred people, who refuse to take the trouble to be civil," while Mrs. Annie White described it as a "beautiful frame which is placed around a valuable picture to prevent its being marred or defaced." The wall or frame functioned as a barrier in two ways: to keep "the coarse and disagreeable at a distance" and to keep respectable women confined.[30]

There are, in fact, remarkable similarities between the prescriptions governing behavior and appearance in the theater or opera house and those constituting street etiquette. Advice on theater- or opera-going covered the topics of salutations, promenading (between the acts), escorts, and dress. Dress became much more formal in the 1880s, and a full toilet was expected. "If she goes in visiting dress, she cannot properly occupy a box, even if one be placed at her disposal, because she would appear like an ugly weed in a gay garden of brilliant blossoms," wrote Mrs. Longstreet.[31] Another manual, written around the same time, advised in similar terms that "a lady goes to the opera not only to see but to be seen, and her dress must be adopted with a full realization of the thousand gaslights which will bring out its merits or defects."[32] On the other hand, conspicuous behavior drawing attention to oneself was frowned upon: "Ladies will not stare around the house through an opera glass. It doesn't look well. Extravagant gesture, loud laughter, a conspicuous use of the fan, all mark a lack of breeding in the lady."[33]

Male spectatorship was also disciplined. As one 1871 etiquette manual stipulated, male "ogling" was an offense against polite society: "Nothing can be more ill bred . . . than ogling a stranger in the streets through an eye-glass . . . or surveying an opposite neighbor at the theatre with a lorgnette."[34] Male escorts came in for a good deal of criticism, especially with regard to their habit of leaving a woman alone in a box during the intermission.[35] One manual reminded men "that a woman is practically a prisoner at such a place, and that each one should be allowed the privilege of choosing whether she shall stay where she is, or walk about."[36] Women were allowed to receive calls in their box under the same rules governing calls at home, but women were not allowed to visit other boxes. At most, they could accompany their male escort on a promenade within the theater, bowing to friends on passing but not allowing other gentlemen to join them, and not stopping to speak with them—just as though they were in a public thoroughfare.[37]

It was also at the opera that débutantes were introduced to the contested nature of appearing in public. The ritualized celebration of coming out in society, for instance, involved putting oneself at the mercy of public scrutiny. At the Metropolitan Opera House, for example, a young woman might find herself the focus of "optical excursions,"[38] perpetrated by the opera glasses "of masculine New York"[39] scanning the boxes for pretty women. Little wonder, then, that débutantes were customarily seated toward the rear of the box—as accurately portrayed in Edith Wharton's fictional description, in the opening pages of *The Age of Innocence*, of old Mrs. Manson Mingott's box at the Academy of Music. In 1905, however, *Town Topics* noted that it had recently become the custom to allow débutantes to take the front seats in the box:

> This, it is to be assumed, is based on the idea of giving the blushing buds more poise and aplomb, and to teach them how to bear unmoved the batteries of staring eyes and whispered comments. Old-fashioned social observers view the change of custom with regret, and do not hesitate to say that there is something incongruous in the spectacle of pretty girls, at the very time of their life when they are supposed to be all maidenly reserve and delicacy, being placed as targets for the curious eyes and cynical lips of the public.[40]

The time spent as a débutante could be fraught with trying to remain within acceptable boundaries of behavior in public, boundaries that they were encouraged to explore during the controlled opportunities for heterosociability, when there was considerable pressure to secure the communally desired outcome of marriage. This was the period in women's lives when their opportunities for display were optimal; after marriage the occasions were somewhat limited and during pregnancy severely restricted. As a married woman, the purpose of display took on a different meaning. It was no longer aimed at attracting male attention with a view to marriage, but was intended to provoke in other men envy of the women's "possessor"—the man who paid for her clothes and jewelery.[41]

The gender dynamics of display and spectatorship in such venues as the opera house is in some ways suggestive of brothel behavior, with men ogling women framed and contained in boxes in darkened auditoriums. Theaters had not entirely rid themselves of associations with prostitution. As already noted, male spectatorship in theaters did undergo a disciplining process, but because it was legitimized within the theater and prosthetically enhanced with the use of binoculars, ogling continued surreptitiously. Women were, of course, spectators too—both of the stage and of each other. Etiquette required that they remain unconscious of being looked at (a tacit sanctioning of male ogling) and not reciprocate the male gaze, as to do so would signal the type of sexual availability associated with prostitution. But society did go to the opera to see and be seen. It would seem, then, that the display of women in a public space at night was charged with all kinds of tensions, especially those of a sexual nature, which perhaps partly accounts for its thematization in both the art and fiction of the times. The nuances of spectacle and display and their embeddedness in gender and class codes have been brilliantly captured by Henry James and Edith Wharton.

Etiquette discourse tended to lag behind social change. This is especially noticeable after 1895, when manuals show little evidence of taking account either of new spaces for nighttime entertainment, such as fashionable supper restaurants, lobster palaces, and cabarets, or of the increasingly fluid boundaries between the *monde* and the *demimonde,* as women became more mobile and began to push against the constraints upon their activities in public space. In fact, as a deeply conservative discourse, etiquette was concerned with social order and the maintenance of social hierarchies. New York's smart or fast set— among the first to embrace a more public and commercialized social life— pushed at "margins of unacceptable thought and behavior," tasting new pleasures and redefining codes of sexual behavior in its pursuit of a more informal lifestyle than that represented by the Four Hundred or its predecessors.[42] Included in the codes of etiquette were prescriptions that held good in the new age of newspaper publicity: The attention to appearance and behavior that promoted self-consciousness, especially among women, lent itself to a commercial aesthetic of display. There was, however, little or no overt acknowledgment of the role of publicity in high-society life. Advice on appearance in public was not given with the press specifically in mind, but rather with reference to the scrutiny of anonymous, ubiquitous eyes. This type of scrutiny was multiplied enormously—albeit vicariously—first with the emergence of mass-circulation newspapers and magazines, and then with the rise of photojournalism. Unintentionally working together, the etiquette manuals and print media mediated both a descriptive and prescriptive discourse of leisure-class femininity, thus inventing the ideal type of society queen. Meanwhile the introduction of photography enhanced the "paradigms for women's production of appearances" visually and transmitted them to a national readership well versed in the codes of female appearance and behavior. As Dorothy Smith argues, women knew where to look for how they should look and how to look at others.[43]

In his 1883 short story "The Siege of London" Henry James reworked the contemporary problem of recognition and the blurring of boundaries between *monde* and *demimonde*. The story opens at the Comédie Française during the first intermission of a play by Émile Augier. A young American diplomat, Rupert Waterville, beguiles his time looking at the rest of the audience through his "dainty but remarkably powerful glass." The story continues:

> He knew that such a course was wanting in true distinction, and that it was indelicate to level at a lady an instrument which was often only less injurious in effect than a double-barrelled pistol. . . . Standing up therefore with his back to the stage, he made the circuit of the boxes, while several other persons, near him, performed the same operation with even greater coolness.
>
> "Not a single pretty woman," he remarked at last to his friend; an observation which Littlemore, sitting in his place and staring with a bored expression at the new-looking curtain, received in perfect silence. He rarely indulged in these optical excursions.

But then Waterville espies what he calls "a kind of beauty," a woman in white with red flowers and diamond earrings "sufficiently large to be seen across the Théâtre Français" and asks his companion whether she is respectable or not.

> "I have made such mistakes—I have lost all confidence," said poor Waterville. . . . Whenever he encountered a very nice-looking woman, he was sure to discover that she belonged to the class represented by the heroine of M. Augier's drama; and whenever his attention rested upon a person of a florid style of attraction, there was the strongest probability that she would turn out to be a countess. The countesses looked so superficial and the others looked so exclusive.

On one level, this might be read as a conventional representation of audience behavior and gender roles, with the emphasis on the "display-value" of the woman and on that ubiquitous symbol of exoscopic enhancement in the hands of a man declaring his right to stare at women in the audience.[44] But a note of discomfiture is introduced with Waterville's inability to distinguish between so-called respectable women and courtesans. The signs of respectability—appearance, manner, carriage—have become unreliable. High-society women and *demimondaines* can occupy the same space, so that even an opera box is no guarantee as a marker of class. As mentioned previously, both classes of women are bearers of multiple meanings, signifying with their bodily presence and appearance male wealth and luxury, and both provoke attention to their sexuality when in public places of entertainment. Indeed, Waterville risks becoming an exhibitionist himself in his search for respectable beauty, which he expects to be on display and claims the right to look at, and makes himself especially vulnerable in this scopophilic act because he cannot tell a courtesan from a countess. Although the narrative hinges on whether the woman in the box is respectable or not, at a deeper level the story is about masculinity and the male code of honor; should a man reveal his knowledge about a woman's private life to others? James was perhaps more sympathetic to the woman's predicament than his French male contemporaries and his story was written specifically as a counter to the plot of *Le Demi-Monde* (1855), a play by Dumas *fils*, in which a woman's past is ignobly revealed by a former lover in the interest of his class.

À la Loge

For society women, then, there were certain settings in which their presence in public space was wholly sanctioned, and this increasingly involved performing as a decorative display for the delectation of the male gaze. Both newspapers and fiction of the period speak to this function of women. Women enacted a spectacle both for viewers and for those who wrote about them; their performance was recorded in detail. Journalists, in particular, wrote in great detail about women's appearance in these sanctioned settings. The more the press made a point of writing about fashionable society, giving attention to what women wore and did, the more women played to the press gallery. Clearly, newspaper publicity could be usefully utilized in social campaigns. The development of society journalism therefore raised the ante for competition and doing things out of the ordinary to attract attention. Writers of fiction reworked and rewrote women's performance of leisure and class, often incorporating it into a narrative of heterosexual desire. At an opera or ball such desire was heightened by the elaborateness of women's costumes, in particular by the décolleté gown, which emphasized women's sexuality. For women, moreover, the art of self-advertisement had to be accomplished within a minefield of conflicting impulses.

Wharton's fiction uses the topos of the opera as a site for pleasure, spectacle, and the performance of class. In contrast to the Jamesian story just referred to, which emphasizes the gentlemanly code of honor, her fiction problematizes the "hyperspecularization" of the woman subject and the sexualization of women's bodies as objects of display.[45]

In a way very reminiscent of Mary Cassatt's series of paintings of women in theater auditoriums, in which the point of focus is women in boxes against a glittering background of other boxes—that is, where the female spectator becomes the object on display—Wharton's novels contain a series of tableaux all featuring women at the opera.[46] The gaze directed at the stage is diverted to the women of the audience in boxes, to women who, according to nineteenth-century "doctrines of femininity," in Dorothy Smith's words, produce themselves "for men as extensions of men's consciousness and as objects of men's desire."[47] This gaze is magnified and intensified through opera glasses, an optical prosthesis primarily intended for surveying performers onstage.

In Wharton's historical novel *The Age of Innocence*, set in the 1870s, the narrative opens with the winter season's first performance of Gounod's *Faust* at the "sociable old" Academy of Music, "cherished . . . for being small and inconvenient, and thus keeping out the 'new people' whom New York was beginning to dread and yet be drawn to . . . [while] the daily press had already learned to describe [the assembled gathering] as 'an exceptionally brilliant audience.'" The self-satisfaction of the "club box" is suddenly disrupted when, during the second act, "a new figure" enters old Mrs. Mingott's box, and "masculine New York" turns its attention away from the stage to bestow it undividedly upon this woman. In the film version of the novel, this moment is captured superbly by Martin Scorsese through a series of rapid pans simulating someone looking through opera glasses. The gaze of the club men is drawn first of all by the appearance of this woman, with her "unusual dress "of dark blue velvet "theatrically caught up under her bosom by a girdle with a large old-fashioned clasp." Its wearer is described as "quite unconscious of the attention it was attracting." Meanwhile, the other female occupants of the box face "their semi-circle of critics with the Mingottian *aplomb*," something that has been "inculcated" by old Mrs. Mingott "in her tribe." This is a *learned* response, designed to resist certain interpretations that may be placed upon the situation. Mrs. Mingott's granddaughter Ellen Olenska, the one who has caused "the commotion," participates in this too, a display of both family and female solidarity. She sits "gracefully in her corner of the box, her eyes fixed on the stage." But the man soon to become her cousin by marriage, Newland Archer, discerns discrepancies in this offstage performance. For one thing, Ellen reveals "a little more shoulder and bosom than New York was accustomed to seeing, at least in ladies who had reasons for wishing to pass unnoticed." Madame Olenska's dress is therefore an offense against "Taste," and her appearance in public, given that her marital status is uncertain, an offense against "Form."[48]

Ellen's unconsciousness—or perhaps false *un*consciousness masking her self-consciousness—feigned or otherwise, can be contrasted with that of Lily Bart, the heroine in *The House of Mirth* (1905). At the start of New York's winter season, Lily is invited to the opening night at the opera by the Jewish financier Sim Rosedale. He has evidently been sent by Gus Trenor, who wishes to contrive a situation so that he can see Lily. Trenor and Mrs. Fisher make up the party in Rosedale's box. Lily takes pleasure in being the center of attraction, of having many eyes "excursing" over her:

> To Lily, always inspirited by the prospect of showing her beauty in public, and conscious tonight of all the added enhancement of dress, the insistency of Trenor's gaze merged itself in the general stream of admiring looks of which she felt herself the centre.[49]

Ever the actress, Lily performs for all men, resisting the possession of any particular man. But in doing so, she risks being classified as promiscuous, forfeiting her respectability.[50] Unknown to her, the gossip in male circles is that she is sexually available. Trenor has paid for Lily's gown and opera cloak and is looking for a return for his financial favors in the form of sexual services:

> He knew only that he had never seen Lily look smarter in her life, that there wasn't a woman in the house who showed off good clothes as she did, and that hitherto he, to whom she owed the opportunity of making this display, had reaped no return beyond that of gazing at her in company with several hundred other pairs of eyes.[51]

However, Lily is completely unaware of the precise nature of the transaction into which she has entered with Trenor by accepting money from him. She believes that he is investing her money for her; in actual fact, he is giving his own money to her. In her ignorance she plays a dangerous game, risking perilous visibility to others on terms she cannot control.[52]

Ironically, Lily is portrayed as a character who prides herself on her ability to control situations. She is a mistress of the art of artifice; she shows an acute awareness of the importance of setting and the need to integrate it with appearance and manner.[53] In fact, she could be said to have bought into the "display aesthetic" of the times, with her concern for lighting effects, the folds of her drapery, the placement of furniture (props), and her persistent, even fatal, desire for luxury. However, Lily's desire for control is undermined by the ability of male characters to define her behavior as promiscuous.

In *The Custom of the Country* (1913) Undine Spragg takes the management of visibility to new extremes in her campaign to scale the social heights of New York. She quickly learns the importance of the opera for making herself visible in New York's high society and begs her father, a midwestern millionaire and newcomer to New York, to buy her a box for Friday nights, so that she can at last be "part of the sacred semicircle whose privilege it is, between the acts, to make the mere public forget that the curtain has fallen." Undine's "consciousness" takes in "the whole bright curve of the auditorium, from the unbroken lines of spectators below her to the culminating blaze of the central chandelier." During the first intermission, "Undine, for the moment unconscious of herself, swept the house with her opera-glass, searching for familiar faces." Indeed, without hesitation or a shadow of self-consciousness, she engages in the scrutiny of other women. Her temporary lack of self-consciousness in her active spectatorship is disrupted, however, when she becomes aware "that she was being intently observed from the neighbouring box," and she turns to be confronted with "the bulging stare" of a well-known society man, Peter Van Degen, and the critical scrutiny of his female companion. Undine is embarrassed—she reddens—when it is obvious that the woman does not remember her. Van Degen, on the other hand, *does* remember her, but this does not elicit from Undine any indication of pleasure or self-gratification. Instead, she refuses to give him "some reciprocal sign of recognition" and quickly engrosses herself in a "haughty study of her programme."[54]

Like Mary Cassatt's painting "Woman in Black at the Opera" (1879), which can be interpreted as ridiculing the exaggerated ogling of the man in the background, Wharton's scene at the opera in *The Custom of the Country* portrays an active female spectator who resists being appropriated by an avaricious, opportunistic male gaze. To have given any sign of recognition to a man to whom she had not been introduced would have been giving him a signal that she did not set great store on social proprieties. And for the most part, Undine is very careful not to make herself a pushover for Van Degen. She wants to be not his mistress but his wife. In fact, she attempts to remain in control of her relations with men, and this brief scene in the opera box encapsulates the contest of wills between Undine and the men in her life. Nevertheless, the narrative as a whole does not elicit sympathy for Undine, who is ruthless in her pursuit of publicity, luxury, and glamor.

What these descriptions of women at the opera provide, then, is a fictional reworking of gender relations in the New York elite with respect to display and spectatorship. Ellen Olenska is "quite unconscious" of the attention she attracts. Being unconscious of such attention is, in fact, the appropriate mode of behavior for a respectable woman. In addition, the ambiguous qualifier "quite" may suggest that she is also a woman of some experience, used to being stared at and able to appear "unconscious."[55] Undine becomes "unconscious" only when she changes her role from that of being the focus of the gaze, male or female, into being a spectator. Seeing and being seen are not mutually exclusive, but in *The Age of Innocence*, these two activities are represented as distinctly gendered—it is men who do the seeing and women who are seen. To reciprocate the gaze or to look at men is to act like a prostitute. The fictional discourse of *The Age of Innocence*, therefore, has the discourse of etiquette current in the 1870s as one of its intertexts. There is nothing self-conscious, however, about Undine's action of spectating. Her action breaks with the prescribed codes of the earlier, more formal period. On the other hand, Undine is embarrassed by her companion's ignorance of how to behave at the opera, by Mrs. Lipscomb's lack of restraint in waving her fan and playbill to attract a man's attention. Undine knows enough from her reading of popular fiction and society columns to realize that a woman must not overtly solicit a man's attention—once again, we are dealing with a boundary demarcating the distinction between respectable women and prostitutes.

In these three novels, Wharton offers us a very pessimistic reading of women's agency, of the extent to which women are able to determine either their own fate or the manner in which they wish to be read in relation to the dominant discourse of femininity. For Wharton, spectacle and display mean only greater opportunities for both social control and surveillance as well as pressure to conform, factors that are not offset by the glamor deriving from hierarchical social relations and from the male production of wealth. In contrast, Dorothy Smith offers us a seductive theory of the feminine subject-in-discourse and "secret agent," contending that women in the process of producing themselves for men are able to experience full agency. She argues that it is in the "back regions" of women's performance of display as an object for male desire that women take pleasure in their preparations and in making decisions.[56] Wharton's characters may take pleasure in their enjoyment of luxury, their wearing of fine clothes, and the evident male approval that this appearance elicits, but they are seen as entrapped, as always subject to the scrutiny of unobserved spectators who have the power to label them as dangerously sexual —with sometimes disastrous consequences.

One further point can be made in order to underscore the significance of Edith Wharton's fictional construction of women and discourse of femininity and her representation of what might be referred to as the "new staging" of female bodies.[57] In this regard, I want to pick up Amy Kaplan's argument about literary realism competing with journalism at the turn of the century. On one level at least, Wharton's novels can be read as a "counterdiscourse," particularly to the consumer-oriented capitalist discourse of mass-circulation daily newspapers and weekly magazines associated with the conspicuous display of leisure and consumption by the nouveaux riches. Her novels attempt to deglamorize this class and to reveal the increasing sexual objectification of women in the competitive display of male wealth. Wharton exposes the gap between how her female characters believe they are presenting themselves to a public audience and how men in that audience view them—something newspapers cannot do because it goes against their self-interest. In doing so, Wharton undermines the dominant scopic regime that privileges men and problematizes women's role, not only in a class that seeks to visually overwhelm spectators with signs of its wealth, but also more generally in a consumer capitalist culture that deploys women's bodies in the commodification of glamor, luxury, and leisure.[58]

Furthermore, she exercises her own agency as a woman writer in exposing how men benefit from the erotics of female display.

By focusing on the opera house, we have seen how the culture of display invaded an urban space to the extent that journalists' reports so concentrated on details of the audience that they sometimes failed to even mention the name of the opera being performed. In fact, the Metropolitan Opera House became a place where the mingling of the older New York patriciate with the "Invaders" occurred, and it thus served a social purpose in widening the circles of the city's elite. As *Town Topics* put it: "The opera box is used as a key to open many doors," and this function was maintained right through 1920.[59] As is clear from both Wharton's work and the activities of the print media, the display of women was integral both to this social merger as well as to the advancement of class interests, and this type of display was consumer-oriented. The print media, as represented in Wharton's fiction, added both to the objectification of women and their surveillance.

"Sinister Eyes"

After 1900 or so, respectability itself underwent redefinition and codes of sexual behavior were modified to embrace a more informal lifestyle. One of the areas of social life in which this emerging transformation was most marked was the theater. The growing respectability of the theater and dramatic productions in the late-nineteenth century was also accompanied by the growing respectability accorded to performers and directors. New York society had never before been noted for aspiring to an intellectual interest in the arts, but the social barriers began to fall at the turn of the century, helped in part by people such as Mrs. Fish, who hired professionals to put on productions at her home. In effect, society hostesses were attempting to break down the gender segregation of social entertainments, a form of segregation that threatened their position and influence. Their very formal world was at risk from the mid-1890s on and in danger of not being taken seriously by their male confreres. To counter this, women had to adapt to developments toward greater informality, and they found that in so doing they opened up opportunities for greater heterosociability.

In the 1890s and 1900s the distinctiveness of high society from the world of the theater began to fade as social barriers against actresses were lowered. Actresses had once been consigned to the *demimonde*, with close associations being made between prostitution and the theater. But as theaters began to appeal to a more refined audience, so too was there a growing respect for the acting profession. There was also a great deal more mingling and blurring of boundaries with the crossing over of actresses into the world of high society, usually through a marital alliance with the scion of a wealthy family or as a result of the fact that some society women took up a career on the stage. Mrs. George J. Gould, formerly Edith Kingdon, had been an actress, for example. In 1908, long after she had left the stage, Frederick Martin, brother of Bradley Martin, put on a short one-act play starring Edith Gould and a current matinee idol in the ballroom at the Plaza Hotel. Other sons of robber baron Jay Gould also showed a fondness for actresses. George's younger brother Howard married Kathrine Clemmons, whom, it was said, he found in Buffalo Bill's Wild West Show, and another brother, Frank, married a Broadway actress, Edith Kelly.[60] Even the next Gould generation showed a penchant for actresses. In 1910 *Town Topics* reported that Jay Gould (grandson of the family founder) had become engaged to Mrs. Beatrice Godfrey, who had been chosen for the London production of *The Dollar Princess* but was unable to take up the part owing to ill health.[61] Meanwhile Elsie de Wolfe, a New Yorker who had been a member of high society in her youth, turned to the stage in the 1890s to rescue her ailing fortunes.

At the turn of the century musical comedies were particularly popular on Broadway and their female casts became the toast of the town. The most famous chorus line of the era was the Floradora sextette, all of whom ended up marrying wealthy husbands.[62] The most famous, or perhaps infamous, actress from the show who married "well" was, however, not one of the Floradora sextette but a young woman who had a small chorus part as a Spanish dancer. Her name was Evelyn Nesbitt and she became the wife of Pittsburgh millionaire Harry Thaw. Prior to her marriage, however, she was fêted by society architect Stanford White, an inveterate man about town. In his biography of White, Paul Baker describes him as "the consummate clubman." He was a member of most of the best clubs in New York, founded several clubs himself, and was an active participant in committees. Apart from this he also designed a number of famous clubs, including the Metropolitan and the Century Association, and he moved with ease between high society and the *demimonde*. His wife, Bessie, was ensconced with their children in their Long Island mansion, Box Hill, from the early 1890s, while Stanford played in the city. He had various hideaways, studios, and apartments for sexual liaisons with models and actresses. According to Baker, he "avoided the lavish so-called lobster palace restaurants around Longacre Square, which many society men frequented openly with actresses and chorus girls." It was to his apartment at 22 West Twenty-fourth Street, located above a toy shop, that White first invited Evelyn Nesbitt in August 1901. And it was at this more discreet address, rather than his better-known residence in the tower of Madison Square Garden, that he conducted his affair with Nesbitt. And it was also here that White would push an unclothed Nesbitt on a red velvet swing so that her feet broke through a Japanese parasol suspended from the ceiling.[63]

The lid was blown off this fantasy land in June 1906, when Harry Thaw shot and killed Stanford White in front of stunned patrons and chorus girls in Madison Square's Roof Garden. For the next month the newspapers were replete with stories about White's predilection for underage actresses and attempts by that indefatigable moral campaigner Anthony Comstock, president of the Society for the Suppression of Vice, to catch White. The *New York World's* metropolitan section ran an article about the chorus girl and the millionaire, two of the "habitués of the all-night restaurants" and "the heterogeneous world that lives upon Broadway and is scarcely awake until the artificial lights replace the sun." In interviews with actresses and theater managers, it was revealed that there was a regular exchange between chorus girls and "rich unprincipled men." White, however, had been regarded by the theatrical community as something of a benefactor who had helped actresses out with money, paid their doctor bills, and sent cabs to take them home from the theater.[64] Meanwhile, Anthony Comstock presented a very different portrait of Stanford White and claimed he had damaging testimony about White and female minors, evidence obtained from men whom he had employed to spy on White at his apartment at Madison Square Garden. Thaw had also had White under surveillance, having hired private detectives to check out White's activities, paying them between $40 and $60 a day. However, the head of the detective agency, John McKenna, told reporters that White had been "much maligned" and was not guilty of improper conduct.[65] As for Thaw, his action elicited little sympathy from a press that variously described him as a maniac, idler, spendthrift, and "champagne and absinthe drinker."[66] The murder of White and the lurid stories about him are, if anything, an illustration of how "male sexual power" had become "institutionalised in public space through its novel integration with modes of spectacle and luxury consumption," something that had become a hallmark of Broadway at the turn of the century.[67]

While the boundary between prostitutes and chorus girls may have been a floating one, the sexual expressiveness of chorus girls was commodified in such a way as to make them a more acceptable representation of sexuality. This sexual expressiveness was kept within certain bounds by the producers of musical comedies in seeking a more respectable audience. The women who appeared in musical comedies became celebrities and were fêted with champagne suppers by society men. As such, actresses came into direct competition with society women. And the competition extended to newspaper publicity as these other "public women" acquired celebrity status. Their photographs appeared in the newspapers, as did photographs of the interiors of their apartments, so that they too "sold" a lifestyle. Another area of competition was in dress fashions. *Vogue* carried a column entitled "Society and Stage" and pointed to the fact that society women sent their maids to the premières of plays in order to take notes on the gowns the leading actresses wore.[68] And the *New York Times* did an item on a play about high society starring Edna May and featuring a "Gibson Girl" chorus. The headline for the article was "Gorgeous Gowns Worn In 'The Catch of the Season' That Interest The Women."[69] This was just one of many plays about society that offered a positive representation of society life and glamorized it both for those within society and for those who looked on enviously.

Elsie de Wolfe, after dabbling with amateur theatricals, became a professional actress when the death of her father in 1889 left the family with no money. She was a member of the Charles Frohman Empire Theatre Stock Company for six years. Though her talents as an actress may have been in doubt, her taste for fine clothes was impeccable. Frohman realized this and used it to his advantage. With Elsie in the cast, he could be assured not only of attracting a respectable patronage for the plays he produced, but also of exciting the interest of those who wanted to see a society woman and her wardrobe. Frohman gave Elsie free rein in choosing gowns for her stage performances, and she made the most of her opportunities by traveling to Paris and striking favorable deals with Paris's leading couturiers. As Elsie herself wrote:

> I became a veritable dressmaker's matinée idol. Always on the first Saturday of any play that I appeared in, they came in a mob, sitting close to the front and jotting down notes about my costumes. One, considered very daring, was spoken of as the "Déshabille Troublante." It was of chiffon in thirty shades of red, beginning in ruffles of deep carmine at the feet and paling gradually to a soft rose at the top. It was made by Madame Gerber of Callot's.

Elsie knew how to market her social credentials and make money from them. She did not lose touch with her friends in high society just because she was on the stage and this too undoubtedly gave her greater cachet with the couturiers. In 1897 she was one of only two professional actresses at the Bradley Martin fancy-dress ball.[70]

Amateur theatricals had long constituted a popular pastime in bourgeois households, and society too had its own elaborate version of these, from plays to *tableaux vivants*. Some mansions, such as Leonard Jerome's, had their own theater.[71] Mrs. Fish was particularly keen on promoting amateur theatricals. And there were sometimes attempts to use amateur theatricals as a form of fund-raising for charity, but in 1920 the season's débutantes broke the mold in staging a show, not in a hotel or rooms where the audience might be confined to their friends and acquaintances, but in a Broadway theater. According to the *World*, midwinter theatricals had become a regular feature of the social program and in January 1920 society women "disported themselves" in *The Runaway*

Girl at the Plaza for the benefit of the Grosvenor Neighborhood House.[72] At the end of the month a group of débutantes put on a musical comedy entitled *What Next!* at the Princess Theater for the benefit of the New York Probation and Protective Association and Girls' Protective League, with seats at $10 and boxes at $150 for the first night, and afterward at $5 and $50 respectively.[73] Following the opening, the society columnist of the *World*, writing in the Sunday edition, described the production as being ambitious in putting novices onstage in competition with professionals, but claimed that it was able to stand on its own merits and was playing to full houses: "a production worthy of its environment in the heart of the White Light district."[74] However, the Saunterer was not as accepting about the idea of society women "disporting themselves" on the public stage:

> "What Next!" Blanketty-blank-blank-dot-blasted if *I* know! With young ladies of high society turning handsprings on the public stage and kicking their toes into the flies for the delectation of the sinister eyes of any sort of mixed audience that pays the price of admission, neither I nor anybody else can tell what *will* happen next. . . .
>
> It was something that should never have been seen outside of a private house, before an invited audience. With the exception of a few of the midnight reviews and cabaret performances, there is hardly a girl and music show on Broadway more frankly unclothed, just as much cloth of gold, tinsel and silk-clad legs. I know I shall be thought a horrible example of that ugly period dubbed Victorian, but I utter the criticism in all sincerity and with the kindliest of feelings, for everyone must realize that a line must be drawn somewhere, that some conventionalities must be observed in society or the whole fabric falls to tatters. I hold that a good place to begin to draw the line is these vulgarizing public performances, which cannot help but have an inimical influence. Had I witnessed such a performance in a private house, of course my lips would be sealed, but a public exhibition is another matter.[75]

This is a very clear statement on the appropriateness of public and private venues and the transformation that accompanies an entertainment when it is shifted from the parlor to the stage. It is also a blatant example of the Saunterer's attempting to draw a line, to demarcate and categorize. What underlies this attempt is the anxiety that society women risked being erroneously classified with actresses and therefore with women of doubtful reputation by making, literally, a spectacle of themselves and by dressing in comparable fashion to Broadway chorus girls. By performing in public, moreover, where there could be few constraints on who constituted the audience, they made themselves available to "sinister eyes"—presumably lower-class ones—and thereby transgressed another taboo boundary in occupying the same public space as men of a lower social class.[76]

What we have seen here are examples from the 1890s of the sexualization of women's appearance in public space. In the nineteenth century, "respectable" women had traditionally been threatened with being misrecognized—and the loss of one's reputation was social death, a loss that was irreversible. An important point to remember is that "respectable" women did not have to engage in prostitution or illicit sexual activities to be labeled prostitutes.[77] What is different about the sexualization of bourgeois women in public in the 1890s and 1900s is the degree to which this is linked with an emerging form of commercialized prostitution. Drawing upon Ruth Rosen's argument, namely that the concern in Progressive America about prostitution was a way of "expressing discontent and anxiety about changes that were corrupting and invading traditional American society"—changes associated with commercialization and the emergence of a consumer-oriented economy, urbanization, and industrialization—I would like to suggest that we see the Saunterer's use of prostitution and living pictures as representing an extreme version of women out of control. The Saunterer wanted to maintain an element of surprise by confining the ultimate revelation of curves to the marital bed. Prostitution was, after all, as Rosen suggests, "the most stigmatized form of female existence outside of patriarchal authority and protection."[78] The prostitute was designated a "disorderly woman," a "public woman," and bourgeois women who left the protective compound of the home and entered into public space—even to shop or engage in club work or social reform—were at risk of being classified as disorderly.

6

Women in the Public Eye

At the turn of the century not only did society women gain greater access to public space, they also became public figures, celebrities whose appearance and activities were often described in minute detail by society journalists. The society page, however, was just as much a contested space as the street or the opera. Society women with high public profiles could control only to a limited extent how their activities and appearance would be interpreted and presented to a reading public. Publicity entailed risks, and yet newspaper publicity became an integral part of life for those active in high society.

From the 1880s on, society journalism was instrumental in bringing about new social relations and practices as part of the more general development of the mass media in society.[1] It created an "imagined community" of readers by informing them about the lifestyle of the leisure class.[2] Indeed, society journalism transformed members of the social elite into celebrities, those who represented "the best" in U.S. society. The Saunterer justified his focus on society by claiming that it was "the flower of civilization, and it must be studied by anyone that has any interest in the history of the human race."[3] In fact, members of the leisure class came to epitomize exemplary success in an allegedly open, democratic society. On the other hand, they could also be regarded as embodying the opposite, that is, social hierarchy and entrenched power, but the overwhelming orientation of society news was, in fact, to present the social elite in a positive light. Indeed, newspapers had a vested interest in publicizing the values of an open, democratic society while simultaneously upholding those of power and privilege. The rapid growth of the newspaper industry and its commercialization automatically aligned it with consumer capitalism, the interests of which were, and are, served by hierarchical social structures.[4] At the same time, society journalism mediated the world of high society to the general public and played an important part in the relationship of the public to the social elite. There were, however, other dimensions involved in the production and reception of "society news," namely the relationship between the press and society, on the one hand, and that between the press and its readers, on the other.

In considering the relationship between the press and society, it is important to note that celebrities and the mass media were dependent on each other. Some women who sought to assert their social leadership undoubtedly made use of the press. This in itself suggests that society celebrities trusted that journalists would present information in acceptable ways. With regard to the relationship between the press and its readers, it may be assumed both from the style of discourse and from the fact that society columns often appeared next to the women's page that the target reader of society news was female (although women were not necessarily the primary purchasers of newspapers). Given that this was the case, such target readers were in all likelihood constructed by editors and journalists as coming from a broader social category than those being written about, to ensure that society columns had a fairly wide appeal concerning matters of taste, fashion, gentility, and women's social influence. Despite this wide appeal, however, newspaper readers were nevertheless conceived of as a homogeneous group having shared understandings about morality, the social structure, and gender roles.

The print media played a powerful role in shaping public opinion and deployed various strategies in order to construct a voice of reason and authority. Implicit in the presentation of reports on fashionable social life were claims to "reproduce events faithfully" and authoritatively. Publishing news about scandals usually promoted sales, but credibility had to be maintained, and this involved a long-term relationship with readers. The denunciations of immorality or hypocrisy committed by people in society could also emphasize the press's role as a defender of public morals. As such, society journalism promoted the alignment of readers with its perspective on high society. That is to say, newspaper stories were sometimes written in such a way as to suggest collusion between the reader and the columnist in glimpsing the exclusive show of fashionable folk.[5]

For the production, transmission, and reception of shared understandings, or symbolic forms, to occur, shared codes had to be available to the participants in high society, the mediators, and the readers of society columns.[6] Such understandings might include class-oriented expectations of how the wealthy or genteel folk should behave, beliefs in equal opportunity and an open social system, or a broad-based conceptualization of what constitutes femininity. At the turn of the century, none of these would have been mutually exclusive. Moreover, such understandings supplemented a growing body of conduct literature in enunciating what was expected of society women. As such, society columns delineated a normative role for women, a role based on traditional values of femininity. However, they also redefined femininity by contributing to broad-ranging processes within consumer capitalism that gave women a new and expansive role in the public world and the culture of display. Nevertheless, in carving out a successful social career, society women still had to negotiate tacit understandings about class and femininity. They had to manage their visibility, that is, give close consideration to how they presented themselves in public.[7]

The Society Page

Frank Luther Mott has associated the period 1885–1905 with the advent of the "great ten-cent magazine"—the illustrated general weeklies such as *Century*, *Harper's*, and *Scribner's*, publications that competed with the Sunday editions of the big city newspapers.[8] *Town Topics*, a New York–based magazine established by E. D. Mann in 1885, was one of these ten-cent weeklies. It included a variety of items, among which were "club news and gossip," financial news from Wall Street, information from the yachting and racing worlds, and reviews of the arts. "All of these will be treated of and written in bright, newsy paragraphs, which is the most popular feature of the journalism of to-day," ran the declaration in the first issue. Indeed, the stated intention of this weekly was to "give its readers matter of a character not treated of in the daily press or given in advance by other publications."[9] At the same time, its society column, "Saunterings," was its best-known department; the column was, in fact, its lead feature. The Saunterer asserted, furthermore, that *Town Topics* was a pioneer of society journalism and that until its appearance, "society in New York received little or no attention from the newspaper press of New York." In addition, in 1891 the Saunterer claimed: "Nearly every Sunday paper in New York now devotes a full page to the movements and habits of society people. The matter is prepared as nearly like mine as possible, being set forth in paragraphs, and, as a rule, my manner of expression is closely imitated."[10] In fact, the Saunterer routinely proclaimed his column to be superior to those of his main rivals, especially with regard to the matter of accuracy. And from time to time he delighted in pouring scorn on the unreliability of the reports contained in the society columns of the dailies. In April 1895, for example, he produced a long paragraph listing not only gross errors of fact but various fabricated stories that had appeared in New York publications. In one particular instance, it was clear to the Saunterer that "the reporter who was assigned to secure these interviews by a city editor more ignorant than himself, probably never went out of the office, and his sentiments were put into the mouths of two people that were abroad and one that does not exist."[11] Certainly, by the 1880s papers such as the *New York Herald*, Joseph Pulitzer's *World,* and the more sedate *New York Times* had all developed Sunday editions that featured at least one main page devoted to society news.[12] By the 1900s, however, society news was packaged very differently in the dailies, especially in their Sunday editions, for by then these had magazine or pictorial sections, whereas *Town Topics* printed neither photographs nor illustrations of the celebrities who featured in "Saunterings."

The emergence of a regular society page in the New York dailies during the winter season in the early 1880s signified that there was sufficient "news" about the activities of the wealthy to sustain the commitment of both newspaper space and staff. It also meant that a steady flow of information had to be maintained. As a rule, society news was increasingly located in certain specific columns in the dailies, and often on whole pages in the Sunday editions. At the same time, unusual or sensational items of news about particular families or individuals, such as divorces, court cases, or suicides, were often brought forward to the front page. This meant that a distinction might be drawn between the regular social activities of the New York leisure class and exceptional events. The murder of society architect Stanford White by Pittsburgh millionaire Harry Thaw in the restaurant at Madison Square Garden in July 1906, for example, was front-page news for weeks, but no mention was ever made of it on the society page in either the *New York Times* or the *New York World*.[13] It is conceivable, therefore, that this was a deliberate attempt to prevent the regular society page from being "contaminated" by the sensational and horrific news of the murder. Clearly, the kind of sensationalism that was regarded as appropriate for the front page had no place on the society page. In the Sunday editions, moreover, the society section was detachable and could be read separately, thus providing male heads of households with the opportunity to keep indelicate material away from their young daughters.

It is possible to see the society page as shaping and defining its readers' impulses, appealing simultaneously to the dream worlds of the masses and to the vanity of the elite. Ultimately, however, this type of journalism represented the interests of the elite. By making high society the subject of mass interest and reporting weekly, if not daily, on the activities of the rich and famous, society news endorsed the lifestyle of the wealthy. At the same time, however, by giving this lifestyle a very public profile, society journalists were also holding it up to public scrutiny. But just as sensational news was kept entirely separate from the society page, so too were the occasionally published criticisms by New York churchmen such as the Reverend Dix, who would take fashionable society to task for its excesses and immorality, for even the comments of churchmen were not allowed to "contaminate," or "break the spell" of, the society news. The intended reader of the society page was presumably anyone who had a fascination with the glamor of the rich or, at the very least, anyone who had an interest in the details of the social life of the leisure class. Criticism was confined to other pages, to sections where, if possible, it appeared alongside items that might reinforce the criticism. On the other hand, there was no guarantee that a reader would make connections between one story and another even when they appeared on the same page. As Richard Terdiman has pointed out: "Newspapers trained their readers in the apprehension of detached, independent, reified, decontextualized 'articles.'" The *New York World*, for example, could produce a front page containing detailed information about Mrs. Astor's mansion on Fifth Avenue side by side with a main news item concerning a violent clash between troops and strikers during the Brooklyn trolley strike of 1895. The two stories occupied the front page by virtue of being categorized as the leading news items for that day as well as the kind of news that would encourage people to buy the paper.[14]

Writers of society pages made appeals to the reader as a regular follower of fashion, as a knowledgeable reader. At the same time, these writers specialized in the use of set rhetorical formulae that would meet readers' stereotypical expectations.[15] Newspapers were also formatted in a systematic way through the use, for example, of different print types so that readers could quickly find the kind of news they were looking for. On the other hand, while headlines and opening paragraphs might confirm for a reader browsing through the paper that particular items were included, those readers requiring detail were enticed into giving their paper closer scrutiny because of the smaller print that succeeded the opening lines or because a story was continued on a subsequent page.

In 1906 the Saunterer's remarks on the unreliability of society reports in the New York dailies came back to haunt him when *Town Topics* became embroiled in a particularly damaging court case involving Justice Deuel, an occasional editor of the weekly.[16] The case was front page news for nine days and was followed with close attention by the daily press.

The case arose following an editorial by Norman Hapgood in *Collier's Weekly*, in which Hapgood alleged both that Justice Deuel was a part owner of *Town Topics*, something that conflicted with his position as a judge, and that *Town Topics* printed scandal about those who were not "cowardly enough" to pay to suppress it. Initially Hapgood's editorial had been prompted by the appearance in *Town Topics* of unpleasant information about Alice Roosevelt, the former president's daughter, which *Town Topics* published. When Hapgood's editorial appeared, Justice Deuel sued him for libel. Ironically, however, the ensuing court case turned into an exposé of *Town Topics*. And, according to the *New York Times*, society thronged to the courthouse to watch the latest entertainment: "Women by the score stepped on each other's heels in their eagerness to gain admission to the court room yesterday morning, and the place was crowded to suffocation. Many of the women were dressed as if for the Theatre."[17]

Predictably, Hapgood's defense counsel argued that the editor had indeed stated the truth about Justice Deuel's active involvement in *Town Topics*—testimony was given about the judge referring to himself as "the censor of *Town Topics*." In addition, however, the defense went on the offensive, as it were, and brought countercharges concerning the blackmailing of social celebrities. Indeed, evidence was presented that pointed to the existence of a list of instructions entitled "Hints to Correspondents of *Town Topics.*" This list included such items as "Remember that ridicule is more effective than abuse" and "Remember that *Town Topics* will pay more liberally than the daily papers for items of news in its own particular line." Charles Stokes Wayne, a former managing editor of *Town Topics*, took the stand and testified that *Town Topics* had a list of forty to fifty so-called immunes, that is to say, people about whom only "pleasant paragraphs" were published. These included, among others, the millionaires William K. Vanderbilt, George Jay Gould, J. P. Morgan, August Belmont, and Stuyvesant Fish. Wayne also exposed the custom of "pairing" paragraphs whereby the first one, the "blind paragraph," would refer to the infelicities of a member of society and the paragraph immediately succeeding it, the "key," would contain the name of the person in question. Wayne also gave evidence to the effect that journalistic "sources" included members of high society, clubmen, servants, and a Newport clergyman. And in his testimony, Robert R. Rowe, a member of the *Town Topics* staff, spoke of how he had disguised himself variously as a telegraph operator, a tambourine player, and a mathematics professor in order to get inside information about society folk. But even more serious allegations came to light. These had to do with Col. William d'Alton Mann, the proprietor of *Town Topics* since 1891, and his blackmailing of prominent society people. Allegedly, Mann's tactic was to dispatch a *Town Topics* agent to solicit substantial subscriptions for an illustrated book entitled *Fads and Fancies of Representative Americans.* If a society celebrity refused to cooperate, "unpleasant things" about them appeared in *Town Topics*; if they concurred, their name was placed on a card index advising journalists as to how they should be treated.

In his summing up for the defense, Mr. Osborne pointed to a mural of the three Fates on the wall of the courtroom. He then drew an analogy between them and *Town Topics*, Justice Deuel, and Col. Mann: *Town Topics* was "the Spinner that wove the light gossip," while Justice Deuel measured the scandal and Col. Mann was the assassin of reputations.[18] After the trial, District Attorney Jerome, who had already made it clear what his position was, referred to *Town Topics* as "a rotten, miserable sheet that ought to be suppressed; the 'Police Gazette' of the Four Hundred; a publication vulgar to refined tastes."[19] Clearly, Hapgood had entered the court in a very strong position, because the prosecutor's comments after the trial indicated that he too was unsympathetic to Justice Deuel's sense of offended honor. In addition, the *New York Times* reporter covering the trial evidently relished, along with so many others, the discomfort of Justice Deuel and Col. Mann on the stand—especially when Mann was cross-examined by Mr. Osborne and interrogated about his financial debts and techniques for "persuading" wealthy businessmen to lend him money. The paper described the scene as "The Court of Mirth"—a "secular" trivialization of Wharton's title—with spectators and lawyers "convulsed with merriment" during the cross-examination. Little wonder, then, that it took the jury a mere seven minutes to decide against the plaintiff.

The Invasion of Privacy

Society simultaneously courted and shunned publicity but ultimately became dependent on it. The difficulty was in attempting to persuade newspapers to respect boundaries between the public and private. Bailey's Beach at Newport, for example, had long been off-limits to reporters, but in 1902 the *New York World* displayed, for the first time, candid photographs of the socially exclusive enjoying leisure in what it regarded as private space.[20] While private beaches no longer guaranteed a refuge from the inquisitive eyes of newspaper photographers, nor did the domestic threshold, it seems, constitute a barrier to the outside world. Some members of society were happy to allow the interiors of their homes to become the subject of photographic essays in Sunday illustrated magazines. To be sure, not all families gave such license to reporters or wished their activities to be reviewed in society news columns, but in the inevitable absence of a collective policy on the treatment of the press, individuals had to do the best they could in determining how far the press should be allowed to go. In truth, it was difficult to simply "switch publicity on and off" and, paradoxically, the press played on high society's desire for publicity while criticizing deliberate attempts by members of society to put themselves on display.

One of the few etiquette manuals to offer guidance on how to deal with newspaper reporters was *Etiquette for Americans* (1898). Its chapter on "Treatment of Reporters" opens with a statement to the effect that "newspaper etiquette"—which is defined as "the exchange of amenities between reporters and their victims"—was of "recent or not yet recognized usage." The manual proposes that newspaper interviews are "an acknowledged evil" and explains that those who "hate notoriety, and consider publicity on any pretext poisonous, must submit to their fate" because of "the thousands with tastes perverted or vitiated who wish to appear in print on any pretext." In doing so, *Etiquette for Americans* constructs its readers as people who should be offended by any attempt on the part of the press to intrude into their private lives. It therefore proceeds by providing guidelines on how to deal with this inevitability of modern life. First, it recommends in the strongest possible terms that reporters who come "to the house of death" should be dismissed "without the faintest concession." Intrusion upon those in mourning is presented as a reprehensible breach

of journalistic etiquette on the part of reporters. The chapter continues by providing advice on how to treat reporters who approach people for "proper"
interviews. It suggests that the reader consider the circumstances of the
reporter, that he or she is "after all, only earning an honest living in a disagreeable way," and that one should adopt the approach appropriate to dealing with
any stranger, that is "to be perfectly polite to them." It recommends that the
best policy is to "give as much or as little information" as one would want them
to have and warns, moreover, that treating a reporter roughly might have damaging consequences. In fact, an interesting parallel is drawn between having to
deal with "rascally servants" and with intransigent reporters, implying that
when such people have a grudge to bear, they are potentially dangerous.
Clearly, the message was that politeness ensures privacy.[21]

Discussion of the press's invasion of privacy had come to the fore in 1890
with the publication of Louis D. Brandeis and Samuel Warren's article "The
Right to Privacy" in the *Harvard Law Review* and the subsequent broader discussion of the issue in magazines such as *Scribner's*. Already it had been noted
that the press was "overstepping in every direction the obvious bounds of propriety and of decency." Brandeis and Warren explored the issue of press invasion in terms of a legal violation of rights, and they pointed, in particular, to the
development of photojournalism: "Instantaneous photographs and newspaper
enterprise have invaded the sacred precincts of private and domestic life." One
of the major problems with newspapers, according to Brandeis and Warren,
was that gossip that had previously been in circulation among "the idle" and
"the vicious" was erroneously dignified through its appearance in print. Not
only was this printed gossip circulated much more widely, but it also had the
potential to produce more harm—both to the individual whose reputation was
at stake and to readers who were led to think mistakenly that such news was
edifying. "Gossip," they claimed, had become

> a trade, which is pursued with industry as well as effrontery. To satisfy a prurient
> taste the details of sexual relations are spread broadcast in the columns of the
> daily papers. To occupy the indolent, column upon column is filled with idle
> gossip, which can only be procured by intrusion upon the domestic circle.

For Brandeis and Warren, then, the issue was one of propriety and the modern
methods of journalism constituted a threat not only to standards of decency but
also to civilization itself:

> The intensity and complexity of life, attendant upon advancing civilization,
> have rendered necessary some retreat from the world, and man, under the refin-
> ing influence of culture, has become more sensitive to publicity, so that solitude

and privacy have become more essential to the individual; but modern enterprise and invention have, through invasions upon his privacy, subjected him to mental pain and distress.[22]

A similar argument had been made earlier in 1890 by E. L. Godkin, editor of *The Nation*. He had written a series of articles for *Scribner's* entitled "The Rights of the Citizen." In the fourth of these Godkin maintained that the right to decide how much knowledge the public could have of one's personal life, activities, tastes, and habits was a natural one. He acknowledged that individuals varied in their desire for privacy but nevertheless privileged those who prided themselves on "personal dignity": "To some persons it causes exquisite pain to have their private life laid bare to the world, others rather like it; but it may be laid down as a general rule that the former are the element in society which most contributes to its moral and intellectual growth."[23] A few years later, in 1894, the editor of *Scribner's* contributed to the ongoing discussion of this issue of privacy when he wrote of the "audacity of American newspapers in the publication of matters essentially private" and of a corresponding "demoralization of the public taste as to privacy and its opposite." He pointed to society hostesses' practice of sending reporters to their dressmaker or caterer for details that were, in effect, printed as free advertisements, thereby transgressing the public/private boundary.[24] Both high society and newspapers, it seems, bore responsibility for the publication of "private" details.

Unsurprisingly, the Saunterer defended the right of the press to invade the privacy of the rich:

> Privacy is something that few of us in the United States desire, and that none of the very rich can have for any price. As for the scions of a pampered and corrupt nobility, it is our duty and pleasure to revile, insult, gibe, sneer at, stare at and crowd them as much as we can. Thus we demonstrate the superiority of our political position and of our manners.

The context for this particular statement was the wedding of Consuelo Vanderbilt to the duke of Marlborough, which took place on 6 November 1895 at St. Thomas's on Broadway. In anticipation of a large, unruly crowd gathering outside the church on the day of the wedding, the Vanderbilt family had requested a large contingent of police to be on duty. The Saunterer was not only scathing that Americans, "a free, virtuous and intelligent people, thoroughly penetrated with the democratic spirit," should wish to gawk at a representative of a "time-corroded aristocracy" and his American bride, but he was also devoid of any sympathy whatsoever for people such as the Vanderbilts:

The very rich in the United States are sincerely to be pitied. There is really no place for them. The social and political conditions are not adapted to them. Unusually, by no fault, they are a little strange, a little alien, in their own country. The life that they lead is necessarily somewhat affected and imitative. Above all, they can hardly enjoy a moment of privacy. They are tracked and hounded by the spies of the press as if they were criminals.[25]

Mrs. Vanderbilt herself was not singled out for criticism by the Saunterer for despairing about the invasion of her family's privacy. Quite the contrary, the Saunterer saw her as being perfectly at ease with her public role: "She has recognized the fact that she does not live for herself alone. The very rich are the royal families of America. Their marriages and divorces are the book of golden deeds that constitutes our court chronicle." Clearly, much of what the Saunterer said was done with tongue in cheek. Nevertheless, he did infer that high society's disdain for crowds amounted to cant.

Managing Visibility

In the late nineteenth century the print media made society women's participation in an increasingly public social life a regular feature of various publications and therefore a subject of intense wider interest. This led to the construction of a new model of femininity insofar as the lifestyle of leisure-class women was paraded before the reading public as an ideal to be emulated. These women's daily and seasonal routines were portrayed in detail, their opinions were sought on matters of household management, and the interiors of their homes were photographed and displayed in magazines and Sunday supplements.[26] By these means, the press sought to "educate" its readers, to have them adopt, albeit on a more modest scale, the lifestyle of the rich and famous. As such, descriptions of leisure-class activities functioned as advertisements for consumer capitalism promoting "progress and civilization" as well as a life of comfort. At the same time and as a matter of routine, such descriptions sold newspapers, kept their proprietors in business, and added prestige to the leisure class by making it a major focus of interest.

Referring to eighteenth-century British periodicals, Kathryn Shevelow has suggested that such publications "often acted as agents for the transmission of 'genteel' codes of conduct, thus aligning themselves with values explicitly associated with the upper classes."[27] Clearly this continued to be the case in the late nineteenth century—and on a massive scale—as society magazines and society columns in daily newspapers took over this function. Needless to say, this had important ramifications for the women whose activities were brought to the attention of millions of readers, for society women had to negotiate the press in their daily life. Careful control of the "impressions they gave off" was necessary in order to maintain a certain presentation of self, involving, in part, apparent conformity to conservative conventions. On the other hand, their activities were seen as trendsetting and this gave them license to explore new directions. Moreover, the interest of the press in their lives conferred upon them a degree of prestige and influence that they could use to various ends in promoting themselves and their family, as well as other of their interests. But press attention also had its negative side: the lack of privacy, unwanted surveillance, the risk of exposure, or misrepresentation.

Society women did have the power to act, to advance their interests, both within an intricate nexus of commercial relationships as well as within the specific social structure of New York City and beyond. They could therefore utilize the mutual interests they shared with society journalism to suit their own purposes. Their high social class made them objects of fascination and public interest, and at the same time they could maintain their claims to distinction through supplying the press with information.[28] Just like business corporations, society women recognized the need for "opinion management" and hired press agents. This was one way of exercising control over what was printed, of ensuring they got the publicity they wanted and disguising what was essentially an act of self-promotion.[29] It is symptomatic of this situation that society illustrator Charles Dana Gibson sought to expose the self-serving relationship between society women and the press in his cartoon "Advertising à la Mode." In this illustration, which appeared in *Life* in May 1905, three society women carry sandwich-boards with the following headlines: "Notice: I Give A Fancy Dress Ball Tomorrow," "Important: I am Going to Europe this Summer," and "We Dine Again Tonight."[30]

In *The Custom of the Country*, Wharton explored the complicity between society journalism and the nouveaux riches. At the outset of her social career in New York City, the female protagonist, Undine Spragg, is shown to have insufficient cultural knowledge. At a dance at the hotel where she is residing with her parents, she is more impressed with a portrait artist, Claud Popple, who seems to be "in the key of the world she read about in the Sunday papers," than with "his more retiring companion," Ralph Marvell, who turns out to be the real "swell." Undine is confused by "unsuspected social gradations" that are not revealed by her major source of information, the newspapers. She is further bewildered by the contradictions she finds at the home of Ralph's sister, "the very stronghold of fashion." Indeed it is while dining here that her fellow guests make fun of Popple's pretentiousness and Undine inwardly winces with embarrassment at her mistake in reversing the social standing of the artist and Marvell. She finds "this world of half-lights, half-tones, eliminations and abbreviations" so puzzling and perplexing that she feels "a violent longing to brush away the cobwebs and assert herself as the dominant figure of the scene."[31]

In order to increase her knowledge of what is considered to be good taste, and in the hope of encountering again some of the people she had met at the dinner, the next day Undine dons her "handsomest furs" and proceeds along Fifth Avenue to the art gallery Mrs. Fairford had mentioned. Undine's instinct for finding the right kind of crowd proves to be impeccable: "Some of the ladies and gentlemen wedged before the pictures had the 'look' which signified social consecration." Sure enough, Undine bumps into a young man whose "grotesque saurian head" looks familiar, and she realizes that she is standing in front of socialite Peter Van Degen, "the hero of *Sunday Supplements.*"[32] It is significant, of course, that Van Degen should be thus designated by Undine, as her knowledge of society comes from newspapers and magazines. By showing how ill-equipped Undine is to enter the upper reaches of New York's rarefied atmosphere insofar as she is totally reliant upon such information, Wharton infers the inaccuracy of newspaper reports. In fact, she writes directly counter to the kind of discourse found on the typical society page and therefore offers a critique of the model of femininity that it promotes.

The kinds of reports on society women's lives that were in circulation at the turn of the century are, in many ways, little different from equivalent articles now current in women's magazines. Such reports shaped and constructed the "ideal woman" and presented her to a readership that was for the most part socially remote from the sphere of high society. As Edward Bok pointed out in one of his editorials for the *Ladies Home Journal*: "The society column of the smallest country newspaper now daily gives reports concerning these folk [the Four Hundred]: their balls, engagements, yachts, gowns and divorces." He also claimed, however, that the Four Hundred was "popularly disliked and jeered at."[33] In contrast, Pulitzer's *New York World* gave prominent profile to society queens in its Sunday magazine feature article "The World Portrait Gallery of New York Society Women," which appeared during the summer season of 1902. In fact, the columnist habitually used masculine metaphors to convey the abilities of society queens to readers. Mrs. Bradley Martin, a conspicuous figure in New York society in the 1880s and 1890s, for example, was described as "a great society general" and a "feminine Alexander" who "has displayed strategic skill that amounts almost to genius." Recounting Mrs. Bradley Martin's twenty-five-year social career, the journalist wrote in terms of her planning a campaign of gourmet dinners leading up to a huge ball in the winter of 1884–85, after which "Mrs. Bradley Martin found herself safely within the lines of New York's Smart Society."[34] The photographs of Mrs. Bradley Martin and her two nieces that accompanied the feature had art nouveau ornamental frames drawn around them.

Mrs. Richard T. Wilson was similarly featured under the headline "The Science of Marrying Well: A Study of a Mother and Three Sisters."[35] This article too offered a retrospective of the past twenty-five years, focusing upon the "brilliant marriages" of the Wilson sisters to Ogden Goelet, Sir Michael Herbert, and Cornelius Vanderbilt respectively. Her children's marital success is attributed to Mrs. Wilson's abilities; her "tact and cleverness," "magnetic force of mind," and "great ambition" are allegedly behind "each signal success." She is portrayed as the ideal mother, who does her best to promote her offspring while displaying a "gentle grace of manner" and "no jarring signs of will power." Once again, Alexander the Great is invoked: "Unlike Alexander, who wept because he had no more world to conquer," Mrs. Wilson is satisfied with "the wonderful result." She thus receives an accolade for being a successful marriage broker, especially as one who does not sacrifice her femininity in furthering her children's social careers. Several years previously the *New York Journal* had similarly praised Mrs. Wilson's matchmaking skills, by means of which she had "brought into her family more money than the original John Jacob Astor or Commodore Vanderbilt gained."[36] Ironically, the apposite metaphor for her success is that of a financier, the one occupation from which she, as a woman, was rigorously excluded. Despite these accolades from the dailies, when Mrs. Wilson died, *Town Topics* incorrectly alleged that she had not been credited by the dailies "for the social advancement of her children," and in order to compensate for this "oversight," the Saunterer lavished praise on "this little Southern woman."[37]

Mrs. Bradley Martin, for one, did not always fare well in the news. During the winter season of 1897–98, when, in the midst of a severe economic recession, she gave a lavish fancy-dress ball, Mrs. Martin was lambasted by the New York press and forced to permanently remove herself and her family to Britain.[38] This was conveniently forgotten by the Saunterer when, on the occasion of her death, he provided a laudatory appraisal of Mrs. Martin's skills as a hostess. Instead, he emphasized that "Mrs. Bradley Martin had the happy faculty of making her largest entertainments serve a semi-public purpose, giving them in years of social dullness and financial depression, and thus giving an opportunity for employment of hundreds of working people." Despite the extensive press coverage she received in *Town Topics*, let alone in the newspapers, in 1920 the Saunterer claimed that "she had no ambitions to become a social power in New York, and yet she may be classed in the same rank, with the late Mrs. Astor, Mrs. O. Mills and Mrs. Fish."[39]

At the turn of the century positive evaluations of society women abounded, all of them replete with what was expected of a wife and mother who was also a social leader. Typical of these is the *New York World*'s feature on Mrs. Clarence Mackay at the time of the death of her multimillionaire father-in-law, John W. Mackay. It described her as a "brunette, tall, with a charming figure" and as someone who was "popular among the young matrons of the fashionable set." It claimed that she was "noted for her intellectuality and for her wit," and pointed to the fact that she personally made clothes for her baby daughter and took an interest in her husband's racing stable. Readers were assured that Mrs. Mackay would make good use of her husband's inheritance, as "she knows how to spend money wisely not only to enhance the enjoyment of those around her, but to increase the happiness of those less blessed than herself." This paragon of a woman, moreover, despite being "an American patrician," was "most democratic and unaffected."[40] What more could one ask of a society queen?

When a woman's visibility was mismanaged, the Saunterer was quick to point out her indiscretions. For example, in 1908 the Saunterer asked: "What devil of perversity is it that urges women and men to abysmal depths of folly?" He continued: "You, sweet reader, may lay aside your Directoire coat and sheath gown, light your Russian cigarette, order a nip of vodka and do the moralizing." He went on to refer to a "beautiful" woman who had been married twice. The first marriage did not last long, for "she was turned loose from the connubial pasture, with a decree of divorce and a cool million." The Saunterer went on:

> Then she flashed her black eyes on the world again and an amorous basilisk could not have played more havoc with the susceptible hearts that came within her range of vision. From among the victims she selected one that pleased her, a big, agreeable, easy-going fellow, who seemed to idolize her, and—she married him. . . . No back and shoulders in all the display of alabaster and pearl powder at the Opera was more exploited, and her "raven hair in its magnificent richness" as Miss Libbey, and the imaginative scriveners of the daily press would say, was a mark of distinction that rose to the proverbial.

Everything, according to the Saunterer, appeared normal on the surface. "But beneath! Oh, the depths of sunny pools! So I am just telling the story in the hope that it will let her know that I know, and, ere it is not too late the lady of the alabaster shoulders, the back and the limpid eyes will awake to the realization of the value of discretion."[41] The Saunterer delighted in such warnings. But it was also a way of calling to task those who had set themselves up as leaders of society.

Of course, married men could get into trouble with their wives when *Town Topics* hinted at their dalliances with other women. We have a rare incidence of a response from one of the anonymous victims of the Saunterer's acerbic tongue. In fact, the victim was connected to the woman with the "alabaster shoulders." According to Cornelius Vanderbilt Jr., son of Grace Wilson and Cornelius Vanderbilt, his father sent the above-quoted article about the lady with the raven hair to Grace, telling her: "I hear the lady is still abroad and that she is expected back this week. She has been away since about the time you sailed and you *must* know how foolish the whole thing is. I am more than sorry to have to bother you with it, but it is only right that you should know. Am really too disturbed but of course you know how ridiculous it is and so does anyone who knows anything about things in New York." It seems that Grace Vanderbilt was profoundly distressed by the article, and in his next letter her husband tried to assure her that *Town Topics* had not pursued the story, even though he thought those connected with the magazine were "such a scoundrelly lot of unprincipled people." He also mentioned that he had consulted a lawyer about the matter and had been advised that there was nothing "legally libellous" in the article. Cornelius believed any public denial would make matters worse.[42]

Publicity could therefore have, and still can have, both favorable and unfavorable consequences for those caught in its beam. Americans struggled with this new force in their lives at the turn of the century and debated its effects. In 1900, for example, the *Ladies Home Journal* carried a series written by "An American Mother" who complained of the way American women had "become crazed with the desire to gain money, social position and power." Newspaper publicity was blamed for unsettling the lives of young American women, of damaging them by both "vulgar notoriety" and "the applause of the public." Young women had become immodest: "Our New Girl lives in the blaze of vulgar publicity. She cannot go to a friend's house, nor ask another girl to visit her in her home, without publishing the fact in the newspapers." And it had now become accepted that a woodcut of her "in her best decolleté gown" would appear in the papers when she began courting and that they would carry detailed reports both of the wedding gifts and her bridal trousseau.[43]

By the 1890s images of women were routinely displayed on society pages in the form of half-tone reproductions of photographs.[44] In the early years of society journalism illustrations had taken the form of sketches that were drawn on wood blocks and then engraved. Charles Dana Gibson was perhaps the best-known illustrator of New York society women, with many people imitating his style; other well-known illustrators included Howard Chandler Christy and W. T. Smedley.[45] By the turn of the century, photography had come into its own. This led to greatly intensified scrutiny of women's appearance, giving rise to all sorts of possibilities for candid rather than posed shots. Just as they had learned how to exert some control over reports about themselves, so society women found ways of harnessing this new facility of society journalism: They offered to pose for cameras or sent in commissioned photographs. From the 1890s on, society pages contained "portrait galleries" of society women, five or six photographs each enclosed in an illustrated frame.

In one sense it was but a small step from portrait paintings to photographic portraits, as both constituted a form of visual representation that displayed women's bodies. However, whereas painted portraits had been intended by and large for private showing, photographic portraits were available to the public.

This distinction no longer existed with the reproduction of painted portraits in newspapers. Indeed, both Wharton and James deal with the painting of portraits as newsworthy, as an occasion for display and self-promotion. In *The Custom of the Country*, the painting of Undine's portrait and its ritualistic unveiling at a tea at the artist's studio gives her an excuse "to telephone her press-agent to do a paragraph." Undine basks in the thought of people crowding in to see her portrait at the spring exhibition. Clearly, her portrait is intended for public consumption.

With her caricature of Claud Walsingham Popple, Wharton adds society portrait painters to her collection of *bêtes noires* of the "Invader" class. Popple's style of painting is described by Mrs. Fairford, a member of the old elite, as "'chafing-dish' art." Early on in her acquaintance with Undine, Mrs. Fairford has made it known that she does not hold Popple in high regard. Her brother Ralph is similarly cynical about Popple's talents as an artist and compares Popple's own description of his ability to "toss off" a picture to the performance of a magician who elaborately points out to the audience that there is nothing up his sleeves. As part of this "dissemblance" aimed at hiding the marks of his craft, Popple goes to a great deal of trouble to pose as a man of leisure, equal in status to his clients. He therefore regards it as inappropriate for his clients to see him at work or marked with indications of work, such as splashes of paint. Consequently, his studio is like a drawing room, complete with a cozy corner, a tea table, and gilt armchairs "of pseudo-Venetian design." In fact, Mrs. Fairford's reference to a "chafing-dish" evokes the bourgeois dining room, with its ornamental tableware—tableware, moreover, that was mass-produced.[46]

Popple's distinction lies in his reputation as "the only man who could 'do pearls,'" the ubiquitous icon of wealth customarily worn in "ropes." As Popple understands so well, the implicit purpose of a portrait is to display wealth; "a long experience in idealizing flesh and realizing dress-fabrics" means that he can satisfy all that fashionable society ever "asked of a portrait," namely "that the costume should be sufficiently 'lifelike,' and the face not too much so." Jim Driscoll, one of the "Invaders," suggests to his "short stout mistrustful wife" that she be painted by Popple for their "new music-room." With a keen eye to his own advantage, as well as to the vanity and pretensions of the nouveaux riches, the artist proposes that he "'work in' a court-train and feathers," and even though Mamie Driscoll has not yet been presented at court, he tells her that the portrait will make "a lovely memento," a memento planned in advance of an event that may never occur. At the same time, Mamie insists that the portrait will have to be commensurate with the predictably large dimensions of their new room. The pretensions of the nouveaux riches, as personified by the Driscolls, are ruthlessly satirized by Wharton in this scene.[47]

The discussion referred to takes place when the Driscolls are attending the unveiling of Popple's portrait of Undine Spragg. While the ornamental role of women represented in wall hangings in either the drawing room or music room is forefronted in the discussion, Undine's portrait suggests yet another dimension to the symbolic function of women's portraits. Popple, who for the most part panders to the material tastes and whims of his clientele, also knows how, when painting a reputed beauty like Undine, to appeal to male sexual desires. Yet Popple feigns innocence in capturing the colors and tones of Undine's flesh in her décolleté gown. "It's a point of honour," he protests to Peter Van Degen, "with the *man* to steel himself against the personal seduction." He explains to the gullible Undine, moreover, that the artist has to wrestle with his "lower and higher natures," but Van Degen, the crude millionaire capitalist, is not fooled by his explanation and praises "old Popp" for his knowledge of "how we live and what we want." Van Degen knows exactly what the difference is between men's and women's portraits. The "great thing," he says, "in a man's portrait is to catch the likeness," but "a woman's picture has got to be pleasing." And he knows that Popple agrees with him, despite the latter's genteel drawing-room performance, as is indicated in his remark to Undine: "Popple always keeps his place at low-neck temperature, as if the portraits might catch cold." Wrapped up in her own narcissism and taking pleasure in the discussion that her portrait evokes, Undine nevertheless manages to take advantage of the situation and secure "a couple of thou'" from Van Degen for the privilege of seeing her in her Empress Josephine fancy-dress costume at a forthcoming ball.[48] Once again, Undine plays with the boundaries between prostitution and respectability.

"A Newspaperized World"

"That mirror of the public mind—the newspaper."[49]

A woman's portrait is also of central significance to Henry James's light comic novel *The Reverberator* (1888), and, as in *The Custom of the Country*, the portrait is the subject of a newspaper article. In *The Reverberator*, the two central characters, Francie Dosson, a young American visiting Paris with her father and sister, and Gaston Probert, a young man who has been brought up in France, meet for the first time in the studio of Charles Waterlow, an artist who has been commissioned to paint Francie's portrait. An analogy is drawn between the notion of the artist "possessing" Francie in the act of painting her and that of a man "possessing" her as a lover. This is indicated by Gaston's sudden feelings of jealousy toward his friend Waterlow, feelings that are intensified when the artist says that he will see Francie "as often as possible—his eye would take possession of her." But later, when the portrait is completed, Gaston no longer begrudges the artist the "insight" that enabled him to "reconstitute the girl on canvas with that perfection." Instead, the portrait is "exactly the way" Gaston "would have chosen that she should be represented," and he "somehow felt proud" of the portrait even though it was no more his property than "the young lady herself." In fact, by this time, he has decided that he does want to "possess" her.[50]

Set in Paris, the novel tells the story of a young American journalist, George Flack, whose job it is "to obtain material in Europe for an American 'society-paper,'" known as *The Reverberator*.[51] This "society-paper" has a substantial circulation of over a hundred thousand, and it is the young man's ambition to make it "the most universal society-paper the world has seen." With this aim in mind, he enlists the help of Francie Dosson, a young woman with whom he is in love. He tells Francie:

> The society news in every quarter of the globe furnished by the prominent members themselves (oh, they can be fixed—you'll see!) from day to day and from hour to hour and served up at every breakfast-table in the United States— that's what the American people want and that's what the American people are going to have. . . . I'm going for the secrets, the *chronique intime,* as they say here; what the people want is just what isn't told, and I'm going to tell it. Oh, they're bound to have the plums! That's about played out, any way, the idea of sticking up a sign of "private" and thinking you can keep the place to yourself. You can't do it—you can't keep out the light of the Press. Now what I am going to do is to set up the biggest lamp yet made and to make it shine all over the place. We'll see who's private then! I'll make them crowd in themselves with the information.[52]

As is evident from this passage, in his choice of title for Flack's society magazine James cleverly evokes the metaphorical association of light with publicity, thus drawing the reader's attention to the main focus of his critique, "the invasion, the impudence, the shamelessness of the newspaper and the interviewer, the devouring *publicity* of life, the extinction of all sense between public and private."[53] The use of the word *reverberator,* which refers *inter alia* to a reflecting lamp, also draws our attention to the problematic issue as to whether society journalism "reflects" society or whether society makes use of the press to act as a "beacon" for its conspicuous activities.

In Paris George Flack befriends the Dossons, a wealthy family of naive Americans who hold newspapers in high esteem. To Mr. Dosson, the newspaper "represented the Mind—it was the great shining presence of our time," while both Mr. Dosson and his two daughters "believed everything that they heard quoted from a newspaper." While Flack is temporarily in the United States to attend to a crisis in the affairs of the newspaper, Francie is courted by Gaston Probert, whose family represents the epitome of privacy. By the time Flack returns to Paris, Francie has become engaged to Probert. And when Flack calls upon Francie at her hotel, it is in the guise of an aggrieved lover who proceeds to ask her about her new life in the *"grande monde."* He does, however, tell her that he needs to "study up" and to take every opportunity to learn. "Every one has something to tell, and I listen and watch and make my profit of it. I hoped *you* would have something to tell." Flack then assumes the position of a close friend who wants to know about the Proberts and is taken by surprise when Francie asks him straight out if he wants to put them in his paper. He takes this question to mean that Francie is not concerned about her information appearing in print and tells her he wants "genuine, first-hand information, straight from the tap." He then maneuvers her into agreeing to go with him to see her portrait at Waterlow's studio, with the stated aim of writing about it in *The Reverberator.* Francie gives him her blessing: "You may say what you like. . . . It will be immense fun to be in the newspapers."[54]

After their visit to the studio, Francie and Flack go out for a drive in the Bois de Boulogne during which Francie speaks without reserve about the Probert family, answering candidly all questions put to her by the newspaperman, unaware that in his mind this conversation is still governed by her instruction that he may say what he likes about her in his paper. Everything that she says appears in one of Flack's articles for *The Reverberator* and when the Proberts read it—a copy is sent to them from the United States—they are mortified by the "vulgar lies and scandal," and "the most odious details" about the Dossons and their family. They feel violated, polluted. The Dossons are baffled by the reaction of the Proberts and cannot see why they are so "affected" by the piece. However, Francie herself begins to wonder whether the different reaction of the Proberts does not indicate that she and her family had "lost their delicacy, the sense of certain differences and decencies." Furthermore, she wonders whether all of the "chatty letters" that she had ever read in the papers had also meant "a violation of sanctities, a convulsion of homes, a burning of smitten faces, a rupture of girls' engagements." Francie's father and sister refuse to let her take any responsibility for the story because to them "the newspapers and all they contained were a part of the general fatality of things, of the recurrent freshness of the universe, coming out like the sun in the morning and the stars at night."[55]

The marriage is saved, but only at the cost of breaking all relations with the Probert family. Gaston casts his lot in with the Dossons and asks them to take him with them anywhere, anywhere except the United States, a country where he finds the solar light too hard, "too much like the scratching of a slate-pencil." He wants to go to a place "where there are no newspapers."[56]

By considering the references to newspapers in this story, then, it is possible see how James positions himself and his art in relation to the news media. As his tale implies, newspapers have the potential to be a destructive force, and yet they disguise their power behind the so-called democratic "need to know," and

seemingly assume that they can unproblematically represent the real and provide objective information. In fact, James places the manipulation of both news
and people at the center of his story.

Wharton too railed against the invasiveness of the press by parodying *Town
Topics* in her representation of a society periodical entitled *Town Talk*, which
appears in both *The House of Mirth* and *The Custom of the Country*. In the latter,
the title of another society paper, *The Radiator,* recalls that of James's
Reverberator. While the collusion between society journalism and the nouveaux
riches is referred to only briefly in *The House of Mirth*, it is integral to the plot of
The Custom of the Country.[57] In the latter, the press is on the side of the
"Invaders." Undine Spragg is shown to be very much at home in the limelight:
She craves attention, publicity, and crowds. On the eve of her entrée into high
society, she sits in her white and gold bedroom with the electric light blazing:

> So untempered a glare would have been destructive to all half-tones and sub-
> tleties of modelling; but Undine's beauty was as vivid, and almost as crude, as
> the brightness suffusing it. Her black brows, her reddish-tawny hair and the pure
> red and white of her complexion defied the searching decomposing radiance:
> she might have been some fabled creature whose home was in a beam of light.

The glare of electric light, let alone publicity, was anathema to Wharton; it
offended her sense of taste and refinement. But Undine is depicted as courting
publicity and using it to her own advantage. When her divorce from Ralph
Marvell is announced, it is her version of events that is circulated, a version that
predictably portrays Ralph as the guilty party. Ralph's sensitivities, like those of
the Proberts, have been so violated that

> for weeks afterward, wherever he went, he felt that blush upon his forehead.
> For the first time in his life the coarse fingering of public curiosity had touched
> the secret places of his soul, and nothing that had gone before seemed as humil-
> iating as this trivial comment on his tragedy. The paragraph continued on its
> way through the press, and whenever he took up a newspaper he seemed to
> come upon it, slightly modified, variously developed, but always reverting
> with a kind of unctuous irony to his financial preoccupations and his wife's
> consequent loneliness. The phrase was even taken up by the paragraph writer,
> called forth excited letters from similarly situated victims, was commented on
> in humorous editorials and served as a text for pulpit denunciations of the
> growing craze for wealth; and finally, at his dentist's, Ralph came across it
> in a *Family Weekly,* as one of the 'Heart problems' propounded to subscribers,
> with a Gramophone, a Straight-front Corset and a Vanity-box among the prizes
> offered for its solution.

The key note in this passage is one of trivialization. The Marvells' divorce is employed to illustrate the hackneyed situation of a husband "Too Absorbed In Business To Make Home Happy," as the initial headline blurts out. With each successive distortion of the story in the print media, ending with its final appearance as a "heart problem," greater credence is ironically given to the cliché of a husband not having enough time for his wife and family. Undine's story, which originally starts out as a way for her to justify her actions, gains wide currency as it gets "reverberated" throughout the media. Meanwhile, Ralph's "reality," his version of events, never gets into circulation, as he would never dream of countering his wife's story in the press. In any case, Undine has already masterfully mobilized public opinion against him.

Generally, moreover, Undine's public persona as a social celebrity is shown to be based on a tissue of lies, as indeed is her version of the breakdown of her marriage to Ralph. And yet it is the newspapers that become not only Ralph's primary source of information about his marital status but also Undine's son's only source of knowledge about his mother. In the penultimate scene of the novel, Mrs. Heeny, the family masseuse, pulls out a newspaper clipping from her bag to verify for the son, Paul, the farcical story about Undine's two-minute divorce from a French count in Reno and her immediate remarriage to Elmer Moffatt. In a brilliant parody of newspaper discourse, Wharton plays on the notion of speed: "No case has ever been *railroaded* through the divorce courts of this State at a higher rate of speed: as Mr. Moffatt said last night, before he and his bride *jumped* onto their east-bound special, *every record has been broken*. . . . Judge Toomey . . . held a night session and *rushed it through* [the divorce]. . . . At the trial Mrs. Spragg–de Chelles . . . gave evidence as to the brutality of her French husband, *but she had to talk fast as time pressed, and Judge Toomey wrote the entry at top speed, and then jumped into a motor* with the happy couple and drove to the Justice of the Peace" (italics added). And so Mrs. Heeny concludes: "There, now you see how it all happened."[58] Just as the novel opens with Mrs. Heeny reading newspaper clippings, so it closes. For Undine, the newspaper remains a useful source of information about others, and she is untroubled by her use of it to present an advantageous representation of herself.

Despite the ambivalence of some members of society toward newspaper publicity, it had become a fact of life by the end of the nineteenth century. Society journalism, moreover, had become an integral part of the general culture of display, and people who sought to assert their claims to high social status made extensive use of newspaper publicity. Because of women's role in testifying to their husband's wealth, society women had to learn how to deal with journalists and how to ensure both favorable and respectable publicity for themselves and their family. It is possible that journalists tried to offset criticism of their invasive methods by exaggerating their representations of society women as models of genteel womanhood. It is also possible that some society journalists were anxious to be regarded as providing respectable accounts of high-society life in order to facilitate their access to members of the social elite. Irrespective of such speculations, however, the end result was the production of a journalistic discourse that reinforced dominant ideals of femininity and encouraged both women's behavior and their appearance to be read as signifying their knowledge of high fashion, their attention to manners, and their husband's business success. As Thorstein Veblen elaborately demonstrated in his *Theory of the Leisure Class* (1899), these constituted shared codes of wealth and status. However, what Veblen did not do in his exposé of the conspicuously rich was to examine the role of the press in mediating shared codes of wealth and status for the general public. On the other hand, Edith Wharton and, to a lesser extent, Henry James convincingly demonstrate how society journalism was implicated in the flaunting of wealth by the nouveaux riches.

Conclusion
Spectacle and Surveillance

At the turn of the century one of the overriding principles in New York's high society was to see and be seen. To provide a spectacle of wealth—to overwhelm "lesser mortals"—was to impose one's power, and this was a principle with a long history, going back to the court society of the ancien régime and beyond. In seeking to claim social distinction for themselves the nouveaux riches emulated both the lifestyle of old New York and that of the European aristocracy, their immediately superior reference groups. By putting their wealth on display through leisure, clothes, expensive entertainments, and houses modeled on European palaces, the nouveaux riches attempted to put as much distance as possible between themselves and their lower-class antecedents. After all, luxury, as Pierre Bourdieu points out, is a "manifestation of distance from necessity."[1]

In seeking to be included in the social elite, the nouveaux riches in New York were confronted by barriers placed against their entry by established members. The class struggle that ensued, involving as it did intense competition in the display of wealth between newcomers and the old elite, is a highly significant theme in Wharton's New York fiction. Indeed, her New York fiction can be said to portray what Bourdieu refers to as "symbolic struggles over the imposition of the legitimate life-style . . . struggles for the exclusive appropriation of the distinctive signs that make 'natural distinction.'"[2] According to Bourdieu, the sites for such struggles include "holiday resorts and restaurants," sites that are very much in evidence in Wharton's fictional representation of the "Invaders" and the "Aborigines." In *The Custom of the Country*, for example, Charles Bowen, a representative of the ascetic old New York elite, somewhat reminiscent of Lawrence Selden in *The House of Mirth*, deplores the noise and crowds wherever fashionable society gathers.[3] Nevertheless, Bowen organizes himself a seat in the corner of a restaurant in good time to observe the room fill with "plumed and jewelled heads":

> The dining-room at the Nouveau Luxe represented, on such a spring evening, what unbounded material power had devised for the delusion of its leisure: a phantom "society," with all the rules, smirks, gestures of its model, but evoked out of promiscuity and incoherence while the other had been the produce of continuity and choice. And the instinct which had driven a new class of world-compellers to bind themselves to slavish imitation of the superseded, and their prompt and reverent faith in the reality of the sham they had created, seemed to Bowen the most satisfying proof of human permanence.[4]

Lacking the security of being accepted as distinctive by those in authority, the nouveaux riches "overdo" it. As Bourdieu explains: "The petit bourgeois is haunted by the appearance he offers to others and the judgement they make of it. He constantly overshoots the mark for fear of falling short, betraying his uncertainty and anxiety about belonging in his anxiety to show or give the impression that he belongs."[5] How the nouveaux riches overdo it is precisely what Wharton illustrates in her fiction, and it is a key component in her critique of social change in turn-of-the-century New York. In Bourdieu's terms, Wharton "enters the game"; she has the cultural knowledge (*connaissance*) in order to do so, supported by her upbringing and education, and she has the "habitus," the predisposition to enter the game as a legitimate player given her position as an insider in New York's high society.[6] In representing the "symbolic struggle" between old New York and the nouveaux riches in her fiction, Wharton ridicules the pretentiousness of social climbers. She lays bare their efforts to appear to be something that they are not—at least in her eyes. Not only does she show them struggling to pass themselves off, as Undine does at Mrs. Fairford's dinner, for example, but she also makes the reader patently aware that the parvenus know nothing of the "real" value of what it is they imitate. Wharton herself does know the value of old New York society. In the first place, she had demonstrated her cultural knowledge with the publication of *The Decoration of Houses* prior to publishing any of her novels or collections of short stories, and she continued to assert her knowledge in other nonfiction works, such as *Italian Villas and Their Gardens*, *A Motor-Flight Through France*, and *The Writing of Fiction*. Second, she affirms this presentation of herself as one of the cultural (and social) elite in her autobiography by attesting to "the formative value of nearly three hundred years of social observance: the concerted living up to long-established standards of honor and conduct, of education and manners." Indeed, "the traditions of three centuries" constituted, in her view, "the moral wealth" of the United States.[7]

By her own admission, Wharton herself had not always appreciated "the moral treasures" of old New York, that is to say, those treasures of "social observance" that she had personally found stifling. But after the First World War, when she had an overpowering sense that *her* New York had been "swept away," she felt the need to "atone" for her "unappreciativeness by trying to revive that faint fragrance." If anything, her historical fiction of the early 1920s, *The Age of Innocence* and *Old New York*, is a further demonstration of her cultural knowledge. She becomes a quasi anthropologist-cum-archaeologist digging up relics, collecting the "smallest fragments" worth preserving and piecing them together.[8] And she does so as one who had known old New York before it had become suddenly and totally extinct. Hers is a privileged perspective; she "captures" the faded past. There is, moreover, an earlier foreshadowing of this self-positioning in her travel book on Morocco, in which she presents herself as a travel writer who provides a glimpse of a land that is destined to change beyond all recognition.[9]

In both her fiction and nonfiction works, then, Wharton asserts her privileged gaze. But, in entering the game, she also participates in the struggle "for the exclusive appropriation of the distinctive signs which make 'natural distinction.'" As Bourdieu argues: "The opposition between the 'authentic' and the 'imitation,' 'true' culture and 'popularization,' which maintains the game by maintaining belief in the absolute value of the stake, conceals a collusion that is no less indispensable to the production and reproduction of the *illusio*, the fundamental recognition of the cultural game and its stakes."[10] In giving voice to the "vanishing denizens of the American continent doomed to rapid extinction with the advance of the invading race"—a dubious analogy at best between old New York and American Indians—Wharton champions a form of high culture.[11] She identifies herself as a writer of serious fiction and distances herself from popular novelists. At the same time, she counters the discourse of society journalism, or at least the part of it that legitimizes the ostentatious display of wealth and mistakes "conspicuousness" for "distinction."[12] She therefore claims superiority over society columnists and popular novelists.[13] Both as a writer of serious fiction, therefore, and as an "authentic" member of New York society, she is someone "in the know." Paradoxically, however, her position is to some extent undermined by the discussion of her novels on the society page and their appropriation by the very forces she criticizes. One reviewer regarded *The House of Mirth*, for example, as a biased and negative portrait of the Four Hundred and accused Wharton of washing society's linen in public. For this particular reviewer, what Wharton had done in writing a novel about high society was no better than adverse newspaper publicity: "In society, we regale ourselves with the latest scandal about Mrs. X, but we don't shout it out in a sub-way car. It is a case of noblesse oblige."[14] Furthermore, Wharton's stance on the vacuousness of fashionable society is adopted by the Saunterer and others as an appropriate judgment of society's "goings-on," so that journalists counteract her attempts to create distance between her novels and what they themselves write.

Ironically, Wharton's writings made visible old New York, a world that prided itself on a high level of invisibility and shunned the glare of publicity. Through her fiction, she held up a model of this social world that was fast fad-ing from view and contrasted it starkly with that of "the pretentious pre-tenders."[15] This contrast is particularly evident in *The Custom of the Country,* in which the nouveaux riches hold sway and their values are promulgated through the daily press while old New Yorkers are marginalized. And in making visible old New York at a time of heightened publicity for those who had millions to spend on leisure and mansions, Wharton contested the new hegemony of the latest class of "world-compellers."

In the early years of *Town Topics,* the Saunterer's position as a self-appointed critic and upholder of standards was not all that far removed from Edith Wharton's.[16] He asserted, for example, that he always had "the lash of satire ready to . . . hand," although he was not fond of using it. "Sometimes, how-ever, I have found it necessary to apply it in order to bring offensive fools to a proper sense of their position, and I have reason to be thankful that the applica-tion has never been ineffective."[17] The Saunterer claimed that he wished only to ridicule those who were "constantly pushing and clawing to get recognition and publicity" and that "the 400 of New York is an element so absolutely shal-low and unhealthy that it deserves to be derided almost incessantly."[18] In the December 1894 holiday issue of *Town Topics,* the Saunterer was scathing about society's languor, conceitedness, and aimlessness. He described it as being wrapped up in its own amusement rather than concerned with the cultivation of the mind. In one sense, this was an attempt to instruct the nouveaux riches on how to conduct themselves appropriately in public, especially as the weekly was read by social aspirants. Such ridicule therefore had an "educative" pur-pose—namely, to modify behavior—with the journal acting, as Shevelow puts it, as "social critic and conduct book, exposing vice and modeling virtue."[19]

The "educative" function of society journalism increased the stakes for women of both the old and new elites who sought publicity for their social activities. Over the years, women's magazines, "Saunterings," and society jour-nalism in general promoted a particular construction of leisure-class femininity. In the Saunterer's view, society women "should be clean, virtuous, stately women, free of all the taints and blemishes that are acquired from ordinary contact with the workaday world."[20] He never ceased to demand adherence to the highest codes of conduct from society. In addition to being held up as a model of femininity, society women were held up as experts in refinement and as "taste makers," so that their participation in entertainments, their hosting of private social events, and their arrangement of food, flowers, and so on were presented by journalists as representing the best and the most fashionable. Such publicity, moreover, put pressure on society women to be seen to be as ultra-fashionable and increased the emphasis placed on fashion as a marker of high social status. But the result of publicity was, of course, to encourage others to adopt the latest trend or to eat at restaurants currently patronized by the wealthy, though once a fashion had been taken up by large numbers of people it no longer had the cachet it had once when it was new or exclusive. And so, as Bourdieu argues, "the sense of good investment . . . dictates a withdrawal from outmoded, or simply devalued, objects, places or practices and a move into ever newer objects in an endless drive for novelty, and . . . operates in every area, sport and cooking, holiday resorts and restaurants."[21] Because of the centrality of their role in the public display of wealth and leisure, women played a vital part in this search for novelty.

The acceptable public image of the society woman was therefore one in which she did not threaten the male world of achievement and business success. Rather, the "ideal" society woman was supposed to enhance her husband's success by her talents as a hostess. Society journalism promoted the construction of such an image. Edith Wharton's Undine Spragg, while not a passionate woman—at least, not in the sexual sense—is a parasite on the male world of business success. She brings financial ruin to both her father and her second husband, Ralph, and jeopardizes the income of her third husband, Raymond. She might almost be regarded as an asexual version of the French courtesans who appear on the pages of Balzac's and Zola's novels, devouring men's money and leaving behind them a trail of destruction. As such, she is a very powerful counterimage to the idealized version of society women constructed by the newspapers. However, in *The Custom of the Country*, it is made patently clear that men are responsible for such out-of-control women. It is men who keep women ignorant about men's work and bribe women with "money and motors and clothes" to keep them out of the way.[22] At least as far as gender relations are concerned, Wharton's novel delivers a powerful critique of modern society and its sham claims to progressiveness.

Over the period from 1870 to 1920, society women experienced both gains and losses with respect to their role in status maintenance or social advancement in the context of the family. The formalization of social rituals in the first half of the period was both enabling and constraining. Their power to monitor access rituals and the marriage market, and the attention and significance given to their observance of manners and their display of leisure, all contributed to an increase in women's informal influence within their family and social class. At the same time, however, their responsibilities in all of these matters demanded a high degree of self-surveillance and conformity. In the second half of the

period in question, the new forces of commercialization and their impact on
the lives of society women were similarly both enabling and constraining. The
heightened emphasis on display increased women's leverage in calling on family
resources to sustain a creditable performance of class. And some women
undoubtedly took pleasure in wearing luxurious gowns and in being admired
by spectators. The opening up of places of high-class commercialized entertainment and recreation increased women's access to public space, and their
role in displaying wealth and leisure at such venues increased the possibilities for
heterosocial activity. The subsequent trend toward informality permitted a
relaxation in the observance of rigid codes of conduct while the new places of
entertainment created opportunities for spontaneity, self-expression, and social
intimacy between married couples.[23] At the same time, both the culture of display and newspaper publicity brought with them the disadvantages of sexual
objectification and external surveillance and extended discourses of control
aimed at disciplining the sexuality of young women. Modernization held out
the promise of certain social freedoms to both men and women, a redefinition
of gender relations even, but in the end it reinscribed patriarchal values.

Women no longer had to be confined to domestic space in order to protect
the patriarchal order. Modern society and technology had now developed
multiple forms of what Michel Foucault called "disciplinary mechanisms" to
monitor women's movements in public space and to ensure their compliance
with codes of morality and respectability, codes that underpinned bourgeois
male power. For those women who were encouraged by the forces of consumer capitalism to pursue a more public social life, society journalism was an
effective means of rendering their activities visible, recording their movements, and comparing society women with each other. For the most part,
therefore, society journalism can be seen as an advanced kind of "discipline
mechanism" that improves "the exercise of power by making it lighter, more
rapid, more effective, a design of subtle coercion for a society to come."[24] The
forms of control that operated in old New York did so "without effusion of
blood." Old New Yorkers "dreaded scandal more than disease" and developed
subtle ways of enforcing their principles of social interaction.[25] Wharton's
views on this are reworked into her fiction and epitomized in an exemplary
manner at the point in *The Age of Innocence* when Newland Archer, seated at
the head of his dining table, looks out at "his captors." Feeling "like a prisoner
in the centre of an armed camp," he suddenly realizes how his own society
enforces conformity as he hears his "captors" communicating to him indirectly
what fate awaits him if he steps out of line. By 1905, however, such bloodless
methods of society were no longer alone in exercising disciplinary control.
Society journalism now broadcast the gossip of private circles, and there was
enormous pressure on women, in particular, to maintain the appearance of
moral probity in public. That this situation could prove problematic for

women is well illustrated by Wharton's description of Lily Bart's exit from the Trenors' house after having narrowly avoided being sexually assaulted by Gus Trenor.[26] And this motif of the problematic exit is taken up again by Wharton in her depiction of the dinner for the duchess of Beltshire at Bécassin's restaurant in the south of France. Significantly, Lily again finds herself in a situation that has the potential to be interpreted in the worst possible light. On this occasion, moreover, a journalist is part of the assembled company. This quite minor figure in the novel, "little Dabham of the 'Riviera Notes,'" whose "little eyes were like tentacles thrown out to catch the floating intimations," has observed "the leave-taking of Mrs. Bry's distinguished guests," and "the whole scene had touches of intimacy worth their weight in gold to the watchful pen of Mr. Dabham." In other words, the society columnist's panoptic gaze has been metaphorically translated into a state of potential instrumentalization—a record of what is occurring may at any moment be on its way to the printing press. Little wonder, then, that when Bertha Dorset publicly insults Lily on leaving the dinner party, Lily's would-be protector, Lawrence Selden, "is mainly conscious of a longing to grip Dabham by the collar and fling him out into the street."[27] Little wonder, too, that Selden's longing is not converted into action. Such is the power of the press.

From a sociocultural perspective, the value of Edith Wharton's New York fiction may well lie in the incisiveness with which she was able to delineate the extent to which women might become the casualties of the very social processes regarded by some as progressive. But innovation has never of itself been a guarantee of emancipation. Living and writing at a time of rapid change, Wharton's achievement was to show how little had *really* changed for women. This was not a popular message at a time when women had high hopes that they would soon be able to participate fully in the public world, but as Wharton's contemporary F. H. Bradley aptly put it: "Where everything is bad it must be good to know the worst."[28]

Notes

Introduction

1. The Saunterer's remarks are in the tradition of George G. Foster, who claimed in *New York by Gaslight* (1850) that "nine-tenths of all crime and suffering" would be abolished if prostitution were done away with (p. 103).

2. *Town Topics,* 11 September 1890, p. 3.

3. "I believe that the possession of great wealth, the presence of continual luxury and an existence of sybaritic ease are sufficient to lead voluptuous natures into a system of sensual gratification more intensely and ingeniously based than is found in humbler and simpler walks of life" (*Town Topics,* 3 December 1891, p. 1).

4. In 1894 the Saunterer protested in strong terms about the "conspicuousness" of the "5 o'clock tea brigade," i.e., "effeminate young men" who flaunted their "indecencies" in public (*Town Topics,* 26 April 1894, p. 5). This was followed a year later by a much more vitriolic piece, at a time of heightened homophobia unleashed by the trial and imprisonment of Oscar Wilde in England. The Saunterer referred back to his earlier "discussion" of "the unspeakable conduct of some of the most conspicuous young men in New York," "our own Oscar Wildes . . . living here in their perfumed bowers" (*Town Topics* 11 April 1895, p. 10):

   > Some means must be soon found to drive the vicious vermin out of our own city. They are here in swarms. They are largely of the wealthy and luxurious class, and they cannot fail, if they are not exterminated, to create in this community a noxious scandal that will disgrace us as a people and seriously poison the moral thought of our youth. London has her shame on view today. New York wears hers under a veil.

   The metaphors of contamination, which the Saunterer also used with reference to prostitutes (p. 188, n. 9), illustrate Mary Douglas's argument that pollution beliefs and purification rituals express "a general view of the social order" (*Purity and Danger,* p. 3).

5. *Town Topics,* 25 April 1895, p. 10.

6. Rosen, *Lost Sisterhood,* p. 62.

7. The Saunterer appears to have taken the position that prostitution was a "necessary evil" (see Rosen, *Lost Sisterhood*).

8. See Susan Buck-Morss, "The Flaneur, the Sandwichman, and the Whore," pp. 99–140, esp. 104–5, 124–25.
9. In other words, that they were acting "unnaturally," neglecting their families and aping men.
10. Society women took up cycling in the summer of 1894 in Newport. At the beginning of the following winter season in New York an exclusive cycling club, the Michaux, was established.
11. *New York World*, 20 January 1895, p. 20.
12. The terms "leisure class," "*haute bourgeoisie*," "bourgeois elite," and "social elite" are used interchangeably throughout this study to refer to those who held the highest social status in New York between 1870 and 1920. Within this socially dominant group there were "fractions" with varying amounts and combinations of economic and cultural capital (see Bourdieu, *Distinction*, pp. 116–20, 260).
13. Kingsland, *Book of Good Manners*, p. 1.
14. Cooke, *Social Etiquette*, pp. 358–59.
15. See, for example, *Daisy Miller: A Study* (1878) and the short story "An International Episode" (1878).
16. James, *The American Scene*, pp. 158–65 and 345–52.
17. Sherwood, *Manners and Social Usages*, pp. 5–6, 10.
18. Rydell, *World of Fairs*, p.19. See also the discussion on the alleged racial degeneration of upper-class American women in Montgomery, *"Gilded Prostitution,"* pp. 187–200.
19. See Morrison, *Playing in the Dark*, pp. 46–47.
20. Bushman, *Refinement of American Culture*, pp. 392, 402–20.
21. Rydell, *All the World's a Fair*, p. 3.
22. The term "mediazation" is used by Thompson, *Ideology and Modern Culture*, pp. 3–4, 12–20.
23. The reference is to Mrs. Stuyvesant Fish; see chapter 3, the section "Formal Sociability in the Home."
24. Shevelow, *Women and Print Culture*, pp. 55–57.
25. See Rojek, *Decentring Leisure*, pp. 22–23.
26. Smith, *Texts, Facts*, p. 193. Although Smith plays on the term "secret agent," the extent to which a subject can be said to be either "secreted" or "fully an agent" deserves further consideration. It is a question, in the first instance, of whether her notion of a "dual subject" (p. 195) does not imply—at least potentially—the need to posit a third subject, one who *reflects* and so on. If so, does her theory of the subject perhaps not then run the risk of a *regressus ad infinitum*? It is, furthermore, a question as to the degree to which, since the advent of psychoanalysis, it can be claimed that, strictly speaking, any subject can be regarded as "fully an agent." Despite these caveats, however, it seems reasonable to assume that, however powerful social constraints and the effects of unconscious ideological complicity may have been, elite women did have some degree of agency.
27. Ibid., pp. 197, 202.
28. Halttunen, *Confidence Men*, pp. xv–xvii.
29. Ibid., p. xv.
30. Ibid., pp. 198 and 207.
31. Ibid., p.196.
32. Bushman, *Refinement of American Culture*, p. 446. Cf. Halttunen: "Proper dress gradually came to be accepted as a legitimate form of disguise; proper etiquette was increasingly viewed as a means of masking and thus controlling unacceptable social impulses; and mourning ritual was coming to be a form of public theater, designed to display the perfect gentility of its participants" (*Confidence Men*, p. 196).
33. Goffman, *The Presentation of Self*, pp. 254, 240, 1–4.

34. As the literary critical term *genre* is both somewhat ill-defined and rather limiting, I prefer to refer, instead, to "types of texts" or "text types" (*Textsorten*). I regard this terminology, which is taken from the discipline of text linguistics or discourse analysis, as comparable with aspects of the more broadly defined area of discourse theory.
35. I base my understanding of "counterdiscourse" on the work of Richard Terdiman.
36. I take these terms from Walkowitz, *City of Dreadful Delight,* p. 21. However, whereas Walkowitz argues that women were more likely to be bearers than makers of meaning, I want to acknowledge the extent to which women entered into the debate about the definition of femininity during this period. One of the important forms of dominant discourse in which femininity was defined was etiquette, and many women writers were involved in writing magazine columns, articles, or books on the subject of etiquette.
37. In discussing Edith Wharton's literary works my aim is neither to provide an exhaustive literary interpretation of any particular text nor to treat any such text as no more than a source for "historical evidence." It is my intention, rather, to increase readers' awareness of the sociocultural dimensions of Wharton's oeuvre.

Chapter 1:
The Social Calendar

1. *New York Times,* 1 January 1905, p. 1, col. 5; 1 January 1915, p. 1, col. 3, and p. 13.
2. *New York Times,* 1 January 1908, p. 1, col. 8. See O'Malley, *Keeping Watch.*
3. Hamlin, *An Albany Girlhood,* pp. 141–42.
4. *Town Topics,* 3 January 1907, p. 3.
5. I build here on the argument contained in Erenberg's *Steppin' Out* and taken up in Taylor's *In Pursuit of Gotham,* pp. 71–75.
6. Wharton, *The Age of Innocence,* ch. 26, p. 1219.
7. *New York World,* 8 January 1905, magazine section, p. 1, col. 2.
8. *Town Topics,* 5 November 1908, p. 3.
9. Kingsland, *Book of Good Manners,* p. 1; see Introduction, p. 7.
10. *Town Topics,* 5 January 1888, p. 2.
11. The aping of European society served its purpose at a time when New Yorkers were forging social ties with members of the European elite. But it should also be noted that European high society itself was changing in response to the rise of business elites in the political and economic power structures.
12. *Town Topics,* 20 February 1886, p. 4.
13. Durkheim, *Elementary Forms,* pp. 10–11.
14. James, *The American Scene,* p. 164.
15. This would qualify for Eric Hobsbawm's and Terence Ranger's category of "invented tradition" as defined in their introduction to *The Invention of Tradition:* "'Invented tradition' is taken to mean a set of practices, normally governed by overtly or tacitly accepted rules and of a ritual or symbolic nature, which seek to inculcate certain values and norms of behaviour by repetition, which automatically implies continuity with the past" (p. 1).
16. *New York Times,* 17 March 1895, p. 11, col. 1.
17. *New York World,* 10 August 1902, Sunday magazine, pp. 6–7.
18. Hall, "Newport and Its Summer Life," p. 5.
19. Thomas, *American Literary Realism,* p. 58.
20. "The Rights of the Citizen," p. 65. For further discussion of this, see chapter 6, the section "The Invasion of Privacy."
21. *New York Times,* 6 August 1905, magazine section, p. 1.
22. Cable, *Top Drawer,* pp. 30–31.
23. This approximates to the itinerary of the Pruyn family.

24. See Montgomery, *"Gilded Prostitution,"* part 3.

25. Mrs. Kingsland wrote of the impossibility of keeping up personal social relations with five hundred to six hundred people and how calling had become a perfunctory obligation but nevertheless one that had to be performed at least once a year. She claimed that it was the New York custom for a married woman in society to call at the beginning of the season and just to leave her own card and two of her husband's, without necessarily inquiring whether the hostess was at home, on the grounds that to make a personal call would leave fashionable women no time for anything else (*Book of Good Manners*, pp. 75, 82–83).

26. A Woman of Fashion, *Etiquette for Americans*, p. 55.

27. Learned, *Etiquette of New York Today*, p. 110.

28. Kingsland, *Book of Good Manners*, p. 74.

29. A Woman of Fashion, *Etiquette for Americans*, p. 59.

30. There are numerous references to the preference for public ballrooms in *Town Topics* during the winter season of 1886. See *Town Topics*, 2 January 1886, p. 3; 23 January 1886, p. 6; and 27 February 1886, pp. 4–5.

31. See, for example, the kind of comment that appeared in society columns: "Gradually, however, with the growth of the city and the visiting list, it was found that the average New York house was too small for dances and balls, and that these could be much better given in some well-equipped restaurant or hotel with ballrooms, and, of course, restaurant facilities, at really not as much expense, and with far greater comfort to hosts and guests; and that entertaining in this way obviated also the necessity of upsetting one's house for days before and after the event" (*New York World*, 7 December 1902, p. 4).

32. See McAllister, *Society As I Have Found It*, pp. 222–23.

33. The Family Circle Dancing Class was another prominent series of subscription balls in the 1870s and 1880s.

34. Levine, *High Brow/Low Brow*, pp. 100–4.

35. Morris, *Incredible New York*, p. 69.

36. Wharton, *A Backward Glance*, chap. 3, pp. 828–31.

37. Sherwood, *Art of Entertaining*, pp. 79–89.

38. Ibid., pp. 401–2.

39. Erenberg, *Steppin' Out*, pp. 10–12.

40. Morris, *Incredible New York*, pp. 234–37.

41. Erenberg, *Steppin' Out*, p. 35.

42. James, *The American Scene*, p. 105.

43. Erenberg, *Steppin' Out*, pp. 34, 40.

44. *New York Times*, 27 January 1895, p. 25.

45. *New York Times*, 3 February 1895, p. 20.

46. *New York Times*, 27 January 1895, p. 25.

47. *New York Times*, 20 January 1895, p. 25.

48. *New York World*, 15 January 1905, metropolitan section, p. 2. Similar criticisms were voiced in Paris. The novelist Edmond de Goncourt wrote: "Social life is going through a great evolution, which is beginning. I see women, children, households, families in this café. The interior is going to die. Life threatens to become public. The club for those on high, the café for those below, that is what society and the people will come to." Interestingly, he alluded to America in lamenting the changes overtaking Paris: "I am a stranger to what is coming, to what is, as I am to these new boulevards without turnings, without chance perspectives, implacable in their straight lines, which no longer smack of the world of Balzac, which make one think of some American Babylon of the future" (Jules and Edmond de Goncourt, *Journal des Goncourts: Mémoires de la vie littéraire*, 9 vols. [1912], quoted in Clark, *The Painting of Modern Life*, pp. 34–35).

49. *Town Topics,* 1 April 1915, p. 5. It was noted that in this season of Lent, Mrs. Oelrichs had earlier in the day been at church "deep in her Lenten devotions."

50. Stanford White to Elsie Clews, n.d., Parsons Papers.

51. See Peiss, *Cheap Amusements,* p. 62.

52. This is prefigured in the novel when Undine is described as enjoying "amusing little dinners at fashionable restaurants" with her husband, Ralph, "and reckless evenings in haunts where she thrilled with simple glee at the thought of what she must so obviously be 'taken for'"(Wharton, *The Custom of the Country,* chap. 12, p. 725, chap. 16, p. 769, chap. 20, pp. 808–9, chap. 12, p. 732).

53. Ibid., chap. 5, p. 666.

54. Quoted in Lewis, *Edith Wharton,* pp. 423–24 (source not given).

55. Wharton, *A Backward Glance,* chap. 21, pp. 824–27.

56. Wharton deals explicitly with family lineages in the second novella, "Old Maid," in *Old New York.*

57. Edith Wharton, "New Year's Day," in *Old New York,* chap. 1, pp. 491–93, 494–95, chap. 5, p. 519.

58. Wharton, "New Year's Day," chap. 7, p. 546, chap. 6, p. 532, chap. 7, p. 547.

59. Wharton, "New Year's Day," chap. 7, pp. 541, 547.

60. This analysis draws on Mary Douglas's identification of different kinds of social environments, in this particular case that of the "high classification" social environment (*Natural Symbols,* pp. 86–91). Mary Ellis Gibson has also drawn on Douglas in "Edith Wharton and the Ethnography of Old New York," pp. 57–69.

61. McAllister, *Society As I Have Found It,* esp. chaps. 10 and 16. In her autobiography, *After All,* Elsie de Wolfe, a New York débutante of the 1880s, recalled McAllister's role as follows: "There was much more glamour to society then than now, and it had a more distinguished quality. Money was not the shibboleth permitting one to enter its carefully guarded gates. Ward McAllister was its monitor, and he blue-pencilled the list of eligibles until the group which they included came to be known as 'The Four Hundred'" (p. 99). Elizabeth Drexel Lehr, another contemporary, recounted in her memoirs, *King Lehr and the Gilded Age,* how seriously McAllister took his responsibilities, devoting his life to "his famous set of rules for the guidance of social New York," reveling "in forms and ceremonies" and turning "his cult of snobbishness" into a quasi religion (p. 11).

62. *Town Topics* was established as a New York–based ten-cent weekly by E. D. Mann in 1885, with a circulation of over fifty thousand by 1890. See chapter 6 for further detail.

63. McAllister, *Society As I Have Found It,* p. 215.

64. Davidoff points to a similar process affecting London society in the early nineteenth century in *Best Circles,* pp. 14–17.

65. Bushman, *Refinement of America,* pp. xii, 413, 419–20. This is a more convincing argument than the one put forward by Jaher in "Style and Status" and evinces a deeper understanding of the social mechanisms that prevailed in the late nineteenth century.

Chapter 2:
The Female World of Ritual and Etiquette

1. Cooke, *Social Etiquette,* p. 358. This extract is a plagiarized version of Mrs. Sherwood's comments on "Women as Leaders" in *Manners and Social Usages,* p. 13.

2. Bushman, *Refinement of America,* p. 440.

3. Sherwood, *Manners and Social Usages,* pp. 16, 51.

4. See Jaher, "Style and Status," p. 275; Davidoff, *Best Circles,* p. 102; and Wecter, *Saga of American Society,* pp. 289–346.

5. See Marriott-Watson, "Deleterious Effect of Americanization upon Women," pp. 782–93, and Van Rensselaer, *The Social Ladder,* pp. 35, 57, 165.

6. John Ruth acknowledged the importance of women's role but then went on to under-mine his own argument: "Women observe all the delicacies of propriety in manners, and all the shades of impropriety, much better than men; not only because they attend to them earlier and longer, but because their perceptions are more refined than those of the other sex, who are habitually employed about greater things" (*Decorum*, p. 24).

7. Van Gennep, *Rites of Passage*, p. 11.

8. Myerhoff, "Rites of Passage," p. 109.

9. Smith-Rosenberg, *Disorderly Conduct*, p. 42.

10. Smith, *Texts, Facts*, p. 197.

11. In this study, I draw on recent work in women's/gender history that has challenged the domination/oppression dialectic and sought to examine women's complicity in their own oppression. Cécile Dauphin et al., for example, have drawn attention to the limi-tations of the domination/oppression dialectic in their article "Women's Culture and Women's Power," pp. 63–88, esp. 64, 66.

12. Ibid., p. 77.

13. Rosaldo, "Women, Culture and Society: A Theoretical Overview," in Rosaldo and Lamphere, eds., *Women, Culture and Society*, pp. 36–37.

14. Sherwood, *Manners and Social Usages*, pp. 37–38.

15. Longstreet, *Social Etiquette*, p. 8.

16. Ibid., pp. 8–9. Compare White: "Etiquette throws a protection around the well-bred, keeping the coarse and disagreeable at a distance, and punishing those who violate her dictates, with banishment from the social circle" (*Polite Society*, p. 12).

17. *Harper's Bazaar Book of Decorum*, pp. 12–14.

18. Kingsland, *Book of Good Manners*, pp. 6–7.

19. *Harper's Bazaar Book of Decorum*, p. 238.

20. Ward, *Sensible Etiquette*, p. 54.

21. *Manners and Rules of Good Society*, p. 37; compare: "Thus to women, as the conductors of social polities is committed the card—that pasteboard protocol whose laws are well defined in every land but our own" (Sherwood, *Manners and Social Usages*, pp. 13–14).

22. *Vogue's Book of Etiquette*, p. 233.

23. Cooke, *Social Etiquette*, p. 71.

24. Longstreet, *Social Etiquette*, pp. 31–33, 50–52.

25. See, for example, Longstreet, *Good Form*, pp. 1–2; this manual was entirely devoted to the subject of card etiquette.

26. Longstreet, *Social Etiquette* p. 47.

27. Cooke, *Social Etiquette*, p. 51. See also Learned, *Etiquette of New York Today*, p. 109.

28. Eighteen Distinguished Authors, *Correct Social Usage*, p. 206.

29. Davidoff, *Best Circles*, p. 37.

30. *New York World*, 15 January 1905, editorial section, p. 6, col.1.

31. Davidoff, *Best Circles*, p. 49.

32. Mrs. Longstreet continues: "He begins by endeavouring to assist his mother at her entertainments, and by being an escort to his sisters on informal evening visits among lady intimates, where his maturity and attractions win for him a future invitation" (*Social Etiquette*, p. 45).

33. Harrison, "The New York Society Girl," p. 7.

34. Longstreet, *Social Etiquette*, pp. 37–39.

35. In actual fact, the term used to designate débutantes in their first season was "buds."

36. *Good Manners*, pp. 166–67.

37. Huybertie Pruyn Hamlin, "The Coming Out Years and Through our Wedding Trip, 1891–1898," typescript (n.d.), p. 4, Hamlin Papers. See also Hamlin, *An Albany Girl-hood*, p. 214.
    Harriet L. Pruyn (1868–1939) was a member of a prominent Albany family with antecedents going back to the days when New York was a Dutch colony. In the late

nineteenth century the Pruyns enjoyed a luxurious lifestyle and had entrée into elite social circles in both the United States and Britain. Over the years, numerous leading New York politicians wined and dined at the Pruyn home, including Grover Cleveland, and many British travelers, often members of the peerage, found a warm welcome at the door of Harriet's widowed mother. When Harriet and later her sister, Huybertie, came of age, Mrs. Pruyn closely adhered to the rituals for presenting daughters to society, both in New York City and Albany, and later arranged for both daughters' presentation at the court of Queen Victoria. During their frequent trips to Europe, Mrs. Pruyn and her daughters mingled with prominent artists and writers, such as Carolus Durand, Oscar Wilde, and Oliver Wendell Holmes, spent weekends at the country estates of titled British aristocrats, and participated in key social events of Parisian and London high society.

38. Wharton, *A Backward Glance*, chap. 4, p. 846.
39. On the other hand, the detail with which Mrs. Hamlin recorded her coming out signifies the importance that was invested in these rituals at the time of their enactment. Their centrality to her personal historical account is also an implicit recognition of their importance. At the end of the typescript for "Some Glimpses of the New York of My Youth in the Eighteen Eighties and Nineties" (1930), she wrote: "It never occurred to me, probably not to many others either, that one day I would be trying to remember these scenes and set them down as a kind of historical picture." The Hamlin Papers are an exceedingly rich source for details of the everyday and ceremonial life of New York women in the bourgeois elite. In the 1930s Mrs. Hamlin, then a widow, drew upon her diaries and letters for her reminiscences, parts of which were published in the 1940s in a regular column entitled "Tattletales of Old Albany" in the Albany *Times-Union*. The reminiscences relating specifically to her début appeared in a local newspaper article entitled "Mrs. Hamlin Recalls Her Debutante Days as Friday's Cotillion Years."
40. Hamlin, *An Albany Girlhood*, p. 213; see also Hamlin, "Some Glimpses," pp. 18–19, Hamlin Papers.
41. Myerhoff, "Rites of Passage," pp. 116–18.
42. Van Rensselaer notes in *The Social Ladder* that Archibald Gracie King was the first man in New York society to hold a ball in a public place when he celebrated his daughter's début at Delmonico's in the early 1870s (p. 37).
43. Longstreet, *Social Etiquette*, pp. 43–44; Ives, *The Social Mirror*, p. 19; White, *Polite Society*, pp. 82–83.
44. *Good Manners*, p. 164.
45. Kingsland, *Book of Good Manners*, p. 116.
46. *Town Topics*, 29 November 1894, p. 6; see also 26 November 1896, p. 3.
47. Hamlin, "Some Glimpses," p. 23, Hamlin Papers.
48. They were not always successful. New York newspapers were full of stories about heiresses being duped by either impoverished European nobles or impostors. See Montgomery, *"Gilded Prostitution,"* chap. 8.
49. See also, for an example of the advice contained in etiquette manuals from the early part of this period, Kingsland: "White is the favorite tint, and when her presentation is made at a ball or party, a diaphanous material is selected, tulle, grenadine, lisse, mull, etc., being suitable. For an afternoon reception or tea she may also wear white, but veiling. fine cashmere, soft Surah and similar fabrics are more suitable than gauzy textures" (*Book of Good Manners*, p. 169).
50. Hamlin Papers, AF 121, Box 13, f. 91.
51. Wharton, *A Backward Glance*, chap. 4, pp. 842–43.
52. Harrison, "The Well-Bred Girl in Society: First Paper—The Young Girl and Dancing," p. 4.
53. Adele Sloane, an heiress and débutante in the early 1890s, captured something of this in her diary entry for November 1894 (*Maverick in Mauve*, p. 180):

It is always just as difficult to unmake a reputation as to make it. If people get it into their heads that one is supposed to be attractive, or wishes to flirt, they start in with that idea and are much nicer to you for the time being than they otherwise would have been. I am not foolish enough to say that I don't want to be liked, because I do want it, but there is a limit at which the line must be drawn. I more than detest that people should simply shrug their shoulders and laugh and say, "Oh, yes! But then she is such a flirt." It is so horribly undignified and makes me feel as mean as dirt.

54. For the role of chaperonage as part of this protection, see Montgomery, "'The Fruit That Hangs Highest,'" pp. 172–91.
55. Harrison, "The Well-Bred Girl in Society: Fourth Paper—Social Laws at Opera, Theatre and Public Places," p. 4.
56. During receptions a débutante was supposed to stand by her mother to receive guests, and young men were introduced to her formally. At supper her brother or father or, in the absence of both, an older male family friend escorted her. Her mother selected her partner for the first dance and she was not to dance with any man more than once. When she received visits from men, she had to be chaperoned. See Longstreet, *Social Etiquette*, pp. 43–45; Ives, *Social Mirror*, pp. 18–21; Kingsland, *Book of Good Manners*, pp. 115–19.
57. Kingsland, *Book of Good Manners*, pp. 191–94.
58. White, *Polite Society*, p. 34.
59. Dale, *Our Manners and Social Customs*, pp. 73–74.
60. Most etiquette manuals had a chapter on this knotty problem. An 1898 manual, *Etiquette for Americans* by A Woman of Fashion, attempted to justify the restraints upon women's behavior thus (pp. 197–98):

> Women, from the moment they are introduced to society as "*débutantes*," to the last day they live on earth, if they stay in society, are hemmed about with many restrictions. It is really a protection and a safeguard to hem them, and many of them are glad to be so protected and guarded. . . . Most women prefer to be inconspicuous; and as tradition has surrounded them always, they do not want what the emancipated call "liberty," and would not know what to do with it if they had it.

Mrs. Kingsland, a firm believer in chaperonage, took a similar line in her *Book of Good Manners*, stating that chaperonage "typifies the sheltering care, the jealous protection, of something very precious. It sets a higher value upon the object by protecting and hedging it round in the eyes of others, and particularly in those of young men who are apt to sigh for the fruit that hangs highest" (pp. 193–94).

61. Sangster, *Good Manners for All Occasions*, p. 81.
62. *Good Manners*, pp. 181, 170.
63. Lears, *No Place of Grace*, p. 27.
64. Ward, *Sensible Etiquette*, pp. 330–31.
65. Douglas, *Purity and Danger*, pp. 38–40.
66. Ibid., pp. 97–98.
67. Sherwood, *Manners and Social Usages*, p. 145; *Good Manners*, p. 171; Kingsland, *Book of Good Manners*, p. 192.
68. Hall, *Social Customs*, p. 179.
69. Sherwood, *Manners and Social Usages*, p. 149.
70. See chapter 4, the section "The Female Tourist."
71. The telegram from Mrs. Clews to her husband read: "Absolutely opposed Adirondacks" (22 August 1897, Parsons Papers, Box 5, f. 9). Attached to the telegram was a letter

from Mr. Clews to his daughter in which he expressed his regret at having to deny Elsie's wish to accompany Herbert and his party, explaining somewhat vaguely: "It is best it should be done—there are some things you can do you know, and there are some things it is not well to do, and this is one of them because the 'World' so decides."

72. Herbert Parsons to Elsie Clews, 1 September 1897, Parsons Papers, Box 4, f. 4.

73. Herbert Parsons to Mrs. Henry Clews, 31 August 1897, Parsons Papers, Box 4, f. 2.

74. A letter from Mrs. Clews to her daughter, dated 21 September 1897, while Mrs. Clews was visiting Europe, contains a reference to the episode: "I enclose an amusing and *specious* letter from Herbert. I answered it at once." A month later, Mrs. Clews once again alludes to the disagreement (Parsons Papers, Box 5, f. 11):

> By the way I have it on my mind to talk a little politics with *you*—that is to say, in regard to the policy of your *independence*. You have made such a bold flight this summer you must feel quite securely intrenched in your *rights*, and not be afraid to *yield* unimportant points simply on the principle it may lead to further oppression.

75. In a chapter entitled "Bringing Out the Daughter," in *Vogue's Book of Etiquette*, the automobile was said to "have been responsible for a great deal of liberty, and it is a far cry from the days when a girl might be allowed a short drive in the well-appointed T-cart of young Midas, with young Midas's groom sitting like a smart image behind, to these when she can step into her own motor and drive whom she will whither she will, without attendant or chaperon" (p. 386). Nevertheless, even in the 1920s, "in this period of emancipation, a girl, properly looked after, though she may sometimes go without parents, takes her maid with her when she goes to parties or goes with a girl who takes a maid, and small rows of these neat attendants may still be seen sitting in the dressing-rooms of private houses or of the restaurant hotels where some dances are given" (p. 390).

76. *Town Topics,* 5 January 1893, p. 6.

77. See chapter 4, the section "The Female Tourist."

78. Brown, *In the Golden Nineties*, pp. 68–70.

79. Longstreet, pp. 127–29; Learned, *Etiquette of New York Today*, p. 127.

80. Sherwood, *Art of Entertaining*, p. 332.

81. Sloane, *Maverick in Mauve*, pp. 181, 182, 184, 192, 194.

82. Hamlin, "The Coming Out Years," p. 69, Hamlin Papers.

83. "As I look back on all the difficulties of dressing in those days, I wonder how we stood it. A maid was a necessity for dressing in the evening as the ball dresses were laced behind. The skirts got filthy on the floors and the cleaning business was most unsatisfactory. . . . It took a maid's time to keep the ruchking clean in the necks and sleeves and the balayeuse renewed under the skirts and the edging sewed on with the wire in it to keep the bottoms of the skirts from flopping in instead of out. This wire velveteen covered edging also kept the edges of the skirts from being cut as they swept the streets. Everything was as elaborate as possible . . . anything to be elaborate and take time to dress" (Hamlin, "The Coming Out Years," p. 69, Hamlin Papers).

84. Thorstein Veblen categorized the function of dress as "an expression of the pecuniary culture." Women's dress, he observed, had to testify to the wealth and social worth of the wearer and her provider; social worth was enhanced by evidence that the wearer could not possibly engage in useful labor. His critique of fashion contrasts sharply with Huybertie's perspective: "That the alleged beauty, or 'loveliness,' of the styles in vogue at any given time is transient and spurious only is attested by the fact that none of the many shifting fashions will bear the test of time. When seen in the perspective of half-a-dozen years or more, the best of our fashions strike us as grotesque, if not unsightly" (*Theory of the Leisure Class*, pp. 120, 125).

85. Kingsland, *Book of Weddings*, p. 45. This sentiment was echoed in other etiquette manuals of the time. For example: "There is no doubt as to one fact; and that is, that it is extremely vulgar, as well as impolitic, to lay in extravagant stores of clothes. . . . The dozens upon dozens of linen petticoats, bodices, and other articles, grow yellow and rot in their desuetude" (A Woman of Fashion, *Etiquette for Americans*, p. 114).

86. Wharton, *The Age of Innocence*, chap. 7, pp. 1159–60.

87. He continues: "When millionaires vie with one another in providing for their children's weddings the richest of floral decorations and the most elaborate and costly music obtainable, people of less wealth will more and more favor the quietest of marriages, on the principle that if one cannot compete well, one had better not try to compete at all" (*Town Topics*, 14 November 1895, pp. 6–7).

88. *Town Topics* reported (20 April 1893, p. 5):

> In America the presence of noblemen is still something to grow excited over, and I know of no city in the world where a chap with a title can create more of a stir than in New York. . . . It supplies quite a study in the effects of republicanism, I should say, this American excitability over the presence of men that sport titles.
>
> The mass of people that turned out for the Bradley-Martin wedding would have led a stranger to believe that some great national event was taking place in the neighborhood of Tenth street last Tuesday noon. Grace Church was taxed to its utmost capacity, yet crowds stood outside in vain trying to gain admittance.

89. See chapter 6, the section "The Invasion of Privacy," for the Saunterer's comments.

90. Balsan, *The Glitter and the Gold*, pp. 41–42.

91. *New York Times*, 4 March 1895, p. 8, and 5 March 1895, pp. 1–2. The marquis commented in his autobiography: "Women journalists laid siege to Anna's bedroom; jewellers and art-dealers lived at my front-door; my valet waxed rich and I waxed angry" (quoted in Brandon, *The Dollar Princesses*, p. 82).

92. It was also possible for women to claim power on the basis of having a lived knowledge of female experience (i.e., mystifying the female world to men and using this both to extend "nonassigned power" and to increase women's call on the family budget). See Lamphere, "Strategies, Cooperation and Conflict," in Rosaldo and Lamphere, eds., *Women, Culture and Society*, pp. 97–111, esp. p. 99.

93. It is interesting to compare the format of etiquette manuals in the period from 1870 to 1917 with those of the postwar period. *Vogue's Book of Etiquette*, for example, retains is vaguely similar in its outline to the Victorian manuals, but places far greater emphasis on social entertainments and recreation, rather than on introductions (pp. 383–84). Calling and cards have virtually disappeared. The chapter on weddings is the longest. There are frequent references to bygone days and quaint customs, such as "carpet-dances," cotillion favors, "At Homes," and ceremonial débuts. The disappearance of the latter is explained thus:

> The great waves of a more democratic society have submerged the old family chiefs. Their word is no longer law; they no longer issue ukases on what shall or shall not be done; who shall or shall not be received. The young 'I will,' coming as it does from a thousand tongues that have been exposed to educations and conditions different from those of their parents, swiftly carries the day. The judgment of youth, whether it is for better or worse, practically admits or refuses social recognition to its fellows. Young people do not, as they used to, make their friends inside the clan. They choose them where they will and bring them home. The best bred boys and girls still preserve, in a measure, their family standards, but they are more lenient to outsiders than their fathers and mothers would be; sometimes too much so for the good of the outsiders themselves.

In discussing the "revolt of the young," *Vogue* proposed that it had not done any great harm but that nevertheless "we must not yield too much to the American mother's desire to efface herself" (p. 388). This points to a major shift in the balance of power within the family, one that focuses on parent-child relations.

Chapter 3: Interiors and Façades

1. James, *The American Scene*, pp. 166–67. This echoes Edmond Goncourt (1891); see p. 174, n. 48.
2. Wharton and Codman, *Decoration of Houses*, p. 115.
3. Ibid., p. 112.
4. James, *The American Scene*, pp. 166–67.
5. Kern, *Culture of Time and Space*, p. 187.
6. Frank Lloyd Wright, "An Autobiography," in *Frank Lloyd Wright: Writings and Buildings*, p. 82, quoted in Kern, *Culture of Time and Space*, p. 186.
7. Wharton and Codman, *Decoration of Houses*, p. 126.
8. See chapter 6.
9. For example, Lucy Hamilton Hooper's article "The Home of Christine Nilsson," for *Ladies Home Journal*, October 1893, p. 1, included photographs of the interior of the famous singer's Parisian home, including shots of her drawing room, library, and dining room; interiors and exteriors of the English country home of the American actress Mrs. Brown Potter appeared in the Sunday magazine section of the *New York World*, 27 July 1902, p. 12; and the Stuyvesant Fishes' Newport mansion was featured in the pictorial section of the *New York Times*, 6 August 1905, p. 1.
10. Wharton, *A Backward Glance*, chap. 3, p. 830.
11. Elias, *Court Society*, p. 43.
12. Wharton, *The Custom of the Country*, chap. 19, p. 803.
13. James, *The American Scene*, pp. 159, 161–62, 163.
14. Ibid., pp. 159, 162–63.
15. Ibid., p. 164.
16. Halttunen, *Confidence Men*, pp. 193–95.
17. Ibid., pp. 102–5, 196.
18. Wharton, *The House of Mirth*, Book I, chap. 14, pp. 168–69, and chap. 9, pp. 114–15.
19. Wharton, *The Age of Innocence*, chap. 2, p. 1025, chap. 4, p. 1036.
20. Wharton, *The House of Mirth*, Book I, chap. 5, p. 61.
21. Wharton, *The Age of Innocence*, chap. 21, p. 1178, chap. 34, pp. 1289–91.
22. Wharton, "The Daunt Diana," in *The Collected Short Stories*, vol. 2, pp. 51–53.
23. Wharton, "The Daunt Diana," pp. 57, 59–60. This quote is a reference to Diana, the moon, coming down from heaven each night to kiss Endymion as he slept on Mt. Latmus (*Lemprière's Classical Dictionary*, p. 250).
24. Tanagra statuettes are figurines of women made of terracotta found in the tombs near Tanagra, city of Boeotia, in ancient Greece (Howatson, *Oxford Companion*, p. 460); they are mentioned in *Decoration of Houses* in the chapter on bric-a-brac, p. 184, as "inexpensive trifles" that become museum treasures in later centuries.
25. Wharton, "The Daunt Diana," p. 54.
26. Saisselin, *Bourgeois and the Bibelot*, p. 53; see chapter 4, "Woman, Desire and the Bibelot." Saisselin goes on to make the connection between bibelots, luxury, and demimondaines, which I pick up in chapter 6. He refers here to Dumas's play *La Dame aux camelias*, which is used by James in "The Siege of London."
27. Saisselin, *Bourgeois and the Bibelot*, p. 67.
28. See, *inter alia*, Schlereth, *Victorian America*, pp. 119–20.
29. Wharton, "Old Maid," in *Old New York*, chap. 3, p. 394.
30. Wharton, *The Age of Innocence*, chap. 5, p. 1042.

31. Wharton and Codman, *Decoration of Houses*, pp. 184–87.
32. Saisselin, *Bourgeois and the Bibelot*, p. 66. American women of the *haute bourgeoisie* did, contrary to the impressions gleaned from reading Wharton's fiction, collect works of art. Kathleen D. McCarthy's study *Women's Culture* has done much to dispel the myths about women's role in the world of collecting. Her study reveals the role of women not only in the collection of the most prestigious forms of art but also in the more neglected realms of decorative arts, the avant garde in the early twentieth century, and American folk art. Louisine Havemeyer, for example, was instrumental in putting together, along with her husband and the assistance of Mary Cassatt, a remarkable collection of Impressionist paintings, which was bequeathed to the Metropolitan Museum of Art in New York in 1929 (p. 108). Millionairess and widow Mrs. Russell Sage was a prominent donor of works of art to the Metropolitan Museum; in 1909 she donated the Bolles collection of early American furniture, containing over six hundred pieces (p. 120). New York born Isabella Stewart Gardner is, however, the ultimate, if solitary, example of a woman who built up a private collection and then planned her home as a museum to display her acquisitions.
33. Wharton, *The Age of Innocence*, chap. 9, pp. 1071–72. According to Wharton's and Codman's own prescriptions, May Welland's and her family's idea of drawing rooms was that of unmitigated discomfort. The drawing room was to be the best room in the house, with "its gilt chairs covered with brocade, its *vitrines* full of modern Saxe, its guipure curtains and velvet carpets." This kind of room, according to these two authorities, was fit only for discharging social duties (*Decoration of Houses*, pp. 124–25).
34. Wharton and Codman, *Decoration of Houses*, p. 189.
35. Matthews, "The Artistic Household," p. 25.
36. Thomson, "Cozy Corners and Ingle Nooks," p. 27.
37. Wharton, *The House of Mirth*, book I, chap. 12, p. 139.
38. Wharton, *The Custom of the Country*, chap. 16, p. 773.
39. Halttunen, "From Parlor to Living Room," pp. 157–90, esp. p. 164.
40. Lears, "Beyond Veblen," pp. 73–98, esp. p. 88.
41. See McCarthy, *Women's Culture*, p. 95.
42. Parloa, "Attractive Cozy Corners."
43. Kingsland, "A Talk About Teas," p. 4.
44. Halttunen, "From Parlor to Living Room," p. 169, quotes Lillian Hart Tryon (quoted in Russell Lynes, *The Domesticated Americans* [New York: Harper and Row, 1963], p. 154): "Life is too full to have patience with formalities. The cry of the time is for few friends and good ones." Therefore, "we are fast becoming a parlorless nation."
45. Hamlin, "Trips to Europe: 2nd Trip, 1885–86," Hamlin Papers.
46. Hattie notes how "plentiful" teas were in the winter season of 1886–87 in Albany, the year she came out. Harriet Pruyn Rice Diary, vol. 8, 3 December 1886, Rice Papers.
47. Hamlin, *An Albany Girlhood*, pp. 63–65.
48. Anna Fenn Parker Pruyn, Diary, 3 April 1878, Hamlin Papers.
49. Rice, Diary, vol. 8, 31 January 1887, Rice Papers.
50. Rice, Diary, vol. 7, 3 January 1883, Rice Papers.
51. Elias, *Court Society*, p. 52.
52. Wharton and Codman, *Decoration of Houses*, pp. 124–25.
53. See Goffman, *Presentation of Self*, pp. 22–30.
54. A Woman of Fashion, *Etiquette for Americans*, p. 80.
55. Crowninshield, *Manners for the Metropolis*, pp. 45–46.
56. Wharton, *The Custom of the Country*, chap. 3, p. 642.
57. Wharton, *The Custom of the Country*, p. 642.
58. Kasson, "Rituals of Dining," pp. 138–39, 141.
59. *Town Topics*, 9 February 1905, pp. 4–5.

60. *Town Topics,* 18 January 1900, p. 3. The season was dull because a number of people had lost fortunes and canceled entertainments (*Town Topics,* 25 January 1900, p. 5).
61. *New York Times,* 21 January 1900, p. 7, col. 4.
62. *Town Topics,* 25 January 1900, p. 3.
63. I am drawing here upon the analysis of Halttunen in *Confidence Men,* p. 186, with regard to parlor theatricals of the 1850s and 1860s.
64. *Town Topics,* 26 January 1905, p. 5; 2 February 1905, p. 5; 9 February 1905, p. 5.
65. *Town Topics,* 3 June 1915, pp. 5–6. It went on to say:

> No one will gainsay that Mrs. Fish's influence was healthy, even if they differed with her and did not approve all she did. She was a devoted wife and mother and a good churchwoman, and she steered clear of all scandals. With Mrs. Astor the old order of society leaders passed away, but Mrs. Fish did keep the clans together. Who can now fill her place?

66. Quoted in Morris, *Incredible New York,* p. 253.
67. Baker, *Stanny,* p. 307.
68. Wharton and Codman, *Decoration of Houses,* pp. 134–35.
69. Wharton, *The Age of Innocence,* chap. 3, p. 1032.
70. Wharton, *The House of Mirth,* book I, chap. 14, p. 169.
71. See, for example, *New York World,* 11 December 1904, editorial section, p. 10, col.1; *Town Topics* also commented frequently on Mrs. Mills's exclusiveness.
72. Howe, *Social Customs,* p. 131.
73. Wharton, *The House of Mirth,* book I, chap. 11, pp. 126–27, and chap. 12, pp. 138–42.
74. One of the working titles for the novel was "A Moment's Ornament" (Lewis, *Edith Wharton,* p. 155).
75. Wharton, *The House of Mirth,* book I, chap. 6, p. 73.
76. This is discussed in detail in Halttunen, *Confidence Men,* pp. 92–123.
77. Goffman, *Presentation of Self,* p. 106.
78. Ibid., p. 78.
79. Ibid., p. 82.
80. Learned, *Etiquette of New York,* p. 273.
81. See, for example, Sherwood, *Art of Entertaining,* p. 206.
82. *New York Times,* 20 January 1895, p. 25.
83. Mrs. Edward Lauterbach also spoke of expecting two servants to remain in the house. She allowed her servants to go out, but any unattended woman was to return by 10:00 or 10:30 P.M. She expressed a preference for Roman Catholic servants, whom she deemed to be of high morals, and for women, whom she regarded as more reliable and willing (*New York Times,* 3 February 1895, p. 20).
84. Ibid.
85. *New York Times,* 10 March 1895, p. 25.
86. *New York Times,* 20 January 1895, p. 25.
87. Sherwood, *Art of Entertaining,* pp. 207–13. Despite the trials and tribulations of the New York society woman, Mrs. Sherwood thought that she managed remarkably well, adding: "She must be the mind, while the Maggies and Bridgets furnish the hands" (p. 23).
88. Seely, *Mrs. Seely's Cook Book,* pp. 12–13, 33, 35–36, 46.
89. *New York Times,* 17 February 1895, p. 25.
90. Dudden, *Serving Women,* p. 123.
91. Reporters from *Town Topics* testified in court in 1906 to getting information from members of society, club members, and servants (*New York Times,* 25 January 1906, pp. 1–2).
92. Howe, "The Vanishing Servant Girl," p. 48.
93. *Vogue's Book of Etiquette,* p. 249.

Chapter 4: Women Abroad

1. Crowninshield, *Manners for the Metropolis,* pp. 3–4.
2. Houghton et al., *American Etiquette,* p. 102.
3. Ruth, *Decorum,* p. 125.
4. *Town Topics,* 5 August 1915, p. 4.
5. See Wolff, *Feminine Sentences.*
6. Amongst the various pieces of advice given to women is the following from Dale, *Our Manners and Social Customs* (p. 139):

   > Ladies of really good breeding will not go upon the streets . . . in flashy attire. On the contrary, they will dress soberly, if elegantly, and their deportment will be such as to attract the least notice. They will walk quietly, seeing and hearing nothing that they ought not to see and hear, recognizing acquaintances with a courteous bow, and friends with cordial, yet not effusive greetings. . . . The very appearance of evil must be avoided, and she is not a true lady who so carries herself in the public thoroughfare that loafers stare as she goes by, and "mashers" follow her with insulting attentions.
   >
   > And this suggests the remark that gentlemen do not congregate at street corners, theatre doors, and on church steps for the purpose of staring at ladies as they pass. Cads do this, and loafers, but no self-respecting or respectable man is ever seen occupying a position which entitles him to the contempt of women, and to the righteous indignation of fathers, husbands and brothers.

7. Walkowitz, *City of Dreadful Delight,* p. 18.
8. Both Walkowitz and Ryan refer to the construction of a metropolis by urban investigators and journalists as a "dark, powerful, and seductive labyrinth" sharply segregated into class zones (Walkowitz, *City of Dreadful Delight,* p. 17; Ryan, *Women in Public,* esp. pp. 68–76). Ryan also refers to the charting of "boundaries of gender" and asserts that "the greatest moral risk that [endangered] women encountered on the public streets" was prostitutes (p. 68); "images of chance meetings and near collisions between virtuous and sinful women were a mainstay of urban gender cartography." Likewise the prostitute was a threat to men (p. 71). Compare Walkowitz, p. 21. While Walkowitz and Ryan refer only to texts by investigators and journalists, I extend the range of text types to include etiquette manuals. Even though such manuals did not as a rule give specific references to places and institutions when offering advice on behavior, they nevertheless "mapped" the city in general terms. See also Stuart M. Blumin's introduction to George G. Foster's *New York by Gas-Light.*
9. Ryan, *Women in Public,* pp. 68–76. In New York at the turn of the century this perception of "social chaos" was accentuated by the influx of southern and eastern European immigrants and African-American migrants from the South.
10. Harvey, "The Urbanization of Consciousness," in *The Urban Experience,* p. 250. This is a revised version of chapter 5 in *Consciousness and The Urban Experience,* pp. 250–76.
11. *New York Times,* 1 January 1905, magazine section, p. 3; see also McCabe, *New York by Sunlight,* pp. 153–54.
12. *New York Times,* 8 January 1905, magazine section, p. 2.
13. McCabe, *New York by Sunlight,* p. 556.
14. Moore, *End of the Road for Ladies' Mile?* p. 23; Resequie, "A.T. Stewart's Marble Palace," pp. 131–32.
15. "The store thrived in an era of bustles, long kid gloves, tall silk hats, horses and buggies, gaslights, costume balls, artistic dinners" (Moore, *Ladies' Mile,* p. 40).
16. Dale, *Our Manners and Social Customs,* p. 137.
17. Zola, *The Ladies' Paradise.*
18. Dale, *Our Manners and Social Customs,* pp. 137–38.

19. McCabe, *New York by Sunlight*, p. 556.

20. Walkowitz refers to similar developments in London shops in the late nineteenth century (*City of Dreadful Delight*, p. 48).

21. The *New York Times* society column mentioned in passing that Fifth Avenue was looking particularly gay in the late morning and early afternoon, with women stopping on their way home from "at homes" to take tea at the Waldorf, Sherry's, or Delmonico's (4 January 1900, editorial section, p. 8, col. 4).

22. *Town Topics*, 15 October 1896, p. 5, and 12 November 1896, p. 4.

23. *Town Topics*, 29 October 1908, pp. 4–5.

24. *Town Topics*, 20 June 1907, pp. 3–4. Cf. p. 171, n. 4.

25. Mrs. Hamlin mentioned the Herman Livingstons, who had an apartment at 20 Washington Square North; the Richard Hunts, also on the square; Misses Julia and Serena Rhinelander, who lived on the corner of Washington Square and Fifth Avenue; the Hampden Robbs, at Thirty-fourth Street before they built 23 Park Avenue circa 1888.

26. Hamlin, "Some Glimpses," p. 16, Hamlin Papers.

27. Baker refers to the Colony Club as "the first clubhouse built for a women's organization in New York City" (*Stanny*, p. 147). The group of women who planned the Colony as a counterpart to a gentlemen's club was headed by Mrs. J. Borden Harriman. The committee included Anne Morgan, daughter of J. P. Morgan; Mrs. Thomas Hastings, wife of the architect; and Helen Barney, daughter of the banker Charles T. Barney, who was chairman of the building committee. He quotes from Florence F. Kelly's 1907 article for *Indoors and Outdoors* with regard to the aims of the club: "to unite in one organization leading women in the business, the social, the artistic, the literary, the theatrical worlds and to give them a club home where they can enjoy social pleasures and athletic privileges." The society belle turned actress Elsie de Wolfe was contracted to design the interior. The Colony Club opened in 1907 on Madison Avenue and was used by prominent members of society for receptions.

28. *New York World*, 1 December 1901, p. 7.

29. *New York Times*, 24 February 1895, p. 11, col. 1.

30. *New York Times*, 21 July 1895, p. 28, col. 1.

31. Parkhurst, "Andromaniacs," p. 15.

32. *Ladies Homes Journal*, March 1895, p. 12.

33. Crowninshield, *Manners for the Metropolis*, p. 38.

34. Dale, *Our Manners and Social Customs*, pp. 139–40.

35. See Weedon, *Feminist Practice*, p. 36.

36. The compromising nature of Lily's two problematic exits, one from The Benedick during the day and the other from Trenor's house at night, are made clear by the prescriptions to be found in etiquette manuals of the late nineteenth century. In his etiquette manual of 1881, for example, John Ruth, who described himself as "an old bachelor," advised ladies on the propriety of calling on gentlemen thus: "A lady never calls on a gentleman, unless professionally or officially. It is not only ill-bred, but positively improper to do so." And with regard to being out after dark, he proposed that: "After twilight, a young lady would not be conducting herself in a becoming manner, by walking alone; and if she passes the evening with anyone, she ought beforehand, to provide some one to come for her at the stated hour" (*Decorum*, pp. 81–82, 119–20). See also Cooke, who wrote: "A lady should not venture out upon the street alone after dark. By so doing she compromises her dignity, and exposes herself to indignity at the hands of the rougher class" (*Social Etiquette*, p. 336). Also Houghton et al.: "A young lady should never walk the streets alone after dark" (*American Etiquette*, p. 103).

37. Lily's knowledge of the demimonde is extremely limited. It is only when she begins her social descent that she encounters other aspects of masculine New York. At the Emporium Hotel, where her employer, Mrs. Hatch, holds court, Lily discovers young

men from her own circle: "This, then, was one of the things that young men 'went in' for when released from the official social routine; this was the kind of 'previous engagement' that so frequently caused them to disappoint the hopes of anxious hostesses" (Wharton, *The House of Mirth*, book II, chap. 19, pp. 294–95).

38. Ibid., book I, chap. 13, p. 156, chap. 14, pp. 166, 170.
39. Wharton, *The House of Mirth*, book II, chap. 13, p. 329.
40. Ives, *The Social Mirror*, p. 58.
41. Howe, *Social Customs*, p. 289.
42. Hartley, *Ladies' Book of Etiquette*, p. 29.
43. White, *Polite Society at Home and Abroad*, p. 36.
44. Rosenzweig and Blackmar, *The Park and the People*, p. 215.
45. Ibid.
46. *New York Times,* 3 June 1906, magazine section II, p. 2.
47. *Town Topics*, 10 May 1906, 3.
48. Hamlin, "Some Glimpses," p. 16, Hamlin Papers.
49. *Town Topics*, 10 May 1906, p. 4.
50. Rosenzweig and Blackmar, *The Park and the People,* pp. 218–19.
51. *Town Topics*, 2 February 1888, p. 5. Remy Saisselin describes the situation in late-nineteenth-century Paris, where *demimondaines* indulged in the "ritual practices" of a "daily appearance, in a carriage, on the Champs Elysées, [a] ride in the Bois de Boulogne, and of course [a] loge in the theater or the opera" (*Bourgeois and the Bibelot*, p. 55).
52. *Town Topics*, 7 December 1905, p. 6.
53. *Town Topics*, 18 May 1905, p. 5.
54. *New York Times*, 1 January 1905, magazine section, p. 6.
55. *New York Times*, 4 August 1895, p. 13, col.3.
56. *New York World*, 20 January, p. 20. *Town Topics* had reported that between forty and fifty cyclists with lanterns had ridden in the lantern ride and that the event had set the seal of fashionable approval on the wheel (20 September 1894, pp. 5–6).
57. *Town Topics*, 21 June 1894, p. 5.
58. *New York Herald*, 8 July 1894, p. 8.
59. *New York Times*, 17 March 1895, p. 1, col. 1. The illustration appeared on p. 14. The costume was named after its designer, Herbert Luey, a ladies' tailor of 303 Fifth Avenue and 202 Washington Park, Brooklyn.
60. *New York Times*, 4 August 1895, p. 13, col. 3.
61. *New York World*, 20 January 1895, p. 20.
62. Hamlin, "The Coming Out Years," p. 91, Hamlin Papers.
63. *New York Times*, 4 August 1895, p. 15, col. 1.
64. Henry G. Barbey to Elsie Clews, 18 and 28 April 1898, Parsons Papers, Box 2, f. 4.
65. Fred V. S. Crosby to Elsie Clews, 26 May 1895, Parsons Papers, Box 2, f. 12.
66. Tom Hastings to Elsie Clews, 16 March 1897, Parsons Papers, Box 2, f. 20.
67. Helen Ripley Benedict to Elsie Clews, Parsons Papers, Box 2, f. 6.
68. Hamlin, *An Albany Girlhood*, pp. 250–51.
69. Whitelaw Reid had been editor of the *New York Tribune* and between 1905 and 1912 was the U.S. ambassador to Britain. He was married to the daughter of the millionaire Ogden Mills.
70. Hamlin, *An Albany Girlhood*, pp. 285–87.
71. Hamlin, *An Albany Girlhood,* pp. 43–44.
72. There is no evidence that the two women actually met, but a letter from Alonzo Potter, son of Bishop Potter and a close friend of Elsie's, indicates that he was staying with the Whitelaw Reids at the time of Huybertie's holiday in the Adirondacks in 1896 and, in fact, mentions that the Pruyns and Parkers of Albany were in the area (Alonzo Potter to Elsie Clews, 18 September 1896, Parsons Papers, Box 2, f. 17). They also appear to have had friends in common, including Alida Chanler.

73. See chapter 2 for a discussion of the problems that Herbert Parsons had when he suggested a camping trip that was to include Elsie.
74. Herbert Parsons to Elsie Clews, 16 August 1895, Parsons Papers, Box 4, f. 2.
75. Hare, *A Woman's Quest for Science*, p. 48.
76. Martens, *Book of Good Manners*, pp. 367–68.
77. See Montgomery, *"Gilded Prostitution,"* chaps. 1 and 4.
78. Burnett, *The Shuttle*, p. 2.
79. See Hamlin, *An Albany Girlhood*, pp. 239–40.
80. Harriet Pruyn Rice, Diary, vol. 10, 2 February 1890, Rice Papers.
81. Wharton, *A Backward Glance*, chap. 6, p. 887, chap. 7, p. 898.
82. Edith Wharton to W. Moreton Fullerton, 22 April 1913, *Letters of Edith Wharton*, p. 298. Fullerton, an American journalist, and Wharton became lovers in 1909.
83. Lewis, *Edith Wharton*, p. 7.
84. Wharton, *A Backward Glance*, chap. 13, p. 1047, chap. 12, pp. 1030–31.
85. Wharton to Fullerton, 22 April 1913, *Letters of Edith Wharton*, p. 298.
86. *Letters of Edith Wharton*, p. 315.
87. Edith Wharton, *In Morocco*, pp. 6, 7.
88. Wharton to Mary Cadwalader Jones, 26 September 1917, *Letters of Edith Wharton*, p. 316.
89. Wharton to Bernard Berenson, 2 October 1917, *Letters of Edith Wharton*, pp. 399, 402.
90. See also Wharton: "Everything that the reader of the Arabian Nights expects to find is here" (*In Morocco*, p. 23).
91. Wharton to Bernard Berenson, 16 April 1914, *Letters of Edith Wharton*, p. 318.
92. Wharton, *In Morocco*, p. 157.
93. Wharton, *In Morocco*, pp. 53, 193–94. Edward Said argues that an important development in nineteenth-century Orientalism was "the distillation of essential ideas about the Orient—its sensuality, its tendency to despotism, its aberrant mentality, its habits of inaccuracy, its backwardness—into a separate and unchallenged coherence" so that the use of the word *Orientalism* evoked an existing body of knowledge regarded as "morally neutral and objectively valid." Further, the work of both scholars and imaginative writers on the Orient in the nineteenth century made this knowledge "more clear, more detailed, more substantial—and more distinct from 'Occidentalism'" (*Orientalism*, p. 205). Wharton uses both *Orient* and *Occident* throughout *In Morocco*, unwittingly falling into the pattern described by Said.
94. Wharton, *In Morocco*, pp. 193–95.
95. Wharton and the other ladies in her party received several invitations to visit harems. Yet Wharton's descriptions of harems contain no references to the difficulties of access or stolen glances of prohibited sights, which characterize her descriptions of sacred places in Morocco. Inevitably her access to Moroccan life was gendered, but for her what was significant was that she was granted such access as a "European" and "unbeliever." Although she was invited into harems, she could only look from aloft on the Merinid court of ablutions in Fez, which "is so closely guarded from below that from our secret coign of vantage we seemed to be looking down into the heart of forbidden things" (Wharton, *In Morocco*, p. 99).
96. Wolff, *A Feast of Words*, p. 299.
97. Wharton, *The Age of Innocence*, chap. 33, p. 1282.
98. *Town Topics*, 8 October 1908, p. 3.
99. Benstock, *No Gifts from Chance*, pp. 183–89. According to Benstock, Wharton's correspondence with Fullerton in Paris that spring shows that "her prime concern was to protect her reputation with her household staff," especially as her husband's valet was her butler in the rue de Varenne apartment. But even when she relocated to her brother's apartment in Paris she felt spied on (p. 183).
100. Lewis, *Edith Wharton*, p. 220.

101. *Town Topics*, 20 May 1915, p. 4.
102. *Town Topics*, 15 April 1915, p. 3.
103. *Town Topics*, 16 May 1895, p. 5.
104. *Manners and Rules of Good Society*, p. 105.
105. Martens, *Book of Good Manners*, pp. 311–12.

Chapter 5:
"Optical Excursions"
1. Martin, *Passing of the Idle Rich*, p. 109.
2. Blair, "Private Parts in Public Places," p. 211.
3. Green, *Spectacle of Nature*, p. 40.
4. Berger, *Ways of Seeing*, p. 47.
5. According to the Saunterer, it was possible to get a private room for two people, "whether they are known or not," in fashionable Parisian restaurants (*Town Topics*, 22 March 1888, p. 1).
6. See Kasson, *Rudeness and Civility*, chap. 7, esp. p. 240.
7. Gilfoyle, *City of Eros*, pp. 232–36. This echoes what William Leach describes as a "new secular carnivalesque" in which people play "at the margins of unacceptable thought and behavior" (see below, pp. 138–39; Leach, "Strategists of Display," pp. 131–32).
8. *Town Topics*, 3 September 1903, p. 4.
9. As, for example, with the following reference to "fashionably dressed" prostitutes taking up their station on "inviting sofas" in the corridor that led to a men's bar in a fashionable hotel: "The management of this very popular hotel would do well to get busy with mops, brooms and detergents and clean out this particular corridor before some scandal breaks that will bring the whole house into distasteful notoriety" (*Town Topics*, 14 October 1915, p. 4).
10. This change in attitudes is represented in Edith Wharton's *The Age of Innocence* by the marriage of Newland Archer's son to Fanny Beaufort, the daughter of Julius Beaufort and his mistress Fanny Ring: "Nothing could more clearly give the measure of the distance that the world had travelled. People nowadays were too busy—busy with reforms and 'movements,' with fads and fetishes and frivolities—to bother much about their neighbours. And of what account was anybody's past, in the huge kaleidoscope where all the social atoms spun around on the same plane?" (chap. 34, pp. 1295–96).
11. Gilfoyle, *City of Eros*, p. 204; see also his map of theaters and brothels in the vicinity of Longacre Square in 1901, p. 208.
12. See chapter 1, the section "Nightlife."
13. Saisselin, *Bourgeois and the Bibelot*, p. 55.
14. This is a reference to one of the Saunterer's commentaries on a society event (*Town Topics*, 29 January 1920, 5). See the section "Sinister Eyes" of this chapter.
15. Kaplan, *Social Construction*, p. 7.
16. Corbin, *Women for Hire*, p. 204.
17. Leach, *Land of Desire*, pp. 9, 61–67; see also Leach, "Strategists of Display," p. 107.
18. Leach, "Strategists of Display," pp. 116, 131–32.
19. See chapter 1, the section "Nightlife."
20. *Town Topics*, 2 April 1896, p. 6
21. Berger, *Ways of Seeing*, p. 133.
22. *New York Herald*, 2 December 1894, fourth section, p. 9.
23. Ibid.
24. Wharton's *The House of Mirth* (p. 294) includes a description of the horse show as an arena of display:

> The Horse Show . . . had produced a passing semblance of reanimation, filling the theatres and restaurants with a human display of the same costly and high-

stepping kind as circled daily about its ring. In Miss Bart's world the Horse Show, and the public it attracted, had ostensibly come to be classed among the spectacles disdained of the elect; but, as the feudal lord might sally forth to join in the dance on his village green, so society, unofficially and incidentally, still condescended to look in upon the scene. Mrs. Gormer, among the rest, was not above seizing such an occasion for the display of herself and her horses; and Lily was given one or two opportunities of appearing at her friend's side in the most conspicuous box the house afforded.

25. *New York World*, 20 November 1904, p. 6.
26. *New York World*, 29 December 1901, p. 5.
27. *New York Times*, 6 August 1905, magazine section, p. 1, cols. 3–5.
28. *New York World*, 10 August 1902, p. 6.
29. Green, *Spectacle of Nature*, p. 34.
30. Longstreet, *Social Etiquette of New York*, p. 8; White, *Polite Society*, pp. 11–12.
31. Longstreet, *Social Etiquette of New York*, p. 181.
32. Ruth, *Decorum*, p. 281.
33. Dale, *Our Manners and Social Customs*, p. 172.
34. *Harper's Bazaar Book of Decorum*, p. 121.
35. Dale, *Our Manners*, p. 172; A Woman of Fashion, *Etiquette for Americans*, pp. 227–30.
36. A Woman of Fashion, *Etiquette for Americans*, pp. 227–28.
37. Dale, *Our Manners*, p. 172.
38. A phrase taken from James. See "The Siege of London," reprinted in *In the Cage and Other Stories*, p. 104.
39. A phrase taken from Wharton. See *The Age of Innocence*, chap. 2, p. 1024.
40. *Town Topics*, 30 November 1905, pp. 3–4.
41. With relation to women being compared to works of art, Saisselin quotes Thomas Graindorge: "They are no longer the dreams which imagination or illusion may embody. What is really wanted of them is possession or exhibition" (*Bourgeois and the Bibelot*, p. 60).
42. Leach, "Strategists of Desire," p. 131.
43. Smith, *Texts, Facts*, pp. 167–71.
44. Garb, "Gender and Representation," in *Modernity and Modernism*, p. 257.
45. Ibid., p. 226.
46. I refer here to *The Loge* (1882), *Lydia Seated in a Loge, Wearing a Pearl Necklace* (1879), and *Woman in Black at the Opera* (1879), which have their parallels in the relevant scenes in Wharton's novels *The Age of Innocence*, *The House of Mirth*, and *The Custom of the Country*, respectively. The last two paintings are reproduced in Garb, "Gender and Representations," pp. 265–66.
47. Smith, *Texts, Facts*, pp. 191–92.
48. Wharton, *The Age of Innocence*, chap. 1, p. 1017, chap. 2, p. 1024, chap. 1, p. 1021, and chap. 2, p. 1026.
49. Wharton, *The House of Mirth*, book I, chap. 10, p. 121.
50. Blair, "Private Parts in Public Places," p. 215.
51. Wharton, *The House of Mirth*, book I, chap. 10, p. 122.
52. Goldner, "The Lying Woman and Social Anxieties," pp. 285–305; Smith, *Texts, Facts*, p. 182.
53. Goffmann, *Presentation of Self*, chap. 1.
54. Wharton, *The Custom of the Country*, chap. 5, pp. 661–63.
55. There is an implied contrast here with May Welland, her cousin, who is a débutante and is seated toward the rear of the box, as was customary until after 1900 when the practice was to seat "buds" in the front. See the "Disciplining the Gaze" section in this chapter.

56. Smith, *Texts, Facts,* pp. 191–202; cf. Green, *Spectacle of Nature,* p. 34; Dauphin et al., "Women's Culture and Women's Power," p. 77.
57. Buci-Glucksmann, "Catastrophic Utopia," p. 224.
58. Leach, "Strategists of Display," p. 116.
59. *Town Topics,* 30 March 1890, p. 1.
60. Simon, *Fifth Avenue,* pp. 166, 197–99; *Town Topics,* 23 January 1908, p. 3.
61. *Town Topics,* 19 May 1910, p. 5.
62. See Morris, *Incredible New York,* p. 267.
63. Baker, *Stanny,* pp. 133–34, 286–89, 321–25.
64. New York *World,* 30 June 1906, metropolitan section.
65. *New York Times,* 29 June 1906, p. 1, col. 4; 1 July 1906, p. 1, col. 1; 4 July 1906, p. 1, col. 7.
66. *New York Times,* 27 June 1906, p. 3, col. 3, and editorial section, 28 June 1906, p. 6, col. 2; *New York World,* 27 June 1906, p. 3, cols. 2–3.
67. Green, *Spectacle of Nature,* p. 40. In referring to Green's work on Paris, I consciously imply a parallel with the urban processes affecting New York at this time.
68. *Vogue,* 18 April 1907, p. 588.
69. *New York Times,* 24 September 1905, magazine section, p. 6.
70. De Wolfe, *After All,* pp. 17–36, 244, 102; Smith, *Elsie de Wolfe,* pp. 53–56.
71. Leonard Jerome was the father of Jennie Jerome, who became Lady Randolph Churchill.
72. *New York World,* 18 January 1920, editorial section, p. 4.
73. *New York World,* 27 January 1920, p. 9.
74. *New York World,* 1 February 1920, editorial section, p. 4.
75. Town Topics, 29 January 1920, p. 5.
76. See Erenberg, *Steppin' Out,* pp. 83–86.
77. As Ruth Rosen has pointed out, in referring to Mark Connelly's work on prostitution in the progressive era, reformers "often extended the familiar label of prostitution to encompass a wide variety of sexual behaviors affronting 'civilized morality,' from engaging in premarital sex to going out with men unchaperoned" (*Lost Sisterhood,* pp. 42–43.)
78. Rosen, *Lost Sisterhood,* pp. 40–46.

Chapter 6:
Women in the Public Eye

1. See, for example, Smith, *Texts, Facts,* esp. chap. 6, pp. 166–70.
2. Anderson, *Imagined Communities,* pp. 15–16, 30–40.
3. *Town Topics,* 2 January 1890, p. 3.
4. I draw here on Roger Fowler's *Language in the News,* chap. 2, esp. p. 20.
5. In reporting the international wedding of Anna Gould to Count Boni di Castellane, the society columnist in the *New York Times* encouraged readers to imagine being a wedding guest: "Why not make believe, then, that you and I have alighted from our cab at the awning stretched from the massive front doors of the residence to the curb" (5 March 1895, p. 1). People's interest in the wedding was evinced by the crowd of onlookers who gathered outside the Gould mansion and the fact that they had to be "kept moving by the police and private detectives" and prevented from glimpsing the family through the windows (*New York Times,* 4 March 1895, p. 8).
6. Thompson, *Ideology and Modern Culture,* pp. 146–54.
7. Ibid., p. 247.
8. Mott, *History of American Magazines,* vol. 4: pp. 1–14, 751–55.
9. *Town Topics,* 3 January 1885, p. 1.
10. *Town Topics,* 17 December 1891, p. 1.

11. *Town Topics*, 11 April 1895, p. 1.
12. *Town Topics* had a circulation of over 50,000 by 1890, in contrast to the *World*'s 350,000 and the *New York Herald*'s 190,000. For further information about New York newspapers and their role in commercial culture, see Taylor, *In Pursuit of Gotham*, pp. 81–83.
13. Even *Town Topics* observed a prolonged silence in the weeks following the murder, but that was because White was on the list of "immunes." White was one of those who had succumbed to the blackmailing tactics of *Town Topics'* owner, Col. Mann, in paying $1,500 for a copy of *Fads and Fancies* (Baker, *Stanny*, p. 288).
14. *New York World*, 20 January 1895, p. 1. See Terdiman, *Discourse/Counter-Discourse*, pp. 121–25.
15. In *Structural Transformation of the Public Sphere*, p. 170, Jürgen Habermas refers to this kind of news as "immediate reward news."
16. This was a criminal libel suit against the editor of *Collier's Weekly*, Norman Hapgood, for criticizing Justice Deuel's treatment of Alice Roosevelt's wedding.
17. *New York Times,* 23 January 1906, p. 1.
18. In Greek mythology the three Fates were Clotho, Lachesis, and Atropos. According to *The Larousse Encyclopedia of Mythology*: "Clotho, the spinner, personified the thread of life. Lachesis was chance, the element of luck that a man had the right to expect. Atropos was inescapable fate, against which there was no appeal" (p. 187).
19. *New York Times,* 19 January 1906, pp. 1–2; 23 January 1906, p. 1; 24 January 1906, p. 1; 25 January 1906, p. 2; 26 January 1906, p. 1; 27 January 1906, pp. 1–2.
20. *New York World*, 10 August 1902, Sunday magazine section, pp. 6–7.
21. A Woman of Fashion, *Etiquette for Americans*, pp. 267–74.
22. Louis D. Brandeis and Samuel Warren, "The Right to Privacy," *Harvard Law Review,* 1890; reprinted in Goldstein, ed., *Killing the Messenger*, pp. 7–21, esp. pp. 8–9.
23. Godkin, "The Rights of the Citizen," pp. 58–67, esp. p. 65.
24. *Scribner's*, April 1894, p. 526.
25. *Town Topics,* 24 October 1895, pp. 5–6.
26. For example, the following appeared in the *New York World* (28 January 1883, p. 5):

    A leaf from the diary of New York society girl at the close of the season of 1882–83 would be an invaluable argument to philosophers who contend that here woman excels man in her powers of physical endurance. But how obtain such a record? For the girl of the period has not time even to keep a diary. A fond mamma, however, who for her own pride and pleasure and for the benefit of her posterity, has kept a record of her daughter's doings of the past week, exhibits with exultation the following resume of a belle's progress for one day: "Rose at 8; took breakfast and read the society news in *The World* until 9:30; went to music lesson at 10; to a photographer's with friends at 11 to have picture taken in tableau costume; attended reading of oriental poetry at Mrs S's at 12:30; thence home to dress and go to luncheon party at Miss B's—forty ladies, little tables, flowers and gaslight, at 3 home to dress again; at 4 to make six calls—thank goodness found everyone out; tea at Mrs B's at 5; reception at Mrs D's at 6; home to dress at 6:45; dinner party at Mrs P's at 7:30; cotillion ball at Delmonico's at 11; to Charity Ball at Academy at 1; home 2:30; talked with Adelaide who waited up for me till 3, then retired."

27. Shevelow, *Women and Print Culture*, p. 2.
28. According to the Saunterer, for example, "Mrs. Astor was most successful in dodging the camera" and her picture appeared only once in the papers, apart from reproductions of her portrait by Duran (*Town Topics*, 5 November 1908, p. 4).
29. See Habermas, *Structural Transformation of the Public Sphere,* p. 194.

30. See Banta, *Imaging American Women*, p. 653.
31. Wharton, *The Custom of the Country*, chap. 2, pp. 363, 639, chap. 3, p. 644, 645. See above, p. 77. Compare this from Bourdieu, *Distinction*, p. 2:

> Consumption is . . . a stage in a process of communication, that is, an act of deciphering, decoding, which presupposes practical or explicit mastery of a cipher or code. In a sense, one can say that the capacity to see (*voir*) is a function of the knowledge (*savoir*). . . . A work of art has meaning and interest only for someone who possesses the cultural competence, that is, the code, into which it is encoded. . . . A beholder who lacks the specific code feels lost in a chaos of sounds and rhythms, colours and lines, without rhyme or reason.

32. Peter Van Degen is the salamander to Undine's water nymph. Wharton, *The Custom of the Country*, pp. 653–54.
33. "Why Bother about the 400?" *Ladies Home Journal*, February 1906, p. 18.
34. *New York World*, 27 July 1902, Sunday magazine section, p. 5.
35. Richard T. Wilson was a southerner who had settled in New York after the Civil War. He and his wife originally came from Georgia.
36. *New York Journal* 1902.
37. *Town Topics*, 4 June 1908, p. 4.
38. See Montgomery, "*Gilded Prostitution*," p. 48.
39. *Town Topics*, 28 October 1920, pp. 3–4.
40. *New York World*, 27 July 1902, p. 3.
41. *Town Topics*, 22 October 1908, p. 3.
42. Vanderbilt, *Queen of the Golden Age*, pp. 223–24.
43. *Ladies Home Journal*, April 1900, p. 19; May 1900, p. 17.
44. Emery, *The Press and America*, p. 341.
45. Pensler, introduction to *Illustrations of W. T. Smedley*, pp. 9–10.
46. Wharton, *The Custom of the Country*, chap. 14, pp. 745, 746. There is a reference earlier in the novel to Popple's mass production of society women's portraits when Mrs. Van Degen mentions that Popple is painting her: "He's doing everybody this year, you know—" (chap. 3, p. 644).
47. Ibid., chap. 14, pp. 745, 750–51.
48. Ibid., chap. 14, pp. 746, 748, 750, 752, 755.
49. *New York Times*, 5 March 1895, p. 1.
50. James, *The Reverberator*, pp. 37, 68–69.
51. The story was loosely based upon the experience of May McClellan, daughter of the Civil War general George McClellan, who had written a letter in 1886 to the *New York World* revealing details about members of Venetian society who had entertained her. See Edel, *Life of Henry James*, vol. 1, pp. 812–14. The phrase "a newspaperized world" comes from James's comments on this particular incident. See James, *The Complete Notebooks of Henry James*, p. 42.
52. James, *The Reverberator*, pp. 14 and 60–61.
53. James, *Notebooks*, p. 40.
54. James, *The Reverberator*, pp. 22, 34, 68, 115, 117, 121.
55. Ibid., pp. 135–38, 198, 158–59.
56. Ibid., pp. 185, 199.
57. Among the guests at Mrs. Wellington Bry's dinner for the duchess of Beltshire at a restaurant in the south of France is the "horrid little Dabham who does 'Society Notes from the Riviera.'" His presence "emphasised the ideals of a world in which conspicuousness passed for distinction, and the society column became the roll of fame" (book 2, chap. 3, pp. 218, 234). See the conclusion for further reference to Dabham.
58. Wharton, *The Custom of the Country*, chap. 12, p. 725, chap. 16, p. 769, chap. 2, p. 635, chap. 23, p. 847, chap. 46, pp. 1008–9.

Conclusion:
Spectacle and Surveillance

1. Bourdieu, *Distinction*, p. 254.
2. Ibid., pp. 249–50.
3. See Wharton, *The House of Mirth*, book II, chap. 4, p. 234.
4. Wharton, *The Custom of the Country*, chap. 19, pp. 802–3.
5. Bourdieu, *Distinction*, p. 253.
6. Ibid., p. 250.
7. Wharton, *A Backward Glance*, p. 780.
8. Ibid., pp. 780–81.
9. See "The Female Tourist," in chapter 4.
10. Bourdieu, *Distinction*, p. 250.
11. Wharton, *The Custom of the Country*, chap. 5, p. 669.
12. Wharton, *The House of Mirth*, book II, chap. 4, p. 234.
13. Kaplan, *Social Construction*, p. 13.
14. As the serialization of *The House of Mirth* in *Scribner's* approached its denouement, advertisements began to appear for the novel. In the *New York Times* "Saturday Review of Books," it was promoted as "the greatest novel of the year." The *New York Times* Sunday magazine section picked up on it in a feature on three novels that were said to hold New York society up to scorn "in the present era of vast wealth and ostentatious display." The society columnist insisted on their verisimilitude: "The smallest details of the picture are recognizable as facts of the life that is pulsing around us in this very hour, and the personages are so lifelike that . . . there will surely be many plausible identifications by readers of the book who are proud of their familiarity with Society." Clearly, such a representation of the novel aligns it with society journalism in pandering to readers' desires to know about high society. The fact that Edith Wharton had "first-hand knowledge" of fashionable society was seen as an important selling factor. A fierce debate ensued in the pages of the "Saturday Review" between two readers who signed themselves as "Newport" and "Lenox." "Newport" was appalled by the novel and saw it as a vulgar caricature society. S/he advised that society's skeletons should be left alone in their closet: "Why mislead the masses by bearing before them only the soiled linen of the Four Hundred?" "Lenox," on the other hand, was all in favor of someone like Wharton critiquing society because of her inside knowledge (*New York Times*, "Saturday Review of Books," 14 October 1905, p. 667; magazine section, 15 October 1905, p. 6; "Saturday Review," 2 December 1905, p. 837; "Saturday Review," 9 December 1905, p. 882).

   Cf. Terdiman, *Discourse/Counter-Discourse*: "This always-frustrated impulse to contradict the discourse of one's antagonist and make the contradiction stick" (p. 12).
15. Bourdieu, *Distinction*, p. 252.
16. Despite the similarities between the Saunterer's sociocritical perspective on society and the sociocultural critique contained in Wharton's fiction, I need hardly emphasize that, as my discussion of discourse and counter discourse indeed suggests, journalistic writings and literary texts usually have quite different discursive functions.
17. *Town Topics*, 26 November 1891, p. 1; compare Bourdieu: "Countless social arrangements are designed to regulate the relations between being and seeming . . . aimed at recalling to reality . . . those who, by exhibiting the external signs of wealth association with a condition higher than their own, show that they 'think themselves' something better than they are, the pretentious pretenders, who betray by their poses, their postures, their 'presentation' that they have a self-image too far out of line with the image others have of them, to which they ought to cut down their self-image ('climb down')" (*Distinction*, p. 252).
18. *Town Topics*, 17 December 1891, p. 1.
19. Shevelow, *Women and Print Culture*, p. 4.

20. *Town Topics*, 6 December 1894, p. 8.

21. Bourdieu, *Distinction*, p. 249.

22. Wharton, *The Custom of the Country*, ch. 15, pp. 757–59.

23. Erenberg, *Steppin' Out*, p. 66.

24. Foucault, *Discipline and Punish*, p. 209.

25. Wharton, *The Age of Innocence*, chap. 33, p. 1282; cf. *The House of Mirth*, book I, chap. 11, p. 130, and *The Custom of the Country*, chap. 23, p. 852.

26. She cannot ring the bell to call for servants for fear of the scandal—"A hideous mustering of tongues." Instead, Lily resolves to leave the house without exciting "conjecture" and puts on a show of normality in front of the Trenors' caretaker in the hall (Wharton, *The House of Mirth*, book I, chap. 13, pp. 155–56).

27. Wharton, *The House of Mirth*, book II, chap. 3, pp. 225–27.

28. F. H. Bradley, quoted by Adorno in *Minima Moralia: Reflections from Damaged Life*, p. 103. Compare "Sorrow is better than laughter for by sadness of countenance the heart is made better. The heart of the wise is in the house of mourning, but the heart of fools is in the house of mirth" (Ecclesiastes 7:34).

Bibliography

Manuscripts

Huybertie Pruyn Hamlin Papers, AF 121, McKinney Library, Albany Institute of History & Art, Albany, New York.

Elsie Clews Parsons Papers, Rye Historical Society, Rye, New York.

Harriet L. Pruyn Rice Papers, AN 162, McKinney Library, Albany Institute of History & Art, Albany, New York.

Published Sources

Adorno, Theodor W. *Minima Moralia. Reflexionen aus dem beschädigten Leben.* Frankfurt am Main: Suhrkamp Verlag, 1951.

Anderson, Benedict. *Imagined Communities: Reflections on the Origin and Spread of Nationalism.* London: Verso, 1983.

Ardener, Shirley, ed. *Women and Space: Ground Rules and Social Maps.* London: Croom Helm, 1981.

A Woman of Fashion. *Etiquette for Americans.* Chicago and New York: Herbert S. Stone, 1898.

Baker, Paul R. *Stanny: The Gilded Life of Stanford White.* New York: Free Press, 1989.

Balsan, Consuelo Vanderbilt. *The Glitter and the Gold.* London: Heinemann, 1953.

Banta, Martha. *Imaging American Women: Idea and Ideals in Cultural History.* New York: Columbia University Press, 1987.

Benstock, Shari. *No Gifts from Chance: A Biography of Edith Wharton.* New York: Charles Scribner's, 1994.

Berger, John. *Ways of Seeing.* Harmondsworth, England: Penguin, 1972.

Blair, Juliet. "Private Parts in Public Places: The Case of Actresses." In *Women and Space: Ground Rules and Social Maps,* edited by Shirley Ardener, pp. 205–28. London: Croom Helm, 1981.

Bourdieu, Pierre. *Distinction: A Social Critique of the Judgement of Taste.* Translated by Richard Nice. Cambridge: Harvard University Press, 1984.

Brandon, Ruth. *The Dollar Princesses: The American Invasion of the European Aristocracy, 1870–1914.* London: Weidenfeld and Nicolson, 1980.

Bronner, Simon J., ed. *Consuming Visions: Accumulation and Display of Goods in America, 1880–1920.* New York: W. W. Norton, 1989.

Brown, Henry Collins. *Brownstone Fronts and Saratoga Trunks*. New York: E. P. Dutton, 1935.

———. *Delmonico's: A Story of Old New York*. New York: Valentine's Manual, 1928.

———. *In the Golden Nineties*. Hastings-on-Hudson, NY: Valentine's Manual, 1928.

Buci-Glucksmann, Christine. "Catastrophic Utopia: The Feminine as Allegory of the Modern." In *The Making of the Modern Body: Sexuality and Society in the Nineteenth Century*, edited by Catherine Gallagher and Thomas Laqueur, pp. 220–29. Berkeley and Los Angeles: University of California, 1987.

Buck-Morss, Susan. "The Flaneur, the Sandwichman and the Whore: The Politics of Loitering." *New German Critique* 39 (1986): 99–140.

Burnett, Frances Hodgson. *The Shuttle*. London: Heinemann, 1907.

Bushman, Richard. *The Refinement of American Culture: Persons, Houses, Cities*. New York: Vintage, 1992.

Cable, Mary. *Top Drawer: American High Society From the Gilded Age to the Roaring Twenties*. New York: Atheneum, 1984.

Clark, T. J. *The Painting of Modern Art: Paris in the Art of Manet and His Followers*. London: Thames and Hudson, 1985.

Cooke, Maud C. *Social Etiquette, or Manners and Customs of Polite Society*. Chicago: National Book Concern, 1896.

Corbin, Alain. *Women for Hire: Prostitution and Sexuality in France after 1850*. Translated by Alan Sheridan. Cambridge: Harvard University Press, 1990.

Crowninshield, Francis W. *Manners for the Metropolis: An Entrance Key to the Fantastic Life of the 400*. New York: D. Appleton, 1908.

Dale, Daphne [Charles Beezley]. *Our Manners and Social Customs: A Practical Guide to Deportment, Easy Manners, and Social Etiquette*. Chicago and Philadelphia: Elliot and Beazley, 1891.

Dauphin, Cécile, et al. "Women's Culture and Women's Power: An Attempt at Historiography." Translated by Camille Garnier. *Journal of Women's History* 1 (1989): 63–88.

Davidoff, Leonore. *The Best Circles: Society, Etiquette and the Season*. London: Croom Helm, 1973.

De Wolfe, Elsie. *After All*. London: Heinemann, 1935.

———. *The House in Good Taste*. New York: Century, 1913.

Deutsch, Sara. "Reconceiving the City: Women, Space and Power in Boston, 1870–1910." *Gender and History* 6 (1994): 202–23.

Douglas, Mary. *Natural Symbols: Explorations in Cosmology*. Harmondsworth, England: Penguin, 1973.

———. *Purity and Danger: An Analysis of the Concepts of Pollution and Taboo*. London: Routledge and Kegan Paul, 1966. Reprint, London: Routledge, 1994.

Dudden, Faye E. *Serving Women: Household Service in Nineteenth-Century America*. Middletown, CT: Wesleyan University Press, 1983.

Durkheim, Emile. *The Elementary Forms of the Religious Life*. Translated by Joseph Ward Swain. 1912. Reprint, London: George Allen and Unwin, 1965.

Edel, Leon. *The Life of Henry James*. 2 vols. Harmondsworth, England: Penguin, 1977.

Eighteen Distinguished Authors. *Correct Social Usage: A Course of Instruction in Good Form, Style and Deportment*. vol. 1. Eighth revised edition. New York: New York Society of Self-Culture, 1907.

Elias, Norbert. *The Court Society*. Translated by Edward Jephcott. Oxford: Basil Blackwell, 1983.

Emery, Edwin. *The Press and America: An Interpretive History of the Mass Media*. Englewood Cliffs, NJ: Prentice-Hall, 1972.

Erenberg, Lewis A. *Steppin' Out: New York Nightlife and the Transformation of American Culture, 1890–1930*. Chicago: University of Chicago Press, 1981.

Foucault, Michel. *Discipline and Punish: The Birth of the Prison*. Harmondsworth, England: Penguin, 1979.

Fowler, Roger. *Language in the News: Discourse and Ideology in the Press*. London: Routledge, 1991.

Foster, George G. *New York by Gaslight*. 1850. Reprint, Los Angeles and Berkeley: University of California Press, 1990.

Fox, Richard Wightman, and T. J. Jackson Lears, eds. *The Culture of Consumption: Critical Essays in American History, 1880–1980*. New York: Pantheon Books, 1983.

Frascina, Francis, et al. *Modernity and Modernism: French Painting in the Nineteenth Century*. New Haven and London: Yale University Press, 1993.

Gallagher, Christine, and Thomas Laqueur, eds. *The Making of the Modern Body: Sexuality and Society in the Nineteenth Century*. Berkeley and Los Angeles: University of California Press, 1987.

Garb, Tamar. "Gender and Representation." In *Modernity and Modernism: French Painting in the Nineteenth Century*, edited by Francis Frascina et al., pp. 219–90. New Haven and London: Yale University Press, 1993.

Gibson, Mary Ellis. "Edith Wharton and the Ethnography of Old New York." *Studies in American Fiction* 13 (1985): 57–69.

Gilfoyle, Timothy. *City of Eros: New York City, Prostitution, and the Commercialization of Sex, 1790–1920*. New York: W. W. Norton, 1992.

Godkin, E. L. "The Rights of the Citizen. IV. To His Own Reputation." *Scribner's*, July 1890: 58–67.

Goffman, Erving. *The Presentation of Self in Everyday Life*. New York: Doubleday, 1959.

Goldner, Ellen. "The Lying Woman and Social Anxieties." *Women's Studies* 21 (1992): 285–305.

Goldstein, Tom, ed. *Killing the Messenger: 100 Years of Media Criticism*. New York: Columbia University Press, 1989.

Good Manners. New York: Butterick Publishing Co., 1888.

Green, Nicholas. *The Spectacle of Nature: Landscape and Bourgeois Culture in Nineteenth-Century France*. Manchester: Manchester University Press, 1990.

Grover, Kathryn, ed. *Dining in America, 1850–1900*. Amherst: University of Massachusetts Press, 1987.

Habermas, Jürgen. *The Structural Transformation of the Public Sphere: An Inquiry into a Category of Bourgeois Society*. Translated by Thomas Burger. Cambridge: MIT Press, 1989.

Hall, Florence Howe. *Good Form for all Occasions: A Manual of Manners, Dress and Entertainment for Both Men and Women*. New York and London: Harper and Bros, 1914.

Halttunen, Karen. *Confidence Men and Painted Women: A Study of Middle-Class Culture in America, 1830–1870*. New Haven: Yale University Press, 1982.

———. "From Parlor to Living Room: Domestic Space, Interior Decoration, and the Culture of Personality." In *Consuming Visions: Accumulation and Display of Goods in America, 1880–1920*, edited by Simon J. Bronner, pp. 157–89. New York: W. W. Norton, 1989.

Hamlin, Huybertie Pruyn. *An Albany Girlhood*. Edited by Alice P. Kenney. Albany, NY: Washington Park Press, 1990.

Hare, Peter H. *A Woman's Quest for Science: Portrait of Anthropologist Elsie Clews Parsons*. Buffalo, NY: Prometheus Books, 1985.

Harper's Bazaar Book of Decorum. New York: Harper and Bros., 1871.

Harrison, Mrs. Burton. "The New York Society Girl." *Ladies Home Journal*, October 1892, p. 7.

———. "The Well-Bred Girl in Society: First Paper—The Young Girl and Dancing." *Ladies Home Journal*, November 1892, p. 4.

———. "The Well-Bred Girl in Society: Fourth Paper—Social Laws at Opera, Theatre and Public Places." *Ladies Home Journal*, February 1893, p. 4.

Hartley, Florence. *The Ladies' Book of Etiquette and Manual of Politeness.* Boston: G. W. Cottrell, 1860.

Harvey, David. *Consciousness and the Urban Experience: Studies in the History and Theory of Capitalist Urbanization.* Baltimore: Johns Hopkins University Press, 1985.

———. *The Urban Experience.* Oxford: Basil Blackwell, 1989.

Hobsbawm, Eric, and Terence Ranger, eds. *The Invention of Tradition.* Cambridge: Cambridge University Press, 1983. Reprint, Canto, 1994.

Holt, Emily. *Everyman's Encyclopaedia of Etiquette: A Book of Manners for Everyday Use.* 2 vols. New York: Doubleday, Page, 1920.

Hooper, Lucy Hamilton. "The Home of Christine Nilsson." *Ladies Home Journal,* October 1893, p. 1.

Howatson, M. C., ed. *The Oxford Companion to Classical Literature,* 2nd ed. 1937. Reprint, Oxford: Oxford University Press, 1989.

Howe, Florence Marion. *Social Customs.* Boston: Estes and Lauriat, 1887.

Howe, Frederic C. "The Vanishing Servant Girl." *Ladies Home Journal,* May 1918, p. 48.

Houghton, Professor Walter R., et al. *American Etiquette and Rules of Politeness.* Indianapolis, IN: A. E. Davis, 1882.

Ives, Alice E. *The Social Mirror: A Complete Treatise on the Laws, Rules and Usages that Govern Our Most Refined Homes and Social Circles.* Detroit, MI: F. B. Dickerson, 1886.

Jaher, Frederick Cople. "Style and Status: High Society in Late-Nineteenth-Century New York." In *The Rich, The Wellborn and The Powerful: Elites and Upper Classes in History,* edited by Frederic Cople Jaher, pp. 219–89. Chicago: University of Illinois Press, 1973.

James, Henry. "An International Episode." In *The Complete Tales of Henry James,* vol. 4. Edited by Leon Edel. London: Rupert Hart-Davis, 1962.

———. *Daisy Miller: A Study.* In *The Complete Tales of Henry James,* vol. 4. Edited by Leon Edel. London: Rupert Hart-Davis, 1962.

———. "An International Episode." In *In the Cage and Other Stories.* Harmondsworth, England: Penguin, 1972.

———. *The Complete Notebooks of Henry James.* Edited by Leon Edel and Lyall H. Powers. New York: Oxford University Press, 1987.

———. *The American Scene.* 1907. Reprint, London: Horizon, 1967.

———. *The Reverberator.* 1888. Edited by Simon Novell-Smith. Reprint, New York: Grove Press, 1979.

Kaplan, Amy. *The Social Construction of American Literary Realism.* Chicago: University of Chicago Press, 1988.

Kasson, John F. "Rituals of Dining: Table Manners in Victorian America." In *Dining in America, 1850–1900,* edited by Kathryn Grover, pp. 114–41. Amherst: University of Massachusetts Press, 1987.

———. *Rudeness and Civility: Manners in Nineteenth-Century America.* New York: Hill and Wang, 1990.

Kern, Stephen J. *The Culture of Time and Space, 1880–1918.* Cambridge: Harvard University Press, 1983.

Kingsland, Mrs. Burton. "A Talk About Teas." *Ladies Home Journal,* October 1892, p. 4.

———. *The Book of Good Manners: Etiquette for All Occasions.* New York: Doubleday, Page, 1906.

———. *The Book of Weddings: A Complete Manual of Good Form in All Matters Connected with the Marriage Ceremony.* New York: Doubleday, Page, 1902.

Lamphere, Louise. "Strategies, Cooperation and Conflict Among Women in Domestic Groups." In *Women, Culture and Society,* edited by Michelle Z. Rosaldo and Louise Lamphere, pp. 97–111. Stanford: Stanford University Press, 1974.

Larousse Encyclopedia of Mythology. Translated by Richard Aldington and Delano Ames. London: Paul Hamlyn, 1959.

Leach, William R. *Land of Desire: Merchants, Power and the Rise of a New American Culture.* New York: Pantheon, 1993.

———. "Strategists of Display and the Production of Desire." In *Consuming Visions: Accumulation and Display of Goods in America, 1880–1920,* edited by Simon J. Bronner, pp. 99–132. New York: W. W. Norton, 1989.

———. "Transformations in a Culture of Consumption: Women and Department Stores, 1890–1925." *Journal of American History* 71 (1984): 319–42.

Learned, Ellin Craven. *The Etiquette of New York Today.* New York: Frederick A. Stokes, 1906.

Lears, T. J. Jackson. "Beyond Veblen: Rethinking Consumer Culture in America." In *Consuming Visions: Accumulation and Display of Goods in America, 1880–1920,* edited by Simon J. Bronner, pp. 73–97. New York: W. W. Norton, 1989.

———. *No Place of Grace: Antimodernism and the Transformation of American Culture, 1880–1920.* Chicago: University of Chicago Press, 1981.

Lehr, Elizabeth Drexel. *King Lehr and the Gilded Age.* London: Constable, 1935.

Lemprière, John. *Lemprière's Classical Dictionary.* London: Bracken Books, 1994.

Leslie, Miss. *The Ladies' Guide to the Politeness and Perfect Manners of Miss Leslie's Behaviour Book.* Philadelphia: T. B. Peterson and Bros., 1864.

Levine, Lawrence W. *High Brow/Low Brow: The Emergence of Cultural Hierarchy in America.* Cambridge: Harvard University Press, 1988.

Lewis, R. W. B. *Edith Wharton: A Biography.* London: Constable, 1975.

Longstreet, Mrs. Abby Buchanan. *Good Form: Cards, Their Significance and Proper Use.* New York: Frederick A. Stokes and Brother, 1889.

———. *Social Etiquette of New York.* Rev. ed. New York: Appleton, 1882.

Lutes, Della Thompson. *The Gracious Hostess: A Book of Etiquette.* Indianapolis, IN: Bobbs-Merrill, 1923.

Manners and Rules of Good Society: A Compendium of the Proper Etiquette to be Observed on Every Occasion. New York: New York Book Co., 1913.

Marriott-Watson, H. B. "The Deleterious Effect of Americanization upon Women." *The Nineteenth Century and After* 54 (1903): 782–93.

Martens, Frederick H. *The Book of Good Manners: A Guide to Polite Usage for All Social Functions.* New York: Social Culture Publications, 1923.

Martin, Frederick T. *The Passing of the Idle Rich.* 1911. Reprint, New York: Arno Press, 1975.

Matthews, F. Schuyler. "The Artistic Household." *Ladies Home Journal,* October 1893, p. 5.

McAllister, Ward. *Society As I Have Found It.* New York: Cassell, 1890.

McCabe, James D. Jr., *New York by Sunlight and Gaslight.* 1882. Reprint, New York: Greenwich House, 1984.

McCarthy, Kathleen D. *Women's Culture: American Philanthropy and Art, 1830–1930.* Chicago: University of Chicago Press, 1991.

Montgomery, Maureen E. "'The Fruit That Hangs Highest': Courtship and Chaperonage in New York High Society, 1880–1920." *Journal of Family History* 21 (1996): 172–91.

———. *"Gilded Prostitution": Status, Money and Transatlantic Marriages, 1870–1914.* London: Routledge, 1989.

Moore, Margaret. *End of the Road for Ladies' Mile?* New York: The Drive to Protect the Ladies' Mile District, 1986.

Morris, Lloyd. *Incredible New York: High Life and Low Life of the Last Hundred Years.* New York: Random House, 1951.

Morrison, Toni. *Playing in the Dark: Whiteness and the Literary Imagination.* London: Picador, 1983.

Mott, Frank L. *American Journalism: A History of Newspapers in the United States Through 250 Years, 1690–1940.* New York: Macmillan, 1942.

————. *A History of American Magazines*. 5 vols. Cambridge: Belknap Press, 1957.

Myerhoff, Barbara. "Rites of Passage: Process and Paradox." In *Celebration: Studies in Festivity and Ritual*, edited by Victor Turner, pp. 109–31. Washington, D.C.: Smithsonian Institution Press, 1982.

O'Malley, Michael. *Keeping Watch: A History of American Time*. New York: Viking, 1990.

Our Manners at Home and Abroad: A Complete Manual on the Manners, Customs and Social Forms of the Best American Society. Harrisburg: Pennsylvania Publishing, 1883.

Parkhurst, Rev. Charles H. "Andromaniacs." *Ladies Home Journal*, February 1895, p. 15.

————. *My Forty Years in New York*. New York: Macmillan, 1923.

Parloa, Maria. "Attractive Cozy Corners." *Ladies Home Journal*, May 1902.

Peiss, Kathy Lee. *Cheap Amusements: Working Women and Leisure in New York City, 1880 to 1920*. Philadelphia: Temple University Press, 1985.

Pensler, Alan S. Introduction to *The Illustrations of W. T. Smedley*. Chadds Ford, PA: Brandywine River Museum, 1981.

Pulitzer, Ralph. *New York Society on Parade*. New York: Harper and Bros., 1910.

Harry E. Resequie, "A. T. Stewart's Marble Palace—The Cradle of the Department Stores," *New York Historical Society Quarterly* 48 (1964): 131–62.

Rojek, Chris. *Decentering Leisure*. London: Sage, 1995.

Rosaldo, Michelle Z., and Louise Lamphere, eds. *Women, Culture and Society*. Stanford: Stanford University Press, 1974.

Rosen, Ruth. *The Lost Sisterhood: Prostitution in America, 1900–1918*. Baltimore: Johns Hopkins University Press, 1982.

Rosenzweig, Roy and Elizabeth Blackmar. *The Park and the People: A History of Central Park*. Ithaca, NY: Cornell University Press, 1992.

Ruth, John A. *Decorum: A Practical Treatise on Etiquette and Dress of the Best American Society*. Chicago: Charles L. Snyder, 1881.

Ryan, Jenny. "Women, Modernity and the City." *Theory, Culture and Society* 11 (1994): 35–63.

Ryan, Mary P. *Women in Public: Between Banners and Ballots, 1825–1880*. Baltimore: Johns Hopkins University Press, 1990.

Rydell, Robert W. *All the World's a Fair: Visions of Empire at American International Expositions, 1876–1916*. Chicago: University of Chicago Press, 1984.

————. *World of Fairs: The Century-of-Progress Expositions*. Chicago: University of Chicago Press, 1993.

Said, Edward. *Orientalism*. London: Routledge and Kegan Paul, 1978.

Saisselin, Remy. *The Bourgeois and the Bibelot*. New Brunswick, NJ: Rutgers University Press, 1984.

Sangster, M. *Good Manners for All Occasions*. New York: The Christian Herald, 1904.

Saunders, Judith. "A New Look at the Oldest Profession in Wharton's 'New Year's Day.'" *Studies in Short Fiction* 17 (1980): 121–26.

Schlereth, Thomas J. *Victorian America: Transformations in Everyday Life, 1876–1915*. New York: Harper, 1991.

Schlesinger, Arthur M. *Learning How to Behave: A Historical Study of American Etiquette Books*. New York: Macmillan, 1946.

Scobey, David. "Anatomy of the Promenade: The Politics of Bourgeois Sociability in Nineteenth-Century New York." *Social History* 17 (1992): 203–27.

Seely, Mrs. L. *Mrs. Seely's Cook Book: A Manual of French and American Cookery with Chapters on Domestic Servants, Their Rights and Duties, and Many Other Details of Household Management*. New York: Macmillan, 1902.

Sherwood, Mrs. M. E. W. *Manners and Social Usages*. New York and London: Harper Brothers, 1884.

————. *Manners and Social Usages*. Rev. ed. New York and London: Harper Brothers, 1918.

————. *The Art of Entertaining*. New York: Dodd, Mead and Co, 1892.

Shevelow, Kathryn. *Women and Print Culture: The Construction of Femininity in the Early Periodical*. New York: Routledge, 1990.

Simon, Kate. *Fifth Avenue: A Very Social History*. New York: Harcourt, Brace, Jovanovich, 1978.

Sloane, Florence A. *Maverick in Mauve: The Diary of a Romantic Age*. New York: Doubleday, 1983.

Smith, Dorothy. *Texts, Facts, and Femininity: Exploring the Relations of Ruling*. New York: Routledge, 1990.

Smith, Jane S. *Elsie de Wolfe: A Life in the High Style*. New York: Atheneum, 1982.

Smith-Rosenberg, Carroll. *Disorderly Conduct: Visions of Gender in Victorian America*. New York: Oxford University Press, 1985.

Susman, Warren I. *Culture as History: The Transformation of American Society in the Twentieth Century*. New York: Pantheon Books, 1984.

Sutherland, Daniel E. *Americans and Their Servants: Domestic Service in the United States from 1800 to 1920*. Baton Rouge: Louisiana State University Press, 1981.

Taylor, William R. *In Pursuit of Gotham: Culture and Commerce in New York*. New York: Oxford University Press, 1992.

Terdiman, Richard. *Discourse/Counter-Discourse: The Theory and Practice of Symbolic Resistance in Nineteenth-Century France*. Ithaca: Cornell University Press, 1985.

Thomas, Brook. *American Literary Realism and the Failed Promise of Contract*. Berkeley and Los Angeles: University of California Press, 1997.

Thompson, J. B. *Ideology and Modern Culture: Critical Social Theory in the Era of Mass Communication*. Oxford: Polity Press, 1990.

Thomson, James. "Cozy Corners and Ingle Nooks." *Ladies Home Journal*, November 1893, p. 27.

Turner, Victor, ed. *Celebration: Studies in Festivity and Ritual*. Washington, D.C.: Smithsonian Institution Press, 1982.

Vanderbilt, Cornelius Jr. *Queen of the Golden Age: The Fabulous Story of Grace Wilson Vanderbilt*. New York: McGraw-Hill, 1956.

van Gennep, Arnold. *The Rites of Passage*. 1908. Translated by M. B. Vizedom and G. L. Caffee. Reprint, Chicago: University of Chicago Press, 1960.

Van Rensselaer, Mrs. May King. *The Social Ladder*. London: Nash and Grayson, 1925.

Veblen, Thorstein. *The Theory of the Leisure Class: An Economic Study of Institutions*. London: Allen & Unwin, 1925; reprint, London: Unwin Books, 1970.

Vogue's Book of Etiquette: Present-day Customs of Social Intercourse with the Rules for Their Correct Observance. New York: Condé Nast, 1925.

Walkowitz, Judith. *City of Dreadful Delight: Narratives of Sexual Danger in Late-Victorian London*. Chicago: University of Chicago Press, 1990.

Ward, Mrs. H. O. *Sensible Etiquette of the Best Society, Customs, Manners, Morals, and Home Culture*. Philadelphia: Porter and Coates, 1878.

Wecter, Dixon. *The Saga of American Society: A Record of Social Aspiration, 1607–1937*. London: Scribner's, 1937.

Weedon, Chris. *Feminist Practice and Poststructural Theory*. Oxford: Blackwell, 1987.

Wharton, Edith. *Italian Villas and Their Gardens*. New York: Century, 1904.

———. *The House of Mirth*. New York: Charles Scribner's Sons, 1905. Reprint, New York: The Library of America, 1985.

———. *A Motor-Flight Through France*. New York: Charles Scribner's Sons, 1908.

———. *The Custom of the Country*. New York: Charles Scribner's Sons, 1913. Reprint, New York: The Library of America, 1985.

———. *In Morocco*. New York: Charles Scribner's Sons, 1920. Reprint, Hopewell, NJ: Ecco Press, 1996.

———. *The Age of Innocence*. New York: Charles Scribner's Sons, 1921. Reprint, New York: The Library of America, 1985.

————. *Old New York*. New York: D. Appleton, 1924.

————. *The Writing of Fiction*. New York: Charles Scribner's Sons, 1925.

————. *A Backward Glance*. London: Appleton-Century, 1934.

————. *The Collected Short Stories of Edith Wharton*. 2 vols. Edited by R. W. B. Lewis. New York: Charles Scribner's Sons, 1968.

————. *The Letters of Edith Wharton*. Edited by R. W. B. Lewis and Nancy Lewis. New York: Collier Books, 1988.

Wharton, Edith, and Ogden Codman Jr. *The Decoration of Houses*. New York: W. W. Norton, 1978.

White, Annie. *Polite Society at Home and Abroad: A Complete Compendium of Information upon All Topics Classified under the Head of Etiquette*. Chicago, Philadelphia, Stockton: Monarch Book Co., 1891.

Wolff, Cynthia Griffin. *A Feast of Words*. New York: Oxford University Press, 1977.

Wolff, Janet. *Feminine Sentences: Essays on Women and Culture*. Cambridge: Polity Press, 1990.

Zola, Émile. *The Ladies' Paradise*. 1883. Reprint, Berkeley and Los Angeles: University of California Press, 1992.

Index